LEAD

AS I LEAD

LEAD
AS I LEAD

ACQUIRING THE LEADERSHIP ATTRIBUTES OF JESUS CHRIST

ROBERT K. REEVE

RED CROWN PUBLISHING

ISBN: 978-0-9821916-1-3

     Reeve, Robert K.

     Lead As I Lead: Acquiring the Leadership Attributes of Jesus Christ / by

     Robert K. Reeve

     Includes index

TABLE OF CONTENTS

FOREWORD

Two stories involving my wife Laurie illustrate the central theme of this book. The first occurred on the Caribbean Island of Saint Martin. It was a beautiful summer day with a bright blue sky covering crystal-blue water. Laurie and I chartered an excursion to an old fort located on a bluff high above the city. We mounted our bicycles along with 10 other vacationers and began the 7-mile round trip. Even though Laurie recently had knee surgery, she was eager to participate. After a mile or so of competing with two-way traffic on a very narrow, winding road, our guide pulled us over into a small parking lot to get us ready for the ascent. He had everyone downshift into "granny," the lowest possible gear so we would have the best chance of reaching the top. He then led out and we followed. Laurie did very well until just before the summit when her knee finally gave out. She stopped and started walking her bike the remaining distance.

What happened next was completely unexpected. Several cars slowed down, rolled down their windows, and shouted words of encouragement! "Good job, you can make it!" "You're almost there, keep going." It was not just the words that were remarkable, it was the friendly, happy tone of their voices spoken with great enthusiasm and with the biggest smiles I have ever seen. Not only did Laurie make it to the top of the next hill, she left Saint Martin with warm feelings and a stronger sense of self-worth, ready to conquer new challenges.

Now, contrast that with the second story which occurred prior to this trip. As Laurie was busily running errands one Saturday, the old family car she was driving died in the middle of the most congested intersection in town. Immediately, the other drivers started honking at her. They too rolled down their windows but shouted obscenities instead of encouragement. They glared, snarled, and gestured to express their anger toward her. There she sat in a dead car amongst newly found enemies with no one to offer help. Gratefully, and probably because of prayer, the car started, and she drove to the nearest parking lot to call me for help. To this very day, she does all she can to

1

avoid that intersection. And when she cannot, deep feelings of anxiety swell within her, almost paralyzing her desire to finish planned activities.

Two powerful stories with opposite results. One encouraged her to future growth while the other left her debilitated. Leadership is using our influence to affect the actions and opinions of others. Whether on a steep hill or at the mill; in the board room, class room, or family room; on a plane, a train, or at the big game, we lead by our influence. With that influence, we can lead people to a better place or stifle their determination to persevere. This book illustrates how Jesus uses His influence to improve lives and situations. By following His example and emulating His attributes, each of us can become a positive influence to lift others to greater attainment and deeper happiness.

INTRODUCTION

Each of us can lead. Each of us *must* lead. Many people feel they must hold an official leadership position to lead. The Savior's pattern of leadership, however, tells a different story. Most scriptural examples from His life show that He simply stepped forward and led out as a single individual trying to make a difference. He encountered people in various situations of daily life and used His influence to help them become better and do better.

The Savior led, first, by becoming someone people would follow voluntarily. Then He mingled among His fellowmen and taught them, ministered to them, and encouraged them to a better way of life. He said, "Follow me" (Matthew 4:19). Then, taking the lead, He guided people forward.

This book draws upon more than 1,100 scriptural references as it discusses 75 attributes Jesus demonstrated as He led people and influenced situations. We can better represent Him as we seek to acquire these attributes ourselves. This book also includes a seven–step process to help us acquire these attributes. Naturally, we have developed some of these attributes more than others, but we can improve each one as we learn from the Savior and emulate His ways.

In the music world, sound engineers use various types of electronic equipment to create the specific sound an artist envisions. One such piece of equipment is a mixing console like the one shown below. The engineer slides the various controls forward or backward to raise or lower the influence that particular control has on the sound.

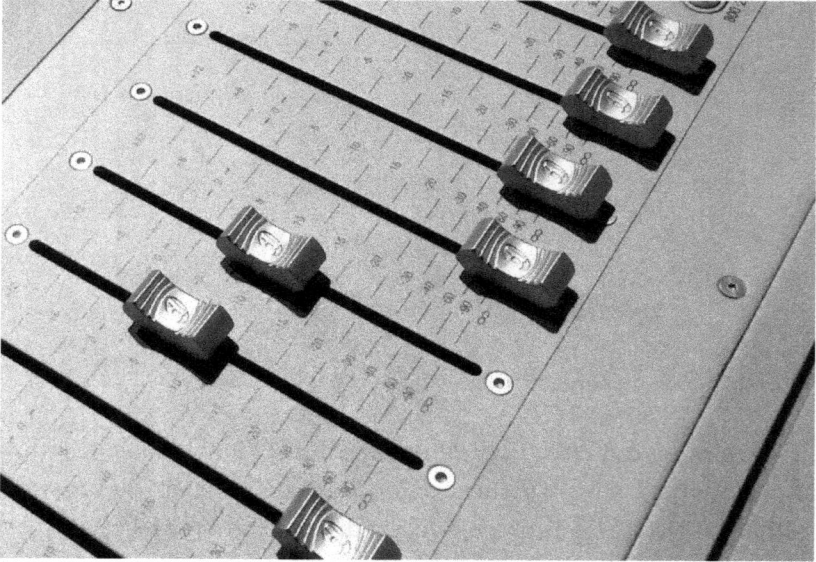

Sound Mixing Console
Imagery for a Leadership Attribute Indicator

We can liken each slider control to one of our leadership attributes. For example, in our current level of development, we may have pushed our slider for *cheerfulness* completely forward signifying that we have done well at developing that attribute. The next slider control might represent *initiates action*, which may be pulled back into the lowest position. Taken together, these two sliders mean we are happy sitting on the sidelines not making much of a difference.

If we could envision a mixing console that represents our current level of attainment for each of the 75 attributes described in this book, we could better see where we need to grow. If we could see a mixing console for one another, we would clearly see that everyone has a different mix of abilities and that everyone has something to offer. I have written this book to help you raise your sliders, or your attributes, so you can have greater influence to bring about good.

Lead As I Lead is a valuable resource for anyone who desires to lift other people, whether or not they hold an official leadership position in the Church or elsewhere. It is particularly helpful for missionaries who represent the Lord Jesus Christ during their ministry. It will help parents as they raise their families. It will help priesthood, Relief Society, and auxiliary leaders who endeavor to develop Christlike attributes in themselves and in others. Indeed, anyone who desires to emulate Jesus Christ and help develop a Zion society will benefit from reading it. As we acquire these attributes, we will find that people are more willing to follow our lead. Then, we can help them be better and do better. By doing this, we will lead as He leads.

CHAPTER 1

THE MEASURE OF A LEADER

If you wish to lead, you first must be someone people want to follow. As President Harold B. Lee stated, "You cannot lift another soul until you are standing on higher ground than he is. You cannot light a fire in another soul unless it is burning in your own soul."[1] By studying the attributes of Jesus, you can learn how to become someone who is standing on higher ground and how to lift others up to that higher ground. To aid in that study, this book discusses 24 attributes that describe *who* He is and 51 attributes that describe *what* He does.

As we study these attributes, it is apparent that His way of leadership is different from how many people think of leaders. Most examples from His life show Him simply leading out as a single individual who was trying to make a difference. Yes, He set up and effectively led an organization, but much of His life was encountering people in various situations of daily life and using His influence to help them become better and do better than they had before.

So often people are reluctant to take the initiative to act on their own. Perhaps this is because they have been told to act only in the position in which they have been appointed. Or, maybe it is fear of punishment for "steadying the ark" as was the case with the ancient Israelites. Regardless of the reason, they seem to wait on the sidelines until called to enter the game. While it is true that some people have been called to specific positions with specific duties, it is also true that everyone has been called to "bring to pass much righteousness" (D&C 58:27) and that "men should be anxiously engaged in a good cause" (D&C 58:27). For as the Savior taught, "it is not meet that I should command in all things for he that is compelled in all things, the same is a slothful and not a wise servant" (D&C 58:26). There is such a need for leaders at home, at work, and in the community. Whether we hold an official leadership position or not, we can use our influence and make a difference.

The concept of leadership implies causing action. As such, there are several words which can describe the way one person causes action in others. Words such as command, force, direct, compel, coerce, intimidate, manipulate, motivate, inspire, and influence could all be used. History books are full of leaders who have used each of these in their version of leadership. However, central to the plan of salvation is the agency of man. Therefore, the word *influence* seems to best describe the type of leadership Jesus uses to cause action in others. Regarding the use of that influence, the Savior explains, "No power or influence can or ought to be maintained . . . , only by persuasion, by long–suffering, by gentleness and meekness, and by love unfeigned; By kindness, and pure knowledge, which shall greatly enlarge the soul without hypocrisy, and without guile" (D&C 121:41–42).

If we measure a leader on who he or she is and what he or she does, then a simple definition of leadership would read something like this: Leadership is influencing yourself and others to be and do the best possible. Implied in this definition is that the leader knows the *best* path to follow and the *best* objectives to obtain. However, having this knowledge alone is not leadership until others follow your lead.

Someone once quipped, "Which way to go, the leader will know." This may be true, but it is incomplete. Leadership also includes attracting followers and then influencing them to become their best and do their best in whatever endeavor the leader is pursuing. For example, the leader on a basketball team often is the best player who also does the best at executing the team plays. If he is to be judged a good leader, then others need to follow him in becoming good players themselves and in executing the game plan properly.

It may seem unusual to include in a definition of leadership the notion that the leader must lead himself. However, it makes sense when we realize that being someone people will follow is a critical element of leadership. The skills needed to lead others are best developed by applying them to ourselves. How can we teach another to be authentic, accountable, forgiving, or perceptive if we have not developed those attributes ourselves? The leader must first be on the path of being and doing his or her best before encouraging others to follow that example.

A mother can be an honorable leader in her family by developing attributes such as love, patience, temperance, and knowledge, and then utilizing those traits consistently each day with family members. If she is someone the family wants to emulate, then she has become an effective leader, a person of tremendous influence.

A young girl can be an honorable leader in her family and social groups by being at peace with herself, being knowledgeable and developing talents, and then influencing others to do the same. People will want to be around her if she lifts them to become better than they have been and do better than they have done.

A scholar can be an honorable leader in his community by developing his mind and heart through study and life's experiences to gain knowledge and wisdom. Then, if students come to learn from him, he can lead them along the same path of discovery that he is following.

Competent gardeners are a good example of leaders. Gardeners do not grow plants and leaders do not grow people. They simply provide the environment and nutrients needed for the seed to grow. Jesus teaches this principle in the parable of the seed growing by itself. "And he said, So is the kingdom of God, as if a man should cast seed into the ground; And should sleep. And rise night and day, and the seed should spring and grow up, *he knoweth not how"* (Mark 4:26–27, emphasis added).

In this parable, the sower plants the seed but the seed grows on its own. The sower does not know how the seed grows nor can he make it grow. His role is to prepare a proper environment, plant the seeds, and let nature take its course. Part of preparing this environment is ensuring there is proper nourishment to facilitate growth. Alma taught: "And behold, as the tree beginneth to grow, ye will say: Let us nourish it with great care, that it may get root, that it may grow up, and bring forth fruit unto us. And now behold, if ye nourish it with much care it will get root, and grow up, and bring forth fruit" (Alma 32:37).

Alma also warned of the dangers of not providing the constant care needed for the continued development of the seed. He said: "But if ye neglect the tree, and take no thought for its nourishment, behold it will not get any root; and when the heat of the sun cometh and scorcheth it, because it hath no root it withers away, and ye pluck it up and cast it out. Now, this is not because the seed was not good, neither is it because the fruit thereof would not be desirable; but it is because your ground is barren, and ye will not nourish the tree, therefore ye cannot have the fruit thereof" (Alma 32: 38–39).

Effective leaders who are attentive will use their strength and resources to cultivate their people, thereby helping them rise to the higher ground that their leaders are putting within their reach.

---

1.   Harold B. Lee, "Stand Ye in Holy Places," *Ensign*, July 1973.

CHAPTER 2

WHAT IS JESUS LIKE?

If leadership is a combination of *who* the leader is and *what* the leader does, and if Jesus is the perfect example of a leader, then we need to better understand who Jesus is. What is He like? From a modern-day Apostle, Elder Orson F. Whitney (1855–1931), we have the following account:

"One night I dreamed . . . that I was in the Garden of Gethsemane, a witness of the Savior's agony. . . . I stood behind a tree in the foreground. . . . Jesus, with Peter, James, and John, came through a little wicket gate at my right. Leaving the three Apostles there, after telling them to kneel and pray, He passed over to the other side, where He also knelt and   prayed . . . : 'Oh my Father, if it be possible, let this cup pass from me; nevertheless not as I will but as Thou wilt.'

"As He prayed the tears streamed down His face, which was [turned] toward me. I was so moved at the sight that I wept also, out of pure sympathy with His great sorrow. My whole heart went out to Him. I loved Him with all my soul and longed to be with Him as I longed for nothing else.

"Presently He arose and walked to where those Apostles were kneeling—fast asleep! He shook them gently, awoke them, and in a tone of tender reproach, untinctured by the least show of anger or scolding, asked them if they could not watch with Him one hour.

"Returning to His place, He prayed again and then went back and found them again sleeping. Again He awoke them, admonished them, and returned and prayed as before. Three times this happened, until I was perfectly familiar with His appearance—face, form, and movements. He was of noble stature and of majestic mien . . . the very God that He was and is, yet as meek and lowly as a little child.

"All at once the circumstance seemed to change. . . . Instead of before, it was after the Crucifixion, and the Savior, with those three

11

Apostles, now stood together in a group at my left. They were about to depart and ascend into heaven. I could endure it no longer. I ran from behind the tree, fell at His feet, clasped Him around the knees, and begged Him to take me with Him.

"I shall never forget the kind and gentle manner in which He stooped and raised me up and embraced me. It was so vivid, so real that I felt the very warmth of His bosom against which I rested. Then He said: 'No, my son; these have finished their work, and they may go with me; but you must stay and finish yours.' Still I clung to Him. Gazing up into His face—for He was taller than I—I besought Him most earnestly: 'Well, promise me that I will come to You at the last.' He smiled sweetly and tenderly and replied: 'That will depend entirely upon yourself.' I awoke with a sob in my throat, and it was morning."[1]

From Elder Melvin J. Ballard (1873–1939), another modern-day Apostle, we have the following account.

"Two years ago, about this time, I had been on the Fort Peck Reservation for several days with the brethren, solving the problems connected with our work among the Lamanites. Many questions arose that we had to settle. There was no precedent for us to follow, and we just had to go to the Lord and tell Him our troubles and get inspiration and help from Him. On this occasion I had sought the Lord, under such circumstances, and that night I received a wonderful manifestation and impression which has never left me. I was carried to this place into this room. I saw myself here with you. I was told there was another privilege that was to be mine; and I was led into a room where I was informed I was to meet someone.

"As I entered the room I saw, seated on a raised platform, the most glorious being I have ever conceived of, and was taken forward to be introduced to Him. As I approached He smiled, called my name, and stretched out His hands toward me. If I live to be a million years old I shall never forget that smile. He put His arms around me and kissed me, as He took me into His bosom, and He blessed me until my whole being was thrilled. As He finished I fell at His feet, and there saw the marks of the nails; and as I kissed them, with deep joy swelling through my whole being, I felt that I was in heaven indeed. The feeling that came to my heart then was: Oh! If I could live worthy, though it would require four-score years, so that in the end when I have finished I could go into His presence and receive the feeling that I then had in His presence, I would give everything that I am or ever hope to be!"[2]

These accounts from Jesus's special witnesses give a view of His personality and character. They show the overarching attributes of love, compassion, and the ability to give personal attention. Together with the following descriptions of Him, we get a better understanding of who He is.

Moroni listed several more attributes of the Savior (Moroni 7:45). These attributes are:

1. Suffereth long
2. Is kind
3. Envieth not
4. Is not puffed up
5. Seeketh not [his] own
6. Not easily provoked
7. Thinketh no evil
8. Rejoiceth not in iniquity
9. Rejoiceth in the truth
10. Beareth all things
11. Believeth all things
12. Hopeth all things
13. Endureth all things

From the Doctrine and Covenants, additional attributes are revealed:

1. Faithful (D&C 4:6)
2. Virtuous (D&C 4:6)
3. Knowledgeable (D&C 4:6)
4. Temperate (D&C 4:6)
5. Patient (D&C 4:6)
6. Kind (D&C 4:6)
7. Godly (D&C 4:6)
8. Charitable (D&C 4:6)

9. Humble (D&C 4:6)
10. Diligent (D&C 4:6)
11. Persuasive (D&C 121:41)
12. Long–suffering (D&C 121:41)
13. Gentle (D&C 121:41)
14. Meek (D&C 121:41)
15. Loving (D&C 121:41)

In addition to these attributes, Jesus gave us counsel that reveals much about His own character. This counsel is applicable to all leaders.

1. Be poor in Spirit (Matthew 5:3)
2. Hunger and thirst after righteousness (Matthew 5:6)
3. Be pure in heart (Matthew 5:8)
4. Let all things be done in cleanliness (D&C 42:41)
5. Delight in chastity (Jacob 2:28)
6. Be a peacemaker (Matthew 5:9)
7. Persecuted for righteousness sake (Matthew 5:10)
8. Do good to them that hate you (Matthew 5:44)
9. Turn the other cheek (Matthew 5:39)
10. Judge not unrighteously (Matthew 7:1)
11. Do not cast pearls before swine (Matthew 7:6)
12. Give good gifts (Matthew 7:11)
13. Build your house on a rock (Matthew 7:24)
14. Be wise as serpents, and harmless as doves (Matthew 10:16)
15. Love thy neighbor (Matthew 22:37–40)
16. Deny yourself and take up his cross, which means to deny yourself of all ungodliness, every worldly lust, and keep His commandments (Joseph Smith Translation, Matthew 16:25–26)
17. Be prepared as in the parable of the ten virgins (Matthew 25:1)

Taken in the whole, these descriptions of Him, and the counsel received from Him, give us an idea of what Christ is like and how His character and personality influence His leadership. Each of God's children is blessed with some level of these attributes, and mortality is designed to be a learning ground for improving them. Through diligent study and consistent effort, great progress can be made during the mortal stage of our eternal progression. If, in some small way, we can learn to become like Him, then we can progress toward leading as He leads.

1.   Orson F. Whitney, "The Divinity of Jesus Christ," *Improvement Era,* January 1926, 224-25.
2.   Melvin J. Ballard, *Crusader for Righteousness*, Salt Lake City: Bookcraft (1966).

CHAPTER 3

NATURAL MAN TENDENCIES

In studying the leadership of Jesus, it is helpful to understand those attributes that are at odds with His example. The pages of this book are best reserved for learning about the Savior's example, but there is benefit in briefly listing those human tendencies that weaken leaders and diminish their ability to be a positive influence on others.

King Benjamin taught: "For the natural man is an enemy to God, and has been from the fall of Adam, and will be, forever and ever, unless he yields to the enticings of the Holy Spirit, and putteth off the natural man and becometh a saint through the Atonement of Christ the Lord, and becometh as a child, submissive, meek, humble, patient, full of love, willing to submit to all things which the Lord seeth fit to inflict upon him, even as a child doth submit to his father" (Mosiah 3:19).

The scriptures tell us much about our carnal desires and tendencies. They show us how and why we should strive to overcome them. They help us replace them with the divine attributes exhibited by the Savior. Following is a partial list of natural man tendencies.

1. Looketh on the outward appearance (1 Samuel 16:7)
2. Exercises unrighteous dominion (D&C 121:39)
3. Lover of their own selves (2 Timothy 3:2)
4. Covets (2 Timothy 3:2)
5. Boasts (2 Timothy 3:2)
6. Proud (2 Timothy 3:2)
7. Blasphemes (2 Timothy 3:2)
8. Disobeys (2 Timothy 3:2)
9. Unthankful (2 Timothy 3:2)
10. Unholy (2 Timothy 3:2)
11. Truce breaker (2 Timothy 3:3)

12. Falsely accuses (2 Timothy 3:3)
13. Incontinent, meaning without self–control (2 Timothy 3:3)
14. Fierce (2 Timothy 3:3)
15. Despises those who are good (2 Timothy 3:3)
16. Traitorous (2 Timothy 3:4)
17. High–minded (2 Timothy 3:4)
18. Loves pleasure (2 Timothy 3:4)
19. Lies (Alma 16:18) (D&C 76:103)
20. Deceives (Alma 16:18)
21. Envies (Alma 16:18)
22. Causes Strife (Alma 16:18)
23. Malicious (Alma 16:18)
24. Reviles (Alma 16:18)
25. Steals (Alma 16:18)
26. Robs (Alma 16:18)
27. Plunders (Alma 16:18)
28. Murders (Alma 16:18)
29. Commits adultery (Alma 16:18)
30. Lascivious (Alma 16:18)
31. Worships graven images (Exodus 20:4)
32. Takes name of Lord in vain (Exodus 20:7)
33. Does not keep Sabbath day holy (Exodus 20:8)
34. Bears false witness (Exodus 20:16)
35. Unbelieving and blind (D&C 58:15)
36. Seeks praise of world (D&C 58:39)
37. Seeks to excel (D&C 58:41)
38. Confesses not, hides sins (D&C 58:60)
39. Pride in their hearts (Helaman 4:12)
40. Oppresses the poor by withholding their food and clothing (Helaman 4:12)
41. Raises great contentions (Helaman 4:12)
42. Boasts in their own strength (Helaman 4:13)
43. Proud, greedy, envious, lustful, gluttonous, and slothful (the seven deadly sins)

These tendencies of the natural man are inherited because of the pre–planned fall of Adam. One purpose of mortality is to understand them firsthand, either from the errors of others or those of ourselves, and then to overcome them. Tendencies of the natural man separate us from God and His influence. Gratefully, the Atonement provides a way to overcome and replace them by following Jesus and acquiring His attributes. Then we can lead as He leads and use our influence to bless lives and improve the many situations we encounter each day.

CHAPTER 4

SEVEN STEPS FOR ACQUIRING CHRISTLIKE ATTRIBUTES

Having a desire to acquire or further develop leadership attributes is a worthwhile objective, but desire alone is not enough. As with all plans for improvement, we need a process that will lead to the desired end. This chapter presents a powerful seven-step process that will help us develop the leadership attributes of Jesus.

Step 1: Have Faith in Christ

Jesus and Lucifer exemplify two contrasting styles of leadership. One is based on principles of righteousness, and the other is based on compulsion and carnal desires as discussed in chapter 3. The first step in acquiring the leadership attributes of Jesus is to have faith that His way is the right way. We must also believe that He will assist us in our quest. Faith in Jesus Christ (Articles of Faith 1:4) is the first principle of the gospel and should be the foundation for all our actions. Because of this faith, we follow Him.

The Bible Dictionary states: "To have faith is to have confidence in something or someone. The Lord has revealed himself and his perfect character, possessing in their fullness all the attributes of love, knowledge, justice, mercy, unchangeableness, power, and every other needful thing, so as to enable the mind of man to place confidence in Him without reservation" (Bible Dictionary, "Faith").

As we learn of Jesus and study His ways, we can develop confidence that His way of leading, His way of teaching, and His way of living constitute the true way we should emulate. His way works for the learned and unlearned and for the experienced and inexperienced. It is attainable by all who accept His invitation to "follow me, and do the things which ye have seen me do" (2 Nephi 31:12).

In Kirtland, Ohio, during the winter of 1834, the Prophet Joseph Smith organized the School of the Prophets to instruct Church leaders in the fundamental principles and doctrines of the gospel. Joseph and other leaders provided that instruction. A portion of these lessons was later published as the *Lectures on Faith.* In these lectures, we learn that in order to have faith in God, we must have "a *correct* idea of his character . . . and attributes."[1] Lecture 3 then identifies fourteen basic attributes: being gracious, showing longsuffering, having an abundance of goodness, being slow to anger, not walking in crooked paths, not lying, being no respecter of persons, showing love, being knowledgeable, having a forgiving disposition, having no variableness, using fair judgment, and being merciful and truthful.[2] The lecture continues, "An acquaintance with these attributes in the divine character, is essentially necessary, in order that the faith of any rational being can center in him."[3]

By becoming acquainted with these attributes, early Church leaders could better emulate Jesus and learn to lead as He leads.

Step 2: Pray

Because we cannot fully develop the attributes of Christ on our own, we all need help from prayer and grace. We can make some progress from our own efforts, but it would be a partial victory. Elder David A. Bednar has taught, "We can in mortality seek to be blessed with and develop essential elements of a Christlike character."[4] However, he further explained, "We cannot obtain such a capacity through sheer willpower or personal determination. Rather, we are dependent upon and in need of 'the merits, mercy, and grace of the Holy Messiah.'"[5]

The Bible Dictionary defines grace as the "divine means of help or strength, given through the bounteous mercy and love of Jesus Christ." Through grace, all mankind can "receive strength and assistance to do good works that they otherwise would not be able to maintain if left to their own means" (Bible Dictionary, "Grace"). Therefore, if we endeavor to perform good works with honest effort and noble intentions, the strength of His mighty hand will compensate for our weaknesses.

The compensation comes because of His great love for those who diligently seek to follow Him.

As we pray for the Lord's help, we might ask for the following:

- Guidance to determine which attributes we should strengthen or develop.
- Understanding of how and when to apply certain attributes.
- Understanding what is going right or wrong with our efforts regarding a particular attribute.
- Help in making a plan for improvement.
- Additional insight.
- Experiences to use in developing a certain attribute.
- Encouragement to continue trying.

During our private prayers, we can be taught and strengthened in ways that can bring tremendous growth and comfort. Throughout each day, we find ourselves in many situations, and we associate with many different people. In each encounter, we have an opportunity to practice the attributes we are trying to acquire. By always keeping a prayer in our hearts, we have a full-time coach available to guide us in each situation. We can tell Him what our plan of action is, and He can help us carry out and, if necessary, modify that plan. Afterward, He can tell us how successful we were. This gives us immediate feedback to aid our learning.

3: Focus on a Few Selected Attributes

Life is too short and human weaknesses are too limiting for us to fully develop all of the Savior's attributes in mortality. The counsel not to "run faster or labor more than you have strength" (D&C 10:4) certainly applies to our quest to develop Christlike attributes. There is wisdom in beginning this journey by selecting a few attributes to focus on that will help you in your current situation and your current responsibilities. The appendix of this book includes a personal attribute assessment form that you can use to evaluate yourself on each of the 75 attributes discussed in this book. Fill out this form and ask

LEAD AS I LEAD

others, such as parents, friends, coworkers, or supervisors, to fill it out on you as well. Evaluating the responses will identify a starting point for developing the Savior's attributes.

Of the 75 attributes discussed in this book, the 24 attributes below describe the core characteristics of Jesus's personality. If we seek to *become* like Jesus, these are the attributes we should emulate.

BECOMING Like Jesus					
Motives		**Demeanor**		**Ability**	
1.	Charity/Love	6.	Optimistic	16.	Confident
2.	Pure in motives	7.	Cheerful	17.	Courageous
3.	Authentic	8.	Dignified	18.	Durable
4.	Selfless	9.	Approachable	19.	Capable
5.	Delights in the success of others	10.	Inclusive	20.	Knowledgeable
		11.	Friendly	21.	Accountable
		12.	Patient	22.	Has integrity
		13.	Compassionate	23.	Diligent
		14.	Kind	24.	Perceptive
		15.	Humble		

Of the 75 attributes discussed in this book, the 51 below describe the actions of Jesus. If we seek to be *doing* as Jesus did, we should emulate these attributes.

DOING		
As Jesus Did		
Governs Himself	**Prepares Followers**	**Honors Relationships**
25. Disciplined	48. Knows followers	69. Obedient
26. Maintains confidentiality	49. Defends followers	70. Submissive
27. Frugal	50. Delegates	71. Loyal
28. Consistent	51. Allows freedom	72. Trusted
29. Endures to the end	52. Avoids favoritism	73. United
30. Prioritizes	53. Overcomes obstacles	74. Respectful
31. Plans ahead	54. Teaches	75. Reports back
32. Prepares Himself	55. Nourishes	
33. Rejuvenates Himself	56. Sets an example	
34. Grows personally	57. Mentors	
35. Labors also		
	Oversees Performance	
	58. Provides hands–on leadership	
Leads Out		
36. Defines objectives	59. Places faith in followers	
37. Lifts vision	60. Expects results	
38. Initiates action	61. Accepts people's best	
39. Visible	62. Follows up	
40. Motivates with persuasion	63. Steps in when needed	
41. Inspires with oratory		
42. Has order	**Judges**	
43. Gives clear direction	64. Is just and merciful	
44. Counsels together	65. Judges righteously	
45. Serves others	66. Disciplines with kindness	
46. Ministers to the one	67. Forgives	
47. Succors the weak	68. Looks on the heart	

Selecting which attributes to work on deserves some forethought. Consider the thought process of Benjamin Franklin as he selected and then prioritized thirteen virtues he wished to acquire. He offers his reasoning for selecting the first eight of those thirteen virtues:

"My intention being to acquire the habitude of all these virtues, I judg'd it would be well not to distract my attention by attempting the whole at once, but to fix it on one of them at a time; and, when I should be master of that, then to proceed to another, and so on, till I should have gone thro' the thirteen; and, as the previous acquisition of some might facilitate the acquisition of certain others, I arrang'd them with that view, as they stand above. *Temperance* first, as it tends to procure that coolness and clearness of head, which is so necessary where constant vigilance was to be kept up, and guard maintained against the unremitting attraction of ancient habits, and the force of perpetual temptations. This being acquir'd and establish'd, *Silence* would be more easy; and my desire being to gain knowledge at the same time that I improv'd in virtue, and considering that in conversation it was obtain'd rather by the use of the ears than of the tongue, and therefore wishing to break a habit I was getting into of prattling, punning, and joking, which only made me acceptable to trifling company, I gave Silence the second place. This and the next, *Order*, I expected would allow me more time for attending to my project and my studies. *Resolution*, once become habitual, would keep me firm in my endeavors to obtain all the subsequent virtues; *Frugality* and *Industry* freeing me from my remaining debt, and producing affluence and independence, would make more easy the practice of *Sincerity* and *Justice*."[6]

Another instructive example comes from the powerful Chinese military leader, Sun Tzu. He is known for his often-quoted book, *The Art of War*. He desired peace, but if war came, he knew how to win through effective leadership. He taught, "Leadership is a matter of intelligence, trustworthiness, humaneness, courage, and sternness."[7] One of Sun Tzu's students, named Du Mu, expounded on these five attributes: "The Way of the ancient kings was to consider humaneness foremost, while the martial artists considered intelligence foremost.

This is because intelligence involves ability to plan and to know when to change effectively. Trustworthiness means to make people sure of punishment or reward. Humaneness means love and compassion for people, being aware of their toils. Courage means to seize opportunities to make certain of victory, without vacillation. Sternness means to establish discipline in the ranks by strict punishments."[8]

Developing these five core attributes is important, but the real power comes from understanding the inter–relationship between the attributes. Another of Sun Tzu's students, Jia Lin, wrote: "Reliance on intelligence alone results in rebelliousness. Exercise of humaneness alone results in weakness. Fixation on trust results in folly. Dependence on the strength of courage results in violence. Excessive sternness of command results in cruelty. When one has all five virtues together, each appropriate to its function, then one can be a military leader."[9]

Learning from a statesman like Benjamin Franklin and a military leader like Sun Tzu may seem out of character in a book centered on the Savior, but they demonstrate the universal application of the leadership attributes Jesus exemplified. From these leaders, we learn to consider the relationship and balance among the various attributes as we select those we wish to develop.

Step 4: Understand the Selected Attributes

To understand an attribute, we must have a clear definition of that attribute and then see how Jesus applied it. For example, what does it mean to be courageous? The definition of *courage* is, "mental or moral strength to venture, persevere, and withstand danger, fear, or difficulty."[10] With that definition in mind, a study of the life of Jesus reveals several examples where He demonstrated courage. For example, while walking in Solomon's porch on the east side of the temple grounds, Jesus was approached by several Jews who said to Him, "If thou be the Christ, tell us plainly" (John 10: 23–24). Jesus replied, "I and my Father are one" (John 10:30). Speaking the plain truth in this situation took great courage, for surely, Jesus knew His pronouncement would cause these men to seek his life. "Then the Jews took up stones again to stone him. Jesus answered them, Many good works have I shewed you from my Father; for which of those works do ye stone me? The Jews answered him, saying, For a good work we stone thee not; but for blasphemy; and because that thou, being a man, makest thyself God" (John 10:31–33).

Another example occurred when Jesus was brought before Pilate, who asked him, "Art thou a king then? Jesus answered, Thou sayest that I am a king. *To this end was I born, and for this cause came I into the world,* that I should bear witness unto the truth" (John 18:37; emphasis added). This bold statement, given in strength yet with humility, must have stunned Pilate and all his court. We can imagine the deathly quiet that filled the royal halls of mortal power, followed by the likely chorus of uncontrolled laughter and condescending jeers. When the questioning continued, Jesus courageously restrained Himself from further defense, for He had already declared the testimony He had come to give.

Then, again with courage, Jesus proceeded to Golgotha, where the purest lamb would suffer for even the most polluted wretch. He carried a heavy wooden cross through hate–filled streets lined with many of His enemies. As He was placed upon the cross and left to slowly die, He demonstrated one lasting example of courage. It was an example His disciples needed to remember because their own courage would be tested if they still chose to follow him.

Step 5: Take Action

As mentioned in Step 2, prayer is a vital component in acquiring an attribute. But prayer, even if offered fervently, must be followed by action. As President Gordon B. Hinckley counseled, "Get on your knees and pray and stand on your feet and do."[11] This *doing* is simply putting into practice what we have studied. It is using our influence to guide people or situations to better outcomes.

In Shakespeare's *Hamlet*, Hamlet gives wise counsel to his mother, Gertrude, who teeters on the edge of sin. To fortify her in a moment of temptation, Hamlet encourages his mother, "Assume a virtue, if you have it not."[12] Using a modern translation of Shakespeare's text,

Hamlet continues, "At least pretend to be virtuous, even if you're not. Habit is a terrible thing, in that it's easy to get used to doing evil without feeling bad about it. But it's also a good thing, in that being good can also become a habit."[13]

The implication is clear. If Gertrude could act virtuous, eventually, she could become virtuous. Shakespeare understood human nature and used Hamlet as a vehicle for teaching this truth: our actions have a powerful effect on our character and vice versa. To change our character, we can change our actions by acting the part of our desired character.

Acting is the enemy of procrastination, which keeps us from doing what we know is worthwhile. Elder Marvin J. Ashton counseled, "Avoid procrastination. We can say with great accuracy procrastination is an unwholesome blend of doubt and delay. Oft-used words of the Savior such as ask, seek, knock, go, thrust, are action words. He would have us use action as we teach and live His principles."[14]

The choice to act is a matter of self-discipline, and it is easier to discipline ourselves if we keep in mind why we wish to act. If we want to lead as Jesus leads, we need to become more like Him so we can have greater influence improving situations and blessing lives.

Step 6: Evaluate Progress

Evaluating progress is an integral part of development. It reveals our improvement and propels us toward future achievement. President Thomas S. Monson said, "When performance is measured, performance improves. When performance is measured and reported, the rate of improvement accelerates."[15] If we truly want to acquire the attributes of Jesus, one of the best ways to do so is to give a progress report in our daily prayers. Jesus sets that example in His great Intercessory Prayer, in which He reported on eleven different points:

1. "I have glorified thee on the earth."
2. "I have finished the work which thou gavest me to do."
3. "I have manifested thy name unto the men which thou gavest me."

4. "They have kept thy word."
5. "They have known that all things whatsoever thou hast given me are of thee."
6. "I have given unto them the words which thou gavest me; and they have known surely that I came out from thee, and they have believed that thou didst send me."
7. "I pray for them."
8. "While I was with them in the world, I kept them in thy name: those that thou gavest me I have kept, and none of them is lost, but the son of perdition."
9. "I have given them thy word."
10. "For their sakes I sanctify myself."
11. "The glory which thou gavest me I have given them; that they may be one, even as we are one" (John 17:1–26).

This was a self-evaluation of the work Jesus had performed. Surely, the need to report to His Father would have guided His actions throughout His mortal life. We too can have such a guide if we establish an evaluation and reporting process.

Many people structure their daily prayers so that they give thanks in the first half of their prayers and ask for blessings in the second half. But effective prayer has a third section—a reporting and discussion section. Morning prayers could be a time to review our selected attributes and think through their definitions and the examples from the Savior's life. Then, we could rehearse how we plan to develop and apply those attributes during the day. Periodic prayers throughout the day can give us strength and insight and help us stay focused on our desired behaviors. During our evening prayers, we could report on our application of selected attributes, recounting circumstances, our actions, and the responses to our actions. Often, during this report, additional insight will flow into our minds so we can see how to be more effective in the future.

In addition to daily prayers, there are other ways to evaluate our progress. Benjamin Franklin, for example, used a process for daily evaluation in his quest to acquire thirteen virtues. He said: "I made a little book, in which I allotted a page for each of the virtues. I rul'd each page with red ink, so as to have seven columns, one for each day of the week, marking each column with a letter for the day. I cross'd these columns with thirteen red lines, marking the beginning of each line with the first letter of one of the virtues, on which line, and in its proper column, I might mark, by a little black spot, every fault I found upon examination to have been committed respecting that virtue upon that day."[16]

Regardless of the method we use, a daily evaluation will keep us focused on improving our behaviors, our minds, and our hearts. This continual evaluation can become more powerful in effecting change if we report our progress to someone.

Step 7: Persist in Pursuing Perfection

A familiar old proverb states, "A journey of a thousand miles begins with a single step." To undertake a notable endeavor, we must first begin. This proverb also teaches that to complete the journey, we must travel a full one thousand miles. To do that, we must stay engaged for the full distance. To develop new attributes, we must begin and then persistently move forward. Often, people begin a noble endeavor only to end prematurely because they lose focus, interest, and determination.

The Savior set an example of helping His followers stay engaged by establishing the sacrament as a weekly reminder of Him and the covenants we have made. The scriptures often repeat the word *remember* because ancient apostles and prophets knew how easy it is to get distracted and step off the path. The Lord has surrounded us with several reminders to help us stay focused on Him. In addition to the sacrament, these reminders include temple ordinances, weekly Church meetings, general conferences, visiting and home teachers, daily prayer, and the scriptures.

Keeping a daily record helped Benjamin Franklin stay engaged until he realized improvement. Later in his life, as he wrote about beginning his quest to acquire virtues, he stated in a moment of introspection, "I was surpris'd to find myself so much fuller of faults than I had imagined; but I had the satisfaction of seeing them diminish."[17] Toward the end of his life, he looked back on his progress of acquiring the attribute of humility and reported, "And this mode, which I at first put on with some violence to natural inclination, became at length so easy, and so habitual to me, that perhaps for these fifty years past no one has ever heard a dogmatical expression escape me."[18] This is the power of staying engaged, of tracking progress and continually evaluating improvement. This effort helped Franklin become a man of tremendous influence because he built his leadership upon attributes he acquired over a lifetime of effort.

In summary, to acquire the leadership attributes of Jesus, we need a process to follow and examples to study. The key to having repeatable success in any endeavor is to apply this motto: "Perfect the process and execute the process perfectly." The seven–step process described in this chapter will help us to the degree that we follow it. Here's a summary of this process:

Step 1: **Have faith** in Christ that His way of leadership is the right way and is attainable.

Step 2: **Pray** for guidance and life experiences that develop His attributes.

Step 3: **Focus** on a few selected attributes.

Step 4: **Understand** the selected attributes.

Step 5: **Take action** by doing what the Savior did.

Step 6: **Evaluate progress** continually.

Step 7: **Persist** in pursuing perfection.

As we perfect our process and execute it perfectly, we will see dramatic improvement in our leadership. Drawing from the scores of examples detailed in this book, we can learn to lead as Jesus leads, and be better able to use our influence more effectively to bless lives and improve situations.

---

1.   *Lectures on Faith* (1985), 3:4; emphasis in original.

2.   *Lectures on Faith* (1985); these are scattered throughout lecture 3.

3. *Lectures on Faith* (1985), 3:19.

4. David A. Bednar, "The Character of Christ," (Brigham Young University-Idaho devotional, Jan. 25, 2003), byui.edu.

5. Bednar, "The Character of Christ."

6. Benjamin Franklin, *Autobiography of Benjamin Franklin*, 1868, 96; emphasis added.

7. Sun Tzu, *The Art of War*, 44.

8. *The Art of War*, 44.

9. *The Art of War*, 44.

10. Merriam-Webster's Collegiate Dictionary, 11th ed., 2003, "courage."

11. Gordon B. Hinckley, regional conference, Santiago, Chile, Apr. 26, 1999; cited in "Inspirational Thoughts," *Ensign*, April 2002, 3.

12. *Hamlet*, act 3, scene 4, page 7 (original text).

13. *Hamlet*, act 3, scene 4, page 7 (Modern text translation; see Sparknotes.com).

14. Marvin J. Ashton, *Be of Good Cheer*, 61.

15. Thomas S. Monson, *Conference Report*, Oct. 1970, 107.

16. Franklin, 97.

17. Franklin, 100.

18. Franklin, 103.

CHAPTER 5

HIS MOTIVES

Attribute 1: Charity/Love

Charity: *Benevolent goodwill or love of humanity. Generosity and helpfulness especially toward the needy.* [1]
Love: *A feeling of warm personal attachment. Affectionate concern for the well–being of others.*

Any discussion of the leadership attributes of Jesus must start with charity for it is the greatest of all attributes. Charity and love are interchangeable words that express the true motive that guides our Savior's actions and the actions of all who lead like Him. Moroni explained how charity is the "pure love of Christ" and taught several ways how this attribute is manifest. "And charity suffereth long, and is kind, and envieth not, and is not puffed up, seeketh not her own, is not easily provoked. . . . Wherefore, my beloved brethren, if ye have not charity, ye are nothing, for charity never faileth. Wherefore, cleave unto charity, which is *the greatest of all,* for all things must fail—But *charity is the pure love of Christ,* and it endureth forever; and whoso is found possessed of it at the last day, it shall be well with him" (Moroni 7:45–47, emphasis added).

In these verses Moroni identified seven characteristics of charity, all of which will be discussed at length throughout this book. There are certainly more than seven and each one further cements in our hearts the greatness of our Savior's love for each of us.

Love, harmony, and goodwill can strengthen any organization and bind top, middle, and lower levels tightly together. This is true for the eternal family of man as well as for the small corner bookstore. There are many scriptures that express the love that binds together our Heavenly Father and Jesus Christ. To the Jews, Jesus said, "The Father loveth the Son" (John 5:20) and "my Father loves me" (John 10:17). To Joseph Smith, the Father declared, "*This is My Beloved Son. Hear Him!*" (JS–H 1:17). To the righteous in the Land Bountiful, He declared, "Behold my Beloved Son, in whom I am well pleased" (3 Nephi 11:7). At the baptism of Jesus, the Father said, "Thou art my beloved Son, in whom I am well pleased" (Mark 1:11). On the Mount of Transfiguration, the Father said, "This is my beloved Son, in whom I am well pleased; hear ye him" (Matthew 17:5).

The relationship between the Father and the Son serves as the foundation upon which we join our love to them. This common thread of love binds together leaders, followers, and everyone associated with them. It forms a powerful union of like–minded people progressing together in a common purpose. Jesus declared:

"As the Father hath loved me, so have I loved you: continue ye in my love.

"If ye keep my commandments, ye shall abide in my love; even as I . . . abide in his love.

"This is my commandment, That ye love one another, as I have loved you" (John 15:9–12).

Love is at the heart of all that Jesus did and it is woven through all that He said. For example, one can feel the love Jesus had for all who lived in His beloved city when He said, "O Jerusalem, Jerusalem . . . how often would I have gathered thy children together, as a hen *doth gather* her brood under *her* wings, and ye would not!" (Luke 13:34). Consider the love Jesus demonstrated to a rich young man who came to Him, as a pupil comes to his teacher. Mark records:

"And when he was gone forth into the way, there came one running, and kneeled to him, and asked him, Good Master, what shall I do that I may inherit eternal life?

"And Jesus said unto him, Why callest thou me good? *there is* none good but one, *that is*, God.

"Thou knowest the commandments, Do not commit adultery, Do not kill, Do not steal, Do not bear false witness, Defraud not, Honour thy father and mother.

"And he answered and said unto him, Master, all these have I observed from my youth.

"Then Jesus beholding him *loved him,* and said unto him, One thing thou lackest: go thy way, sell whatsoever thou hast, and give to the poor, and thou shalt have treasure in heaven: and come, take up the cross, and follow me" (Mark 10:17–21, emphasis added).

This was not a rebuke of a wicked man but a response to one who lived a good life and wanted to live the better life the Savior offered. Jesus, ever the teacher, revealed out of love the "one thing" this young man still lacked.

In His final hours with the Apostles, Jesus taught of love and He taught with love. He wanted these future leaders to understand that love is the foundation of all they are called to do. John records, "Now before the feast of the passover, when Jesus knew that his hour was come that he should depart out of this world unto the Father, having *loved his own* which were in the world, *he loved them unto the end"* (John 13:1, emphasis added). Jesus then went on to teach them, "A new commandment I give unto you, That ye *love* one another; as I have *loved* you, that ye also *love* one another. By this shall all men know that ye are my disciples, if ye have *love* one to another" (John 13:34–35, emphasis added).

Love is at the heart of the type of leadership Jesus practiced. He taught this principle throughout His ministry and demonstrated it by His example. Now that He renewed this principle during the Last Supper, Jesus set the stage for one lasting example of His love. That example would be demonstrated in Gethsemane and Calvary.

No mortal has offered a greater example of love than when Jesus fulfilled His own words, "Greater love hath no man than this, that a man lay down his life for his friends" (John 15:13). He did what He said He would do, "I lay down my life for the sheep" (John 10:15). Alone in Gethsemane, in humble submission and with perfect love for His Father and all His Father's children, Jesus humbly bowed and said, "*nevertheless not as I will,* but as thou *wilt"* (Matthew 26:39). Surely, this is the greatest expression of love ever offered!

Examples of Righteous Leaders

Leaders who love their people and spend their whole lives in their service will find that love reciprocated. Just as with the Savior, so it was with Nephi. Near the end of Nephi's life, his brother Jacob records, "The people . . . loved Nephi exceedingly, he having been a great protector for them, having wielded the sword of Laban in their defence, and having labored in all his days for their welfare" (Jacob 1:10).

This one verse of scripture says so much about leadership. People love a leader who protects them, defends them, and serves them. It is such a simple formula but very effective. Nephi sought the will and word of God, then taught that to his people. He relocated them when enemies threatened their lives and taught them how to live after the manner of happiness. He did it with love and because of love. He did it for all his people and for all his days. Nephi followed the example of the Savior and was loved for it.

Occasionally, a leader comes along that demonstrates such love that it seems the whole world weeps at his passing. Below is a tribute Elder Matthew Cowley gave of one such leader, President George Albert Smith.

"All those million miles which he traveled during his lifetime were used in distributing love wherever he went. Only a few weeks ago I went to the hospital to inquire about his health. On hearing that I was out in the hall he sent for me to come in, and when I went in, I walked up to his bedside and he reached out and took me by the hand, and gripping my hand firmly he said. 'Young man, remember all the days of your life that you can find good in everyone if you will but look for it.' The last message, the last instruction to me—'Remember always you can find good in everyone if you will but look for it.'

"He loved everyone because he could see the good within them. He did not look upon sin with the least degree of allowance, but he loved the sinner because he knew that God was love, and that it is God's love that regenerates human souls and may, by that process, transform the sinner into a saint.

"Maybe there are sinners who mistook his love for respect. He didn't respect the sinner, but he loved him. I am sure that love found response in the hearts and in the lives of those whom he loved."[2]

Leaders like President Smith truly influence others to be their best and to do their best. Through their love alone, they lift people and give them the encouragement to lift themselves. William Shakespeare said, "They do not love that do not show their love."[3] President Smith did show that love. He practiced what Benjamin Franklin once said, "If you would be loved, love, and be loveable."[4] President Smith was a reflection of this truth.

Mother Teresa was one of the world's great leaders because her influence touched so many people. Her life's work was to remove the sick and dying from their desperate situations and move them to a comfortable place where she could care for them. Though she died in 1997, she is still looked upon as a great example of one who practiced love for her fellow man. She also used her influence to attract others to help in her cause which started in the streets of Calcutta, India then grew throughout the world. Despite this worldwide influence, she said, "Don't look for big things, just do small things with great love."[5]

Though none of us are yet able to love as Jesus loves, our Heavenly Father has created a means for us to develop this central attribute. He organized His children into families where parents could develop love by sacrificing much of their best years of mortality in the service of their children. This sacrifice starts with the original nine months of pregnancy, to the 24 hours of daily care during infancy, and then through the challenging teenage years. Often this sacrifice continues into adulthood. Being a parent helps develop love as we put the needs of another person before our own. It helps us love someone more than ourselves.

Summary of Examples

- Charity, the pure love of Christ that never fails, is manifest by long suffering, kindness, and by avoiding envy, pride, and being easily provoked as described by Moroni.
- A relationship between leaders and followers that is based on love binds each level together to form a solid foundation for a productive organization, as demonstrated by the Father and

the Son, and as taught by Jesus when He said, "As the Father hath loved me, so have I loved you: continue ye in my love" (John 15:9).

- Honorable leaders teach and correct their followers in love, because of love, as Jesus did with the rich young man.
- The love between leaders and followers is not for short-term convenience or mutual benefit but is to last to the end, as demonstrated by Jesus who "loved them unto the end" (John 13:1).
- Honorable leaders and followers live their lives for each other, as Jesus does for His disciples and His disciples do for Him.
- Honorable leaders and followers develop a love for each other as they look for the good, as taught by George Albert Smith when he said, "You can find good in everyone if you will but look for it."
- Serving others develops love, as demonstrated by parents.

Questions for Personal Reflection

- How long does your love endure for those who seem to always fall short of your expectations?
- Is love your driving motive, as it is with the Savior?
- How many of those you lead would say they love you?
- How are you showing love for your leader to your associates?
- How are you fostering love among those you influence, rather than combativeness?
- Are you more concerned for the welfare and success of those you lead than for your own rank advancement?

Attribute 2: Pure in Motives

Motive: *Something that causes a person to act. A stimulus to action.*

The scriptures teach two basic motives of the Savior. The first is explained when He said, "Father, thy will be done, and the glory be thine forever" (Moses 4:2). Jesus expanded on this motive as He told the Jews, "I seek not mine own will, but the will of the Father" (John 5:30). A second motive was "to bring to pass the immortality and eternal life of man" (Moses 1:39). Surely, these are the purest of motives, to glorify His Father and bless the lives of His Father's children.

Overlooking the Sea of Galilee, Jesus taught His disciples about pure motives when He said, "Blessed *are* the pure in heart: for they shall see God" (Matthew 5:8). He could teach this because He lived it. As President David O. McKay taught, "The Savior's constant desire and effort were to implant in the mind right thoughts, pure motives, noble ideals knowing full well that right words and actions would inevitably follow."[6] All leaders would do well to follow the counsel of Nephi who taught that we should "follow the Son, with full purpose of heart, acting no hypocrisy and no deception before God, but with *real intent*" (2 Nephi 31:13, emphasis added).

There is never a hint in recorded scripture that Jesus had ulterior motives or sought personal glory. His perfectly pure heart will forever stand in stark contrast to that of the adversary who from the beginning had deceit infesting his heart. It was Satan, who in the Council in Heaven declared, "Behold, here am I, send me, I will be thy son, and I will redeem all mankind, that one soul shall not be lost, and surely I will do it; *wherefore give me thine honor*" (Moses 4:1, emphasis added). Lucifer's only motive was to bless himself. Jesus's motive was to bless everyone else.

Examples of Righteous Leaders

President Dallin H. Oaks, a modern Apostle, and himself an example of one with pure motives, taught that some motives are better than other motives. Regarding what motivates us to serve others, he describes a hierarchy of motives that gradually improve from good, to better, to best. They are:

1. Hope for earthly reward
2. Good companionship
3. Fear of punishment
4. Sense of duty
5. Hope for an eternal reward
6. Charity, the pure love of Christ[7]

The last of these motives can be described by what the scriptures call "a more excellent way" (1 Corinthians 12:31). It is the highest form of motivation. It is a sincere desire to bless the lives of others. Such was the desire of the sons of Mosiah. The scriptures record their pure love for their brethren, the Lamanites. "Now they were desirous that salvation should be declared to every creature, for they could not bear that any human soul should perish; yea, even the very thoughts that any soul should endure endless torment did cause them to quake and tremble" (Mosiah 28:3).

These sons had such pure motives that Mosiah granted them permission to embark on a dangerous but noble mission to bring Lamanites to Christ. Their mission was tremendously successful, and they improved the lives of many Lamanites. They emulated the attributes of Jesus such as; charity, confident, durable, courageous, diligent, initiates action, labors also, teaches, serves everyone, and so forth.

Summary of Examples

- Honorable leaders with pure motives give the acclaim for his successes to his leader who gave him the opportunity to serve in the first place, as Jesus did who said, "Father, thy will be done, and the glory be thine forever" (Moses 4:2).
- Honorable leaders with pure motives focus on the task he has been given, rather than the benefits from doing that task, as demonstrated by Jesus in bringing salvation to all.

- Honorable leaders help move their people up the hierarchy of good motives to better motives until they reach the purest of motives; that of charity, as taught by Elder Oaks.
- Honorable leaders with pure motives of charity and love can lead many people away from their lives of wickedness to lives of righteousness, as did the sons of King Mosiah.

Questions for Personal Reflection

- Are you honest with yourself about your true motives?
- Do you want to succeed for your own benefit rather than to cause a competitor to fail?
- Is your desire to be a leader motivated by love, and a sincere desire to help others?
- Did you join your organization because you believe in its objectives?
- Can you refrain from manipulating circumstances, facts, or other people to elevate yourself?
- When you speak of the struggles of another person, is it because you have a genuine desire to help, rather than a ploy to make them look bad?

Attribute 3: Authentic

Authentic: *Being actually and exactly what is claimed. Implies actual character not counterfeited, imitated, or adulterated. Conforming to an original so as to reproduce essential features.*

Jesus was exactly what He claimed to be, the literal Son of God. He was what He declared when He said, "I am the way, the truth, and the life" (John 14:6). He was the authentic reproduction of essential features of His Father and leader. He told Philip, "He that hath seen me hath seen the Father" (John 14:9). This was more than just a physical likeness but mirrored His purpose, priorities, and personality.

God the Father personally verified the authenticity of His Son, Jesus Christ. It was His voice sounding forth from "a bright cloud" that proclaimed, "This is my beloved Son, in whom I am well pleased; hear ye him" (Matthew 17:5). Those who did hear Jesus were taught that His works would authenticate Him as the Son of God and their rightful leader. He declared, "The works which the Father hath given me to finish, the same works that I do, *bear witness of me*, that the Father hath sent me" (John 5:36, emphasis added). He then added, "If I do not the works of my Father, believe me not" (John 10:37).

Jesus invited further scrutiny of His authenticity by encouraging people to "Search the scriptures . . . they are they which testify of me" (John 5:39). An even more dramatic invitation for scrutiny came when He appeared to the Nephites. The result was a perfect knowledge that He was who He said He was: He was the authentic Son of God.

"Arise and come forth unto me, that ye may thrust your hands into my side, and also that ye may feel the prints of the nails in my hands and in my feet, *that ye may know that I am the God of Israel*, and the God of the whole earth, and have been slain for the sins of the world.

"And it came to pass that the multitude went forth, and thrust their hands into his side, and did feel the prints of the nails in his hands and in his feet; and this they did do, going forth one by one until they had all gone forth, and did see with their eyes and did feel with their hands, and did know of a surety and did bear record, that it was he, of whom it was written by the prophets, that should come.

"And when they had all gone forth they *witnessed for themselves*" (3 Nephi 11:14–16, emphasis added).

Followers will always evaluate the authenticity of their leader because they do not want to follow an imposter. Sometimes it takes a while for a leader's true self to be revealed and when it is, followers must decide if they still are willing to follow. Many people followed Jesus because they "did eat of the loaves, and were filled" (John 6:26) but when He declared, "I am the living bread which came down from heaven" (John 6:51), they judged Him to be an imposter and "walked no more with him" (John 6:66). Unfortunately, they judged wrongly.

The scriptures show how Jesus taught His disciples about authenticity. In the parable of the talents, three servants were willing to do as their master requested, but only two proved authentic by increasing their master's worth. In the parable of the good Samaritan, the Samaritan showed authenticity because he was the only one who actually served his fellow man. By contrast, the Lord used the barren fig tree to show a lack of authenticity because its leaves announced that it had fruit when indeed it did not.

A lack of authenticity has destroyed many relationships, partnerships, and friendships. Some people act a certain way in an attempt to be successful, but their outward persona is no reflection of their underlying character. External influences such as illness, bankruptcy, stress, or persecution can break the façade and reveal the hidden character that often is much different than what is portrayed. Not so with Jesus. His authenticity was never more illuminated than during those dark hours on the cross, or in the lonely and deeply painful Gethsemane.

Those agonizing events did reveal His true, authentic self, and it was much greater than mortal understanding. Who else could say, during the greatest trials known to man, "Sleep on now, and take *your* rest" (Matthew 26:45) or, "Father, forgive them; for they know not what they do" (Luke 23:34). Yes, His true authentic character was revealed. He was exactly what He claimed to be, the very Son of God. This truth was amplified by the thunderous convulsion of nature itself that cried out as its creator paid the ultimate price that no counterfeit could pay.

One of the most difficult questions for all of us is if we are authentic. Is our view of ourselves accurate? Are we better than we present ourselves, or are we not as good? Would our spouse agree with our assessment? Would our boss, neighbor, siblings, or parents agree with who we represent ourselves to be? Or are we imposters?

Elder W. Eugene Hansen observed that soldiers have stripes on their shoulder and medals on their chest that broadcast their level of experience, knowledge, and accomplishments. These stripes and medals authenticate the soldier. By comparison, each of us earns stripes and medals as we gain life experience and knowledge. Often it takes a while for others to see our "stripes." They are less noticeable in civilian life, but they are just as real and important. Unfortunately, some people profess stripes they do not have, but those who have authentic stripes will find people are more likely to follow their lead.

Examples of Righteous Leaders

Being an authentic leader means you have paid the price to understand what you are asking others to do. Authenticity brings credibility and trust, which often are the attributes that persuades people to follow your lead. Elder Neal A. Maxwell exemplified the cost and the power of authentic leadership. The last eight years of his life was consumed by a battle with leukemia that was played out in the public eye. Despite the cost to himself, his battle led thousands of sufferers along their own personal journey through the refiner's fire. At one point in his journey, this noble Apostle received the sweet assurance from his Lord that his struggle had purpose, not just for his own refinement but for the others he would influence. The Spirit whispered to him, "I have given you leukemia that you might teach my people with authenticity."[8] Of his example, President Dallin H. Oaks, also of the Quorum of the Twelve Apostles, said of Elder Maxwell, "His courage, his submissive attitude in accepting his affliction with cancer, and his stalwart continued service have ministered comfort to thousands and taught eternal principles to millions. His example shows that the Lord will not only consecrate our afflictions for our gain, but He will use them to bless the lives of countless others."[9]

At Elder Maxwell's funeral, President Gordon B. Hinckley said: "He has accomplished more in these past eight years [of his illness] than most men do in a lifetime . . . He comforted, blessed, and encouraged his fellow sufferers. Their oppressive burdens were made lighter by this good Samaritan who bound up their wounds and brought the sunlight of hope into their lives . . . Like the Master whom he loved, he 'went about doing good'" (Acts 10:38).[10]

Another example of authenticity is George Frideric Handel, one individual who has influenced millions of people for over 250 years. He wrote almost 50 operas and nearly 30 oratorios, all of which lifted the souls of men and women, but it was his *Messiah* that has had the greatest influence. He acknowledged that this oratorio, largely composed in a three–week period, was guided by heaven for, "God has visited me."[11] This hallmark of his career came between two severe strokes and numerous financial and health related setbacks. Through his suffering, he became personally acquainted with the very Messiah who was at the center of this majestic composition.

Having experienced human suffering himself, "Handel stipulated that profits from . . . all future performances of *Messiah* 'be donated to prisoners, orphans, and the sick. I have myself been a very sick man, and am now cured,' he said. 'I was a prisoner, and have been set free.' Following the first London performance of Messiah, a patron congratulated Handel on the excellent 'entertainment.' To this, Handel replied, "My lord, I should be sorry if I only entertained them, I wish to make them better.'"[12] Spoken as the true leader he was, Handel used his influence to improve lives. Having become more like the Savior through his personal experiences, he lifted and continues to lift millions of people to the higher ground to which he was lifted.

Summary of Examples

- The authenticity of a leader is often testified of by his leader, as the Father did for Jesus.
- The authenticity of a leader is substantiated by the fruit of his labors, as taught and demonstrated by Jesus.
- The authenticity of a leader is further substantiated by close

examination of him personally, as demonstrated by Jesus serving among the Jews and the Nephites.

- The authentic leader has paid the price for personal understanding, as did Elder Neal A. Maxwell and George Frideric Handel.

Questions for Personal Reflection

- Are you truthful in your own self–evaluation?
- How real are the credentials you advertise?
- Does your outward persona reflect the same person as your true inward character?
- Do you recognize that your close associates know your true character better than you think they do?
- Have you paid the price to have wise understanding?
- Do you live the same gospel principles throughout the many situations you encounter each day as you profess to on Sundays?

Attribute 4: Selfless

Selfless: *Concerned more with the needs and wishes of others than with one's own. Having little or no concern for oneself, especially with regard to fame, position, money.*

The life of the Savior is a perfect example of a selfless leader. All that He did and all that He taught was for the benefit of others. He had already achieved greatness and perfection; He did not need to elevate Himself any higher. Instead, He took on a mission to elevate each of us and devoted His entire efforts to that selfless cause. His selflessness is revealed in His words, "I can of mine own self do nothing . . . because *I seek not mine own will,* but the will of the Father which hath sent me" (John 5:30, emphasis added).

Moroni reinforced this principle when he described charity as "the pure love of Christ" (Moroni 7:47). "And charity suffereth long, and is kind, and envieth not, and is not puffed up, *seeketh not her own*" (Moroni 7:45, emphasis added). This phrase, "seeketh not her own" suggests a selfless intent in the motives of those possessing charity.

The attribute of selflessness can be found in most of the actions and teachings of Jesus. For example, at the end of His 40–day fast, when He was "an hungred" (Matthew 4:2), the adversary came to tempt Him. After He cast Satan away, Jesus learned that John had been cast into prison. Instead of being concerned with His own needs, His thoughts turned outward toward John "*and he sent angels,* and behold *they* came and ministered unto [John]" (Joseph Smith Translation, Matthew 4:11).

Some of the most noteworthy examples of selflessness occurred towards the end of Jesus's life. These examples teach us that when we go through our own trials, we can be strengthened by focusing on the needs of others. One such example occurred in the upper room where the feast of the Passover was celebrated. Shortly after identifying Judas as His betrayer, Jesus focused on the needs of His faithful Apostles. Instead of anticipating the great suffering He would soon endure in Gethsemane,, He offered comforting words to these dear associates. He said, "Peace I leave with you, my peace I give unto you: not as the world giveth, give I unto you. Let not your heart be troubled, neither let it be afraid" (John 14:27). Jesus then offered His great intercessory prayer as He prayed for His disciples rather than for Himself.

The next example of selflessness came after His suffering in the Garden of Gethsemane. He was approached by "a band of men and officers from the chief priests and Pharisees" (John 18:3), who had come to take him. John records, "Then Simon Peter having a sword drew it, and smote the high priest's servant, and cut off his right ear" (John 18:10). Jesus, who must have been weakened by the suffering He just endured and knowing the time of His Crucifixion was fast approaching, set aside His own circumstances and addressed the wounded man. "And Jesus answered and said, Suffer ye thus far. And he touched his ear, and healed him" (Luke 22:51). One can only imagine the feelings of this healed man as he watched his healer being led away by men with "torches and weapons" (John 18:3).

Examples of Righteous Leaders

The life of a true leader is indeed the life of a selfless shepherd who lives and gives his life for his sheep. He does all that is in his power to lift, encourage, teach, and protect His sheep. Jesus and Joseph Smith both lived their lives for their sheep, and in the end, they even gave their life for them. President Thomas S. Monson tells the story of Joseph this way:

"In Carthage Jail he was incarcerated with his brother Hyrum and others. On June 27, 1844, Joseph, Hyrum, John Taylor, and Willard Richards were together there when an angry mob stormed the jail, ran up the stairway, and began firing through the door of the room they occupied. Hyrum was killed, and John Taylor was wounded. Joseph Smith's last great act here upon the earth was one of selflessness. He crossed the room, most likely thinking that it would save the lives of his brethren in the room if he could get out . . . and sprang into the window when two balls pierced him from the door, and one entered his right breast from without. He gave his life; Willard Richards and John Taylor were spared. 'Greater love hath no man than this, that a man lay down his life for his friends.'"[13]

50

The Prophet Joseph was selfless to the end, just as his mentor was, the Lord Jesus Christ. The character of their hearts and the integrity of their souls remained intact even as they gave their lives for their friends.

Elder David S. Baxter said, "Selfless service is a wonderful antidote to the ills that flow from the worldwide epidemic of self–indulgence. Some grow bitter or anxious when it seems that not enough attention is being paid to them, when their lives would be so enriched if only they paid more attention to the needs of others."[14] Not everyone has discovered this path to a more enriching life, but it has been found by some. For example, President Gordon B. Hinckley told of a group of selfless doctors and nurses who initiated action by providing neonatal resuscitation training to nearly 19,000 professionals in 2003. The result was saving thousands of babies.[15]

These leaders were just a small group of well–trained men and women who led out and used their influence to improve lives. These are they who do not draw attention to themselves but they do as Jesus taught, "Let your light so shine before men, that they may see your good works, and glorify your Father which is in heaven" (Matthew 5:16).

Jesus has shown us a better way. Through His selfless life, He has shown how to turn our thoughts and actions outward to serve others, rather than inward to serve ourselves. In doing so, He shared two great secrets to happiness. The first is when we lift others, we ourselves are lifted. The second is when we seek the happiness of others, we also find it ourselves.

Summary of Examples

- The selfless leader focuses outwardly on others, rather than inwardly on himself, as Jesus did repeatedly. Such as when He showed greater concern for John in prison, or when He focused on training the Twelve before His Crucifixion, or for the high priest's servant, or for the duty–bound soldiers.
- The selfless leader focuses on elevating each of his people

rather than himself, as Jesus did when He gave His intercessory prayer, or said, "Let not your heart be troubled" (John 14:27).

- The selfless leader serves others even when it is not convenient, as did Jesus and Joseph Smith.
- The selfless leader lives his life for others, as did Jesus and Joseph when they ministered unto their fellowmen.
- The selfless leader endures hardships and steps in to save his people, as did Jesus in Gethsemane and Joseph in Carthage.
- The selfless leader finds opportunities to serve rather than waiting to be asked, as did the doctors and nurses who provided neonatal resuscitation training.

Questions for Personal Reflection

- Are you willing to sacrifice some personal advancement so you can use your energies and resources for the advancement of those you hold dear?
- Can you help a friend in need when doing so takes away from addressing your own needs?
- Can you help others succeed without desiring any credit for their successes?
- Are you engaged in a noble cause to lift others, such as promoting literacy and education for everyone?

Attribute 5: Delights in the Success of Others

Delights: *Great joy or pleasure.*

In just five words, the Savior revealed much about His style of leadership. Those five words were "the glory be thine forever" (Moses 4:2). They were spoken to God the Father as His plan for our salvation was presented. Jesus had offered to be the sacrificial lamb required for that plan to be efficacious and deferred all the praise and glory that would come because of His efforts. In doing so, He demonstrated that a significant attribute of leadership is to delight in the success of others. He did not want or need the credit. He did not envy someone who did get the credit. Even though He would do much of the work required for the Plan of Salvation to succeed, His only desire was for His Father's success and our growth. This is in stark contrast to the natural man tendencies so common among us. The natural man desires to take credit that would lift us up in the eyes of others.

While preaching in Galilee, the Savior was approached by a leper who knelt down and beseeched Him to heal his leprosy. Jesus, moved with compassion, straightway healed him. Then He charged him to "say nothing to any man" (Mark 1:40–44). If the Savor had wanted to glorify Himself He would have given a much different response. Sometime later, Jesus was found ministering in the coasts of Decapolis, an area populated mainly by Greeks with a mix of Syrians, Arabs, and Jews. There, a deaf man was brought before Him to be healed. The Savior "took him aside from the multitude" and "straightway his ears were opened, and the string of his tongue was loosed, and he spake plain" (Mark 7:33). Then, "he charged them that they should tell no man" (Mark 7:35–36). Jesus could have displayed His power before a large multitude and glorified Himself. Instead, He ministered in private and asked that His works remain private.

Jairus was a prominent man in the community and a ruler of the synagogue. When his twelve–year–old daughter lay dying in his house, he came to the Savior, fell at His feet, and pleaded that He heal her. Jesus went to His house and "suffered no man to go in, save Peter, and James, and John, and the father and the mother of the maiden" (Luke

8:51). Again, He did not want a public spectacle. This was a private, sacred experience meant for a selected few. The Savior reached down and took the daughter by the hand, and she arose. The "parents were astonished: but he charged them that they should tell no man what was done" (Luke 8:56).

As these examples attest, the Savior did not seek credit for healing the sick, or any other miracles He performed. Rather than taking credit, He gave all the glory and thanks to His Father, the true source of His power. For example, when He was about to feed the 5,000 with five barley loaves and two small fish, He first paused to give thanks to His Heavenly Father (John 6:11). In doing so, He publicly acknowledged His Father rather than elevating Himself. Similarly, when He turned six pots of water into good wine in Cana of Galilee, He simply said to the servants, "draw out now" (John 2:8). This miracle was performed to help His mother be successful, for apparently, she was the host on this occasion. Jesus provided the needed help but did it privately, so that the "ruler of the feast" (John 2:9) and other guests were unaware of where the wine came from. Only a few close associates knew of His works.

Not only did the Savior avoid taking credit, He chastened those who did or those who did not defer credit to the proper source. Moses learned this lesson in the desert of Zin when the congregation of Israel was gathered together and there was no water for them or their animals. In desperation, "they gathered themselves together against Moses and against Aaron." Then, Moses and Aaron went "unto the door of the tabernacle of the congregation, and they fell upon their faces: and the glory of the Lord appeared unto them." Moses was told to take a rod and speak unto a rock and it would give water. Moses then took the rod, smote it twice and "water came out abundantly." Because Moses did not sanctify Jehovah "in the eyes of the children of Israel," he was chastened, "therefore ye shall not bring this congregation into the land which I have given them." It is likely this was an unintentional oversight by Moses but he had failed to acknowledge the true source of the miracle (see Numbers 20:1–11).

In addition to not seeking credit, leaders must avoid envying the success of others. Jesus was aware of the vicious nature of envy, for His life was shortened by its influence. When Pilate was considering the release of Jesus, he manifested his awareness of the nature of Jesus's accusers. Mark records, "But Pilate answered them, saying, Will ye that I release unto you the King of the Jews? For he knew that the chief priests had *delivered him for envy*" (Mark 15:9–10, emphasis added). Many leaders in power at the time of Christ had a resentful awareness of His capability and popularity. They envied Him because of His noble stature, wisdom, knowledge, and inherent power. They were afraid of Him and the masses He attracted.

During the earthly ministry of Jesus, there were two sources of power that seemed to exceed His. The first was Caesar who represented earthly rule, but instead of envying him, Jesus said to render to Caesar that which belonged to him. The second source of power was God the Father who represented heavenly rule. Jesus could have avoided any mention of His Heavenly Father, who was truly the one being greater than Himself. Instead, Jesus told the Jews, "My Father . . . is greater than all" (John 10:29). Later He said, "My Father is greater than I" (John 14:28). These are not statements made by someone whose heart is full of envy.

Following the Savior's 40–day fast, Satan came to tempt Him because he envied what Jesus had, and did everything possible to get Him to fall. Most leaders will face this same problem. They will be envied for what they have, for who they have become, and for what they have accomplished. It has been said that "jealousy is the tribute that mediocrity pays to success." This jealousy, spawned from envy, can consume all the energy and resources of those within its influence. Wise leaders can be perceptive to its corrosive influence and take precautionary and corrective action as needed. Then, they can harness the power of their people to become more successful in their endeavors.

Examples of Righteous Leaders

The story of Joseph and his brothers who sold him into Egypt is replayed daily in the lives of millions of people. It is replayed in business, education, politics, sports, and many homes. It is the story of one person who shines a little brighter than others, and then is extinguished lest he or she become a star employee or a ruler over them. The story of Joseph reveals that "Israel loved Joseph more than all his children, because he was the son of his old age: and he made him a coat of many colours" (Genesis 37:3). To make matters worse, Joseph shared with his family some dreams he had been given. These were interpreted to mean he would rule over them. Stephen, in the book of Acts, summarized what would happen next: "And the patriarchs, *moved with envy*, sold Joseph into Egypt" (Acts 7:9, emphasis added).

As this story is replayed over and over today, many capable people are quietly moved out of the spotlight by those who are envious. They destroy their reputations, make them unavailable for choice assignments, or dilute the esteem their leader has for them. Elder Jeffrey R. Holland gives this insight into envy: "It has been said that envy is the one sin to which no one readily confesses, but just how widespread that tendency can be is suggested in the old Danish proverb, 'If envy were a fever, all the world would be ill.' The parson in Chaucer's Canterbury Tales laments it because it is so far-reaching—it can resent anything, including any virtue and talent, and it can be offended by everything, including every goodness and joy. As others seem to grow larger in our sight, we think we must therefore be smaller. So, unfortunately, we occasionally act that way."[16]

Natural tendencies toward envy can be mitigated as we remember that each person has some gifts, but not all gifts. "For all have not every gift given unto them; for there are many gifts, and to every man is given a gift by the Spirit of God. To some is given one, and to some is given another, that all may be profited thereby" (D&C 46:11–12). Patience is an effective antidote for envy if we remember that while one person may shine now, we may yet have opportunities in the future. We are reminded of the familiar words, "To every *thing there is* a season, and a time to every purpose under the heaven" (Ecclesiastes 3:1). By removing envy from their own lives, leaders are better prepared to help remove it from others. Then, the energies of his or her people can go toward progression rather than retaliation. This can happen if the leader truly delights in the success of others.

Summary of Examples

- Honorable leaders give credit for their success to the one who gave them the opportunity to serve, as did the Savior when He said, "the glory be thine forever" (Moses 4:2).
- Honorable leaders who do not seek the credit often serve behind the scenes where no one is watching, as Jesus did when He performed His miracles.
- Honorable leaders need to be careful not to imply they are the source of good actions that originate from either their leader or subordinates, as demonstrated by Moses with the rock.
- A leader who is free from envy is not afraid of power going to another person, as it did to Caesar.
- A leader who is free from envy is not hesitant to acknowledge the greatness of his own leader, as Jesus did for His Father.
- A leader who is free from envy rejoices in the success of his people, as does Jesus.
- A leader who is free from envy does not maneuver to remove people who are a potential threat to his own power, as the patriarchs did to Joseph.
- A leader can minimize envy by avoiding "favored son" treatment as was given to Joseph of old.

Questions for Personal Reflection

- Can you listen to a person tell of their past accomplishments and refrain from "one–upping" them by telling of your even more grand accomplishments?
- Do you avoid any amount of "leveling" where you pull others who are successful down to a lower level?
- Can you be happy for the successes of those you lead without feeling resentful, especially if you feel you have not been properly acknowledged?
- Can you surround yourself with people more talented than you and be a help for their continued growth instead of a hindrance?

- When someone is called to serve in a position you would like to have, do you feel envy?
- Are you leading children to having feelings of appreciation rather than resentment for peers who accomplish great things?
- As your children succeed, can you keep the spotlight on them rather than the fine job you did in raising them?

---

1. Definitions used to define each attribute in this book come primarily from the *Merriam-Webster's Collegiate Dictionary, 11th edition.* These definitions are occasionally augmented by words or phrases from other dictionaries that include the *Riverside Webster's II Dictionary*, Dictionary.com, and the Oxford English Dictionary at oed.com. No other reference will be made for the remaining definitions in this book.

2. Matthew Cowley, *Conference Report*, April 1951, "Third Day—Solemn Assembly," 166.

3. William Shakespeare, *Two Gentlemen of Verona*, act 1, scene 2, line 31.

4. Benjamin Franklin. BrainyQuote.com, Xplore Inc, 2015. http://www.brainyquote.com/quotes/quotes/b/benjaminfr1034 55.html, accessed January 4, 2015.

5. Brian Kolodiejchuk, *Mother Teresa : Come Be My Light: The Private Writings of the Saint of Calcutta*, (2007).

6. David O. McKay, *Conference Report*, October 1951, "First Day—Morning Meeting," 4.

7. Dallin H. Oaks, "Why do We Serve?" *Ensign*, November 1984.

8. Bruce C. Hafen, *A Disciple's Life: The Biography of Neal A. Maxwell*, 2002, 562.

9. Dallin H. Oaks, "Give Thanks in All Things," *Ensign*, May 2003.

10. "Elder Neal Ash Maxwell: A Promise Fulfilled," *Ensign*, September 2004.

11. Stefan Zweig, *The Tide of Fortune: Twelve Historical Miniatures* (1940), 121. Cited in Spencer J. Condie, "Handel and the Gift of Messiah," *Ensign*, December 2010.

12. Donald Burrows, *Handel: Messiah* (1991), 28; Cited in "A Tribute to Handel," *Improvement Era*, May 1929, 574. Cited in Spencer J. Condie, "Handel and the Gift of Messiah," *Ensign*, December 2010.

13. Thomas S. Monson, "The Prophet Joseph Smith: Teacher by Example," *Ensign*, November 2005.

14. David S. Baxter, "Faith, Service, Constancy," *Ensign*, November 2006.

15. Gordon B. Hinckley, "I Was an Hungred, and Ye Gave Me Meat," *Ensign*, May 2004.

16. Geoffrey Chaucer, *The Canterbury Tales*, ed. Walter W. Skeat (1929), 534-35. Cited in Jeffrey R. Holland, "The Other Prodigal," *Ensign*, May 2002.

CHAPTER 6

HIS DEMEANOR

Attribute 6: Optimistic

Optimistic: *An inclination to put the most favorable construction upon actions and events or to anticipate the best possible outcome.*

Lehi explained to his young son Jacob that "there is an opposition in all things" (2 Nephi 2:11). The word opposition comes from the root *opposite* which means the Lord has created an environment where we can choose between opposites. Two of the most common opposites are optimism and pessimism. Some people adopt an optimistic view of life as they continually look for the more positive and happy sides of things, while others choose the pessimistic perspective.

Jesus displays optimism as He works "to bring to pass the immortality and eternal life of man" (Moses 1:39). He anticipates the best possible outcome for each of us as we implement His teachings in our lives. His very Atonement is a great expression of optimism. It is a gift He willingly offered because He believed many would take advantage of His sacrifice.

It was this optimistic view that led Jesus to say, "In my Father's house are many mansions. . . . I go to prepare a place for you" (John 14:2). He went ahead to prepare a place in anticipation that many would qualify for those mansions. However, He recognized that all would not immediately follow Him. Again, anticipating the best possible outcome, Jesus counseled His servants to keep trying. "For unto such shall ye continue to minister; *for ye know not but what they will return and repent,* and come unto me with full purpose of heart, and I shall heal them; and ye shall be the means of bringing salvation unto them" (3 Nephi 18:32, emphasis added).

In the parable of the mustard seed, Jesus taught that the kingdom of God was like a mustard seed, which is the smallest of seeds but can grow into the greatest of herbs. This optimistic view of the growth of His kingdom is parallel to His view of each of us. We are so small in our development but can grow into the greatest of people.

In a more recent time, Jesus continued this theme by helping His infant Saints to anticipate the best possible outcome when He said, "Ye cannot bear all things now; nevertheless, *be of good cheer,* for I will lead you along. The kingdom is yours and the blessings thereof are yours, and the riches of eternity are yours" (D&C 78:18, emphasis added). Given such humble and turbulent beginnings, it would have been hard for these early Saints to see the future greatness of the Lord's Kingdom. But with faith, they persevered and lent their efforts in building that which their leader anticipated.

Examples of Righteous Leaders

The Prophet Joseph knew that one of the important roles of a leader was to be optimistic even when things looked troubling. Throughout his life, he continually carried an air of optimism that helped his followers have the strength to endure their trials. On one occasion, he visited the home of his cousin, George Albert Smith, who was deeply afflicted with inflammatory rheumatism. This illness caused painful swelling in his legs, arm, and shoulder. In his journal, George recounts: "I suffered the most excruciating pain and although the winter was very cold I could suffer no clothes on me except a very light blanket. Cousin Joseph came to see me. I told him I was almost discouraged being afraid my joints would be drawn out. He told me I should never get discouraged whatever difficulties might surround me. If I was sunk in the lowest pit of Nova Scotia and all the Rocky Mountains piled in on top of me, I ought not to be discouraged but hang on, exercise faith and keep up good courage and I should come out on the top of the heap."[1]

This optimistic perspective helped George through his recovery and it kept the Saints moving forward in setting the foundation for the Kingdom of God on earth. Without optimism, that effort would have been even harder.

In more modern times, trials continue and so does the need for an optimistic leader. President Gordon B. Hinckley proclaimed, "I am an optimist! . . . My plea is that we stop seeking out the storms and enjoy more fully the sunlight. I am suggesting that as we go through life, we 'accentuate the positive.'"[2] Every situation in life has opposing dimensions, part is positive and part is negative. If we feed the positive, the negative seems to shrink from view. A leader who can encourage his or her people to be positive infuses them with energy and strength that are unavailable to the pessimist.

We all know that life can change in the blink of an eye. We also know that bad things happen to good people. In some cases, these good people use those bad things to become better people. In doing so, they become someone with tremendous influence. One such person is Becky Reeve who was a missionary serving with her whole heart when tragedy hit at 35 miles per hour.

Early one morning, she and her companion left their New Mexico apartment for the 100–mile journey to zone conference. There was a heavy frost on the road, so they proceeded carefully. Wanting to test the condition of the road, Sister Reeve gently touched her brakes and the car immediately began to fishtail. Soon the car left the road, flipped two and a half times, and landed on its top. Sister Reeve was ejected, landed on her head, broke her neck, and was permanently paralyzed. She is confined to a wheelchair but refuses to have her influence also confined to that wheelchair. She uses her experience to lift as many people as possible who are suffering from their own version of paralysis.

In her effort to influence others, she recorded this story in her book, *The Spirit Knows No Handicap*. In the preface of that book she said, "I heard the prophet Spencer W. Kimball in his closing remarks in the April 1979, general conference say, 'Seemingly small efforts in the life of each member could do so much to move the Church forward as never before.' These words sank deep into my heart and I wondered, *What could I do?* I decided to share some of my personal experiences, hoping that others might be strengthened by my testimony that you can trust the Lord, that even in a wheelchair life can be rich and rewarding if you want it to be, because the spirit knows no handicap."[3]

This is the Savior's way of leadership. It is using your influence to lead people to a better place. It is being optimistic, lifting vision, being courageous, and initiating action. The encouragement of President Kimball was a call for individual people to lead out and make a difference. Through his influence, he encouraged Becky Reeve to lead out and use her influence to bless the lives of as many people as she could. Through her optimistic attitude, the countless firesides, her book, and her personal ministry, she leads like the Savior and improves lives.

Summary of Examples

- It takes optimism to act as though each of your people can be successful, as Jesus does by striving "to bring to pass the immortality and eternal life of man" (Moses 1:39).
- It takes optimism to prepare for success rather than failure, as Jesus does by focusing on preparing mansions rather than prisons.
- It takes optimism to continue developing and serving your people even though progress may be hard to detect, as Jesus taught the Nephites to "continue to minister" unto them.
- It takes optimism to see great potential from a meager beginning like a mustard seed.
- It takes optimism to believe that despite tremendous odds things will work out, as Joseph Smith encouraged George Albert Smith.
- It takes optimism to turn personal tragedy into an opportunity to lift and encourage others, as Becky Reeve did following her paralyzing car accident.

Questions for Personal Reflection

- Do you view life as an opportunity rather than a trial?
- Do you view setbacks as learning experiences or as thieves of your happiness?

- Have you felt the energy–draining effects of negative comments from negative people?
- Do you influence others by portraying optimism during periods of great difficulty?
- Are people drawn to you because they feel good being around you?
- What are the blessings you enjoy by living in our current civilized society?
- When you encounter people complaining about the weather, the government, or other people, what have you done to lead them to positive thoughts?

Attribute 7: Cheerful

Cheerful: *Promoting or inducing cheer; pleasant; bright. Noticeably happy and optimistic.*

A leader who is cheerful goes beyond feeling optimistic inside, he displays that feeling on the outside for others to see. In this way, he promotes cheer and pleasantness in those around him. Proverbs gives us wise insight on the value of cheerfulness. "A merry heart maketh a cheerful countenance: but by sorrow of the heart the spirit is broken" (Proverbs 15:13). Also, "A merry heart doeth good *like* a medicine: but a broken spirit drieth the bones" (Proverbs 17:22). In addition, "Heaviness in the heart of man maketh it stoop: but a good word maketh it glad" (Proverbs 12:25).

Lehi taught his son Jacob, "Men are, that they might have joy" (2 Nephi 2:25). This must have been a refreshing doctrine to Jacob, who was Lehi's "first–born in the days of [his] tribulation in the wilderness" (2 Nephi 2:1). This tribulation was in part because he "suffered afflictions and much sorrow, because of the rudeness of [his] brethren" (2 Nephi 2:1). Not only did Jacob suffer, but many in his family also did, and each could have been encouraged by Lehi's words. Jacob's brother Nephi understood the principle of having joy and led his people to live "after the manner of happiness" (2 Nephi 5:27). He influenced them to build a stable foundation for their lives so that security could produce happiness. Happy people want to become better people and they want to do better things. Happy people more easily overcome the trials of life, and often turn misfortune into personal growth and understanding.

In the scriptures, we find the Lord's reassurance, "Wherefore, *be of good cheer,* and do not fear, for I the Lord am with you, and will stand by you" (D&C 68:6, emphasis added). He also said, "These things I have spoken unto you, that in me ye might have peace. In the world ye shall have tribulation: but *be of good cheer;* I have overcome the world" (John 16:33, emphasis added). These words surely strengthened the Apostle Paul who endured much because of his testimony of Christ. Despite great tribulation, he tried to remain cheerful.

"*We are* troubled on every side, yet not distressed; *we are* perplexed, but not in despair; Persecuted, but not forsaken; cast down, but not destroyed" (2 Corinthians 4:8–9). Undoubtedly, a cheerful heart was soothing medicine to an oft wounded soul.

There are many short quotes about being cheerful that circulate freely because of the constant need to avoid discouragement. Examples include, "A smile will increase your face value"; "If you are happy, don't forget to tell your face"; and "Some bring happiness wherever they go, others whenever they go." Also, "Wherever you go, no matter what the weather, always bring your own sunshine."[4] James Barrie, the author of *Peter Pan,* said, "Those who bring sunshine to the lives of others cannot keep it from themselves." And finally, "In the depth of winter, [we find] within [us] an invincible summer."[5] Poets and authors have brought us so much material to help us be cheerful. Now we need leaders who can incorporate this elevating attribute as they use their influence to bless lives.

Examples of Righteous Leaders

The Prophet Joseph Smith often lifted the hearts of the Saints during their times of trial. Usually he was enduring great difficulty himself such as when he was incarcerated in the Liberty Jail. From that cold and damp cellar, his thoughts were constantly with his people who also were suffering. Seeking to lift and encourage them, he wrote these words of encouragement, "Therefore, dearly beloved brethren, let us cheerfully do all things that lie in our power; and then may we stand still, with the utmost assurance, to see the salvation of God, and for his arm to be revealed" (D&C 123:17). Rather than complain to them about his plight, he sought to cheer them up and influence them to greater resiliency.

Stories of the strength, action, and influence of pioneer woman are many. They endured much, learned much, and taught much. One inspiring example is Mary Fielding Smith, widow of Hyrum Smith and mother of President Joseph F. Smith. President Smith recounted in his later years how one day during the exodus from Nauvoo, their journey west was in peril when their yoke of ox went missing near the Missouri river. Though just a young man, he searched feverishly for several hours with the aid of his uncle but could not find them. Then around noon, he came back to camp and found his mother, Mary, on her knees in fervent prayer.

Joseph F. Smith recorded, "When she arose from her knees I was standing nearby. The first expression I caught upon her precious face was a lovely smile which, discouraged as I was, gave me renewed hope and an assurance I had not felt before. A few moments later, Uncle Joseph Fielding came to camp, wet with the dews, faint, fatigued, and thoroughly disheartened. His first words were: 'Well, Mary, the cattle are gone!' Mother replied in a voice which fairly rang with *cheerfulness*, 'Never mind; your breakfast has been waiting for hours, and now, while you and Joseph are eating, I will just take a walk out and see if I can find the cattle.'"[6]

Mary Fielding Smith was led to find the cattle who were hidden in the bottom of a deep gulch near the river. Her family was then able to resume their journey to Zion. Mary was doing more than leading their journey, she was using her influence to mold her young son who one day would use his influence to guide millions of Saints as president of the Church. The role of motherhood is one of the greatest leadership positions in society but often is not recognized as such. If leadership really is using your influence to help others become better and do better, what greater example of a leader is there than a mother? Especially a cheerful mother who leads in the midst of deep trials as did Mary Fielding Smith.

The poet Ella Wheeler Wilcox wrote:

It is easy enough to be pleasant
When life flows by like a song
But the man worth while is one who will smile
When everything goes dead wrong.[7]

Martha Washington, wife of George Washington, held a similar view. She said, "I am still determined to be cheerful and to be happy in whatever situation I may be for I have learned from experience the greatest part of our happiness or misery depends upon our disposition and not upon our circumstances."[8] These great people remind us of this eternal truth: happiness and cheerfulness are a choice, and if chosen, lifts hearts and energizes souls.

Summary of Examples

- Mortality is designed for each person to be happy, as Lehi taught his son Jacob that "Men are, that they might have joy" (2 Nephi 2:25).
- It takes a cheerful demeanor to keep a happy heart in trying times, as Jesus taught His disciples and as Lehi taught his son Jacob.
- A happy life is built upon principles of stability and security, as taught by Nephi who led his people to live "after the manner of happiness" (2 Nephi 5:27).
- A cheerful heart can soften the effects of trials, as taught by Paul as he endured great tribulation.
- A cheerful demeanor should be a way of life that accompanies all our actions, as taught by Joseph Smith.
- A cheerful heart is more in tune to the promptings of the Holy Ghost, as demonstrated by Mary Fielding Smith.

Questions for Personal Reflection

- Can you portray cheerfulness even when you are feeling sick, hurt, overloaded, overlooked, rejected, attacked, or discouraged?
- Does your voice carry a cheerful tone?
- Can you cheer up yourself, or do you expect others to do it for you?
- Are you more cheerful at work or at church than at home? Do you come home and greet family cheerfully? Do you continue to be cheerful throughout the evening?
- Are you cheerful with those you lead, rather than projecting a "tough" image?

Attribute 8: Dignified

Dignified: *Showing a composed manner that is worthy of respect. Stately, formal reserve or seriousness of manner, appearance, or language.*

Those who have had personal association with Jesus would have noticed that He carried Himself with dignity that was worthy of respect. They would have noticed His composed and stately manner, whether He was walking along the seashore, climbing the steps of the temple, riding in triumphal entry into Jerusalem, kneeling in Gethsemane, or hanging on the cross at Calvary.

Elder Orson F. Whitney has given us a treasure as he described the appearance and demeanor of the Master from his own experience. In an account of his vision of the Lord in Gethsemane, Elder Whitney said, "He was of noble stature and of majestic mien [demeanor]—not at all the weak, effeminate being that some painters have portrayed—a very God among men, yet as meek and lowly as a little child."[9] When Elder Whitney viewed the Savior attempting to awaken His Apostles who were to watch with Him, His demeanor was "in a tone of tender reproach, untinctured by the least suggestion of anger or scolding."[10] There was no manifestation of impatience, annoyance, or condescending language. Even during His greatest trial, He remained dignified and noble.

When Nephi and his brother Lehi were imprisoned, they and those with them heard a voice from heaven. "And it came to pass when they heard this voice, and beheld that it was not a voice of thunder, neither was it a voice of a great tumultuous noise, but behold, it was *a still voice of perfect mildness*, as if it had been a whisper, and it did pierce even to the very soul" (Helaman 5:30, emphasis added). This is the voice of the Master. A dignified voice, stately and calm. A reflection of His life where He ministered with poise and lived without haste or anxiety.

The Gospel of Luke records the tender story of Jairus, "a ruler of the synagogue," who "fell down at Jesus's feet, and besought Him that he would come into his house: For he had one only daughter, about twelve years of age, and she lay a dying." The account then continues, "But as he went the people thronged him." While the throng pressed upon him, another woman with an "issue of blood . . . touched the border of his garment." Jesus stopped to minister to her, "And he said unto her, Daughter, be of good comfort: thy faith hath made thee whole; go in peace." There is no indication that Jesus was annoyed with her or that He was busily hurrying to His next appointment. After He ministered to her needs, He continued walking toward the young woman's bedside when word was received that she had died. Again, in a dignified, calm, and reassuring manner He simply said, "Fear not: believe only, and she shall be made whole" (Luke 8:41–44, 48, 50).

When Jesus learned that His friend Lazarus was sick, He "abode two days still in the same place where he was" (John 11:6). By the time He arrived at where His friend lay, Lazarus had been dead four days. Again, Jesus remained calm and measured, for there were lessons He would teach from this situation. One lesson was that a leader can soothe and stabilize others as He portrays dignity and poise during tragedy.

Before cleansing the temple of moneychangers, Jesus visited the temple the night before. His dissatisfaction with the activities going on in His Father's house must have bothered Him for months. Now it was time to teach the Jews the sanctity of the temple. Surely, He determined in His mind what actions He would take the following day. He then retired with His disciples in Bethany for the evening. The next day He returned to Jerusalem and cleansed the temple of those activities that defiled it. He did not act in haste or in an uncontrollable fit of anger. He acted with dignified strength and measured actions as He removed the impurities and taught the doctrine of holiness (Mark 11:11–15).

One of the great challenges for leaders is to stay calm and dignified through the storms of life. People take their cues from their leaders and stability breeds stability. The Savior demonstrated such dignified stability and poise in a real-life storm on a windswept sea. This account has become an oft-quoted story to show how a leader restores calm during great turbulence.

"And when he was entered into a ship, his disciples followed him.

"And, behold, there arose a great tempest in the sea, insomuch that the ship was covered with the waves: but he was asleep.

"And his disciples came to *him*, and awoke him, saying, Lord, save us: we perish.

"And he saith unto them, Why are ye fearful, O ye of little faith? Then he arose, and rebuked the winds and the sea; and there was a *great calm* "(Matthew 8:23–26, emphasis added).

Leaders do not restore calm during a storm by being a storm themselves. They are first dignified and calm, then use that calming influence to tame the great tempests of life.

When Jesus was brought before Pilate with His life hanging in the balance, He again demonstrated great dignity by keeping His actions measured and controlled. Standing with poise and strength and covered with humility, He quietly withheld His defense of Pilate's charges, thereby setting the stage for His Crucifixion.

"And when he was accused of the chief priests and elders, *he answered nothing.*

"Then said Pilate unto him, Hearest thou not how many things they witness against thee?

"And he answered him to never a word; insomuch that the governor marvelled greatly" (Matthew 27:12–14, emphasis added).

The dignity that He carried during His life was not abandoned in His final hours. What example of nobility did He give to those who scourged His body in the cold dungeons of the wicked? What dignity did the crowds observe as the cruel crown was driven down into His scalp? How stately did He wear the robe of mockery? Surely, each who witnessed His final hours saw the majesty of the King of kings even as He was confined in chains, nailed to a cross, and hung in the most undignified manner. That image of greatness amid suffering must have been burned deep into their minds to be remembered all their days.

Examples of Righteous Leaders

In November of 1838, the Prophet Joseph Smith and several of his associates where imprisoned in a cold, unfinished court house in

Richmond. There they were surrounded by guards that Parley P. Pratt described as "composed generally of the most noisy, foul–mouthed, vulgar, disgraceful rabble that ever defiled the earth."[11] In that deplorable, wretched condition, these noble leaders were subjected to immense physical and emotional abuse as the jailers boastfully told of the atrocities being committed against the Saints. It was in this setting that Elder Pratt, who also was incarcerated, described the Prophet Joseph as showing great dignity as he stood up in defense of his beloved people.

"On a sudden he arose to his feet, and spoke in a voice of thunder, or as the roaring lion, uttering, as near as I can recollect, the following words: 'SILENCE, ye fiends of the infernal pit. In the name of Jesus Christ I rebuke you, and command you to be still; I will not live another minute and bear such language. Cease such talk, or you or I die THIS INSTANT!'

"He ceased to speak. He stood erect in terrible majesty. Chained, and without a weapon; calm, unruffled and dignified as an angel, he looked upon the quailing guards, whose weapons were lowered or dropped to the ground; whose knees smote together, and who, shrinking into a corner, or crouching at his feet, begged his pardon, and remained quiet till a change of guards.

"I have seen the ministers of justice, clothed in magisterial robes, and criminals arraigned before them, while life was suspended on a breath, in the Courts of England; I have witnessed a Congress in solemn session to give laws to nations; I have tried to conceive of kings, of royal courts, of thrones and crowns; and of emperors assembled to decide the fate of kingdoms; but dignity and majesty have I seen but *once*, as it stood in chains, at midnight, in a dungeon in an obscure village of Missouri."[12]

This single act of demonstrating dignity, strength, and courage during great tribulation set an example that has emboldened countless others, both contemporaries, and future generations.

Consider another prophet many years later who demonstrated dignity in another difficult situation. That prophet was President Howard W. Hunter and the date was February 7, 1993. President

Hunter was standing at the rostrum in front of some 17,000 students assembled at the Brigham Young University Marriott Center. He was addressing a worldwide audience when a 27–year–old man rushed to his side with a briefcase he said contained a bomb. He held what he claimed to be a detonator to President Hunter's head and demanded he read a three–page letter releasing the Quorum of the Twelve Apostles and proclaiming himself as the new head of the Church in place of President Hunter. But things went differently than planned.

President Hunter just stood still, looking neither to the right nor left but stood resolute in dignity and with calmness. Almost immediately the congregation began singing the beloved hymn, "We Thank Thee, O God, For a Prophet." This singing caught the young man off guard, and he was apprehended by several students and then by security personnel. Without missing a beat, President Hunter then delivered his intended message, titled "An Anchor to the Souls of Men." As he did so, he personally demonstrated how strong, dignified leadership can be an anchor to the souls of men.

Summary of Examples

- It takes a dignified leader to remain poised and stately during trials, as Jesus was in Gethsemane.
- It takes a dignified leader to portray dignity even in speech, as Jesus did to the imprisoned Nephi and Lehi.
- It takes a dignified leader to be unruffled when others in distress are clamoring for attention, as was Jesus when the woman "touched the border of his garment" (Luke 8:44).
- It takes a dignified leader to remain calm when tragedy strikes, as Jesus did when Lazarus died.
- It takes a dignified leader to take bold, decisive action while maintaining self–control, as Jesus did when cleansing the temple.
- It takes a dignified leader to be calm and in control during turbulent storms in life, as demonstrated by Jesus upon the windswept sea.

- It takes a dignified leader to be poised when under attack, as Jesus did before Pilate and President Hunter before an assailant.

Questions for Personal Reflection

- Have you influenced others by remaining poised and restrained while being criticized?
- Do you carry an air of confidence and self–control while still being approachable?
- Have you ever calmed an unruly person or ended an argument by intervening with composure and dignity?
- When you find you have been misrepresented or undermined by another person, can you keep your composure both in your immediate and long–term responses?
- Can you respond to disappointment with dignity?
- Can you portray cheerfulness in a dignified manner?

Attribute 9: Approachable

Approachable: *Accessible and easy to meet or deal with. Friendly and easy to talk to.*

The Savior demonstrates His approachability with one simple and welcoming invitation, "Come unto me" (Matthew 11:28). With out-stretched arms, He signals that the greatest of all is accessible to the least of all. And He is always accessible whether day or night. This need to be constantly accessible was taught by Jesus to His disciples as part of a lesson on prayer. This lesson started when He offered what is now known as "The Lord's Prayer." Jesus then gave the parable of the friend at midnight (Luke 11:5–8) to teach that through prayer, we can always approach the throne of God whenever we are in need. The Savior's message was that in order for leaders to influence others, they need to be both approachable and accessible, even at inconvenient times.

In this parable, Jesus taught that God "is available at any time and under any circumstance, to respond to our earnest petitions. He will do what is necessary to help us, when we go to him with honest and sincere hearts, even if we have put off or delayed approaching him."[13] Nephi taught that Jesus, like His Father, is always welcoming and approachable as well. He said, "Behold, doth he cry unto any, saying: Depart from me? Behold, I say unto you, Nay; but he saith: Come unto me all ye ends of the earth, buy milk and honey, without money and without price" (2 Nephi 26:25). The invitation has been made, the arms have been opened, and His voice is welcoming. Now we only need to approach Him and allow ourselves to be influenced by Him. The hour is never too late nor is His schedule too busy.

Throughout His Judean ministry, Jesus was approachable to individuals as well as to large groups. He was approachable for Nicodemus and for the rich young man who visited Him by night. He was approachable for the woman who touched the hem of His garment as He walked through the crowd. He also was approachable to the 5,000 and many other large groups who came to hear Him preach. Today, He continues to be approachable for He says, "draw near unto me, and I will draw near unto you" (D&C 88:63). Those who accept this invitation will receive His influence in helping them become better and do better than ever before.

Following His Crucifixion, Jesus immediately began to make Himself accessible to His followers who had endured so much because of their love for Him. When He appeared to His disciples in Jerusalem, they were understandably "terrified and affrighted, [for they] supposed that they had seen a spirit" (Luke 24:37). He responded warmly by inviting them to approach Him when He said, "Behold my hands and my feet, that it is I myself: handle me, and see; for a spirit hath not flesh and bones, as ye see me have" (Luke 24:39).

A similar experience occurred in the Americas when He visited those gathered in the Land Bountiful. He beckoned to them and said,

"Arise and come forth unto me, that ye may thrust your hands into my side, and also that ye may feel the prints of the nails in my hands and in my feet, that ye may know that I am the God of Israel, and the God of the whole earth, and have been slain for the sins of the world.

"And it came to pass that the multitude went forth, and thrust their hands into his side, and did feel the prints of the nails in his hands and in his feet; and this they did do, going forth one by one until they had all gone forth, and did see with their eyes and did feel with their hands, and did know of a surety and did bear record, that it was he, of whom it was written by the prophets, that should come.

"And when they had all gone forth and had witnessed for themselves, they did cry out with one accord, saying:

"Hosanna! Blessed be the name of the Most High God! And they did fall down at the feet of Jesus, and did worship him" (3 Nephi 11:14–17).

Jesus continued this invitation when He said, "And ye see that I have commanded that none of you should go away, but rather have commanded that ye should come unto me, that ye might feel and see" (3 Nephi 18:25). The Savior does not send any away who wish to come to Him. He welcomes them whenever they feel the need to approach Him. Then He can use His influence to lift and guide them.

Examples of Righteous Leaders

The Prophet Joseph Smith emulated the approachability of Jesus as he made himself available to everyone, friend and foe, elderly and young, saint and sinner. His accessibility was thought by some to be a weakness. They felt a prophet and leader should be somewhat aloof. Speaking of Joseph, President Dallin H. Oaks said, "the Joseph Smith I met in my reading and personal research was a man of the frontier—young, emotional, dynamic, and so loved and approachable by his people that they often called him 'Brother Joseph.'"[14] Joseph knew that if you want to influence others, you must be approachable and accessible as was Jesus.

Summary of Examples

- It takes approachability for followers to feel comfortable in coming to their leader even when it is inconvenient, as taught by Jesus in the parable of the friend at midnight.
- It takes approachability for a leader to allow his followers to get to know him personally, as Jesus did with Nicodemus, the rich young man, and others.
- It takes approachability for a leader never to send a follower away, even when busy, as demonstrated by Jesus with the woman who touched the hem of His garment.
- It takes approachability for a leader to be available to everyone, whether friend or foe, saint or sinner, as demonstrated by Joseph Smith throughout his life.

Questions for Personal Reflection

- How often do family members or friends approach you at inconvenient times, such as late at night?
- When was the last time you delayed an important appointment to give personal attention to someone in need?
- Are you reclusive or welcoming?
- Do you put on an air of importance that tells others to keep their distance?

- Can you make a less talented person feel like a peer during your interactions?
- Do you avoid being associated with a restrictive clique?
- How often do people of other faiths come to you for association?

Attribute 10: Inclusive

Inclusive: *Comprehensive embracing. A relation between two classes that exists when all members of the first are also members of the second. Not excluding any section of society or any party involved in something.*

In three simple words, the Lord issued an all–inclusive invitation to "Come unto me" (Matthew 11:28). This invitation did not exclude anyone, for "he inviteth them all to come unto him and partake of his goodness; and he denieth none that come unto him, black and white, bond and free, male and female; and he remembereth the heathen; and all are alike unto God, both Jew and Gentile" (2 Nephi 26:33). He goes even a step further when teaching the Nephites, "And ye see that I have commanded that *none of you should go away,* but rather have commanded that ye should come unto me, that ye might feel and see; even so shall ye do unto the world" (3 Nephi 18:25, emphasis added).

Jesus invites all to learn of Him and emulate His ways. He said, "I the Lord am willing to make these things known unto all flesh . . . For I am no respecter of persons" (D&C 1:34–35). He "eateth . . . with publicans and sinners" (Matthew 9:11). He taught the wealthy young man, the leper, the learned, the powerful, the blind, the Samaritan, and the Jew. He taught His disciples to follow His example and be inclusive as well. He said, "But when thou makest a feast, call the poor, the maimed, the lame, the blind" (Luke 14:13). His desire was to encircle His arms around everyone, for "all men are privileged the one like unto the other, and none are forbidden" (2 Nephi 26:28).

In addition, Jesus taught, "let not the head say unto the feet it hath no need of the feet; for without the feet how shall the body be able to stand? Also the body hath need of every member, that all may be edified together, that the system may be kept perfect" (D&C 84:109–110). This is the challenge to leaders, to help all in the organization have a place of worth and to function fully in that place. Their role is to create a relation between various classes, such as the head and the feet, so that all members feel included. This is the pattern set by the

Master Shepherd who includes everyone in His invitation to be a part of His fold, that all "may be edified together" (D&C 84:110).

Examples of Righteous Leaders

In the Book of Mormon, the prophet Alma explained that he had been called to preach the Gospel of Christ to everyone, for none were to be excluded. He said, "And now I say unto you that this is the order after which I am called, yea, to preach unto my beloved brethren, yea, and every one that dwelleth in the land; yea, to preach unto all, both old and young, both bond and free; yea, I say unto you the aged, and also the middle aged, and the rising generation; yea, to cry unto them that they must repent and be born again" (Alma 5:49).

Alma had been called to represent Christ and teach His gospel to all within his reach because the Savior desires to influence everyone. He set the pattern of inclusion for us to emulate in all our dealings with our fellow man.

Summary of Examples

- An inclusive leader reveals all he can to each person without regard to rank or tenure, as Jesus did, for He was "no respecter of persons" (D&C 1:34–35; Acts 10:34).
- An inclusive leader does not turn away anyone who wishes to join with him, as taught by Jesus to the Nephites when He said, "none of you should go away" (3 Nephi 18:25).
- An inclusive leader associates with everyone from top management down to entry level people, as Jesus did who ate "with publicans and sinners" (Matthew 9:11).
- An inclusive leader associates with those of all levels of accomplishment, as Jesus did with the learned men in the temple as well as the "poor, the maimed, the lame, the blind" (Luke 14:13).

Questions for Personal Reflection

- Are you willing to include in your circle of friends those who need your help more than you need their help?
- Do you draw others to you who are in different circumstances than you, such as those who are single, childless, younger, older, less educated, and so forth?
- Are you able to accept those of more or less ability and position into your circle of friends?
- Whom among your peers can you draw into your circle of influence?
- When was the last time you led out and forgave someone who had offended you and allowed them back into your friendship?

Attribute 11: Friendly

Friendly: *Kind and pleasant, accommodating. Showing kindly interest and goodwill. Inclined to approve, help, or support rather than being hostile or at variance.*

In one short, four–word sentence, Jesus taught much about the relationship between leaders and followers. He simply said, "ye are my friends" (D&C 84:63). This statement shows a feeling of acceptance, unity, and respect. Clearly, we are not on equal footing with Him, He knows that and we know that, but He is fostering a relationship of inclusiveness. Jesus allows us to have self–respect because it is difficult to grow in an intimidating and groveling environment.

Jesus taught how relationships should be established on love and friendly feelings when he gave "the great commandment."

"This is my commandment, That ye love one another, as I have loved you.

"Greater love hath no man than this, that *a man lay down his life for his friends.*

"*Ye are my friends,* if ye do whatsoever I command you.

"Henceforth I call you not servants; for the servant knoweth not what his lord doeth: but *I have called you friends;* for all things that I have heard of my Father I have made known unto you" (John 15:12–15, emphasis added).

By acknowledging us as His friends, Jesus demonstrates a relationship between leader and follower that is so different than what many leaders practice. It is, however, consistent with the teachings of the prophet Jacob who encouraged his people to "Think of your brethren like unto yourselves, and be familiar with all" (Jacob 2:17). This type of relationship places the leader out among the people where his or her influence can be felt rather than in the elevated chambers of isolationism. It also creates a better environment for growth during difficulty. Joseph Smith once lamented, "I will try to be contented with my lot, knowing that God is my friend. In Him I shall find comfort."[15] One may ask, "How many of us find friendship with our leaders?" Those who can say "yes" have a leader who has developed the proper setting for enhanced performance and growth.

Examples of Righteous Leaders

One of the great leaders in the old world was King David. Through his influence, he united all of Israel and led them to their greatest strength and prosperity. Before becoming king, David developed his leadership skills first as a young shepherd and then as a courageous opponent to Goliath. His influence expanded greatly when King Saul placed him "over the men of war" (1 Samuel 18:5). There was something unique about David and his leadership. The Bible states "he was accepted in the sight of all the people" (1 Samuel 18:5) and "all Israel and Judah loved David" (1 Samuel 18:16). Yes, he was a hero for defeating Goliath, but there seems to be more that led all people to love him and unite behind him. We know "David behaved himself more wisely than all the servants of Saul" (1 Samuel 18:30) but still, it seems there was more. It appears David also had the ability to be friendly with those he led and he became a beloved leader among them.

David's friendship with Jonathan, King Saul's son forms one of the great stories of friendships in all scripture. Jonathan was in line to the throne but because he loved David "as his own soul" (1 Samuel 18:3), he took off his royal robe, his garments, his sword, his bow, and his girdle, and gave them all to David. This was done as an expression and a covenant of their friendship (1 Samuel 18:4). Even when Saul sought David's life, Jonathan defended him and protected him. Later, Jonathan's love for David was expressed when he said, "The Lord shall be between you and me, and between your children and my children forever" (1 Samuel 20:42). What better expression of friendship could he have given? Jonathan demonstrated the application of the words found in Proverbs, "A friend loveth at all times" (Proverbs 17:17).

Today, in a Church setting, there are many ways to foster a friendly atmosphere. For example, one Relief Society president felt she could use her influence to foster friendships among her neighbors. She asked each woman in the neighborhood to write something nice about

10 other women in the neighborhood. Perhaps they noticed some characteristic or action they appreciated, or maybe they had been recipients of their goodwill and kindness. These comments were then compiled into one personal letter for each woman. Remarkably, each woman in the neighborhood received comments from many different people so that each personalized letter contained several uplifting and encouraging comments. Actual statements from these anonymous letters are as follows:

- "You see the best in others."
- "You come from a large family and learned that by working together the job can get done more quickly."
- "You always make me laugh, and I love talking to you."
- "You make everyone feel like they are your friend."
- "You are a great friend who is easy to talk to, who listens and loves me for who I am."
- "You emulate so many qualities of the Savior."
- "You make people a priority. [You are] loving, caring, serving, [and] everyone's friend."
- "You make me feel like we've been best friends for years, even when I first met you."
- "You are talented at taking something simple and making it gorgeous."
- "You are a great mother . . . it's obvious your children adore you."
- "I love that you are a fun mom and can play with your children."
- "You are a down-to-earth girl who can relate to everyone."
- "I love hearing about your life experiences."
- "You are so much fun to be around that you always draw a crowd."
- "I have never heard you say a negative thing about anyone."
- "I know you have had your share of trials, but through whatever you deal with in life, you exude joy!"
- "You are such a cute mom."
- "You always have a smile and care about how I am doing."

- "Happiness and joy! That's what I feel from you."
- "Everyone feels better after spending any time with you."

The results were as expected; many women shed tears of appreciation as they read their letters repeatedly. Smiles were plentiful and happiness was expressed on every face and in every heart. One sister framed her letter and hung it on her wall so she could be reminded daily of the special characteristics others saw in her. A simple project perhaps, but through it, one leader brought a neighborhood together in friendship.

Summary of Examples

- A friendly leader is friendly to each person, even though they are not as capable, experienced, or of similar rank, as Jesus demonstrates with each of us.
- A friendly leader is one whose followers will find comfort in, as Joseph found comfort in God.
- A friendly leader is friendly even to those who may be promoted over them, as Jonathan was to David.
- A friendly leader creates an environment where others can draw together in friendship, as demonstrated by the Relief Society President.

Questions for Personal Reflection

- Do you still make new friends as you did when you were younger?
- Do you lead by taking the first step in bringing others inside the circle of your influence?
- How often are you friendly with those of other beliefs or lifestyles?
- What do you know about the personal lives of those lower in your organizational chart?
- Can you disagree without being disagreeable?
- Can you be friendly to both those who can benefit you and those who have seemingly nothing to offer you?

- Do you take the lead by being friendly first to people you meet each day such as fellow commuters?
- How well do you refrain from taking advantage of others by trying to get the best seats or move to the head of the ticket line?

Attribute 12: Patient

Patient: *Able to accept or tolerate delays, problems, or suffering without becoming annoyed or anxious. Steadfastness despite opposition, difficulty, or adversity.*

Abraham gives one of the most detailed accounts of the creation of the world. At one point in that narrative he records, "And the Gods watched those things which they had ordered *until they obeyed*" (Abraham 4:18, emphasis added). This seems to suggest the Gods put into motion a process that took some time for the things they ordered to come together. There is no hint of impatience but rather an understanding of the developmental process. They remained watchful and patiently allowed all things to take their normal course.

This practice of allowing things to take their normal course is beautifully described in the Lord's parable of the barren fig tree. The parable begins: "A certain man had a fig tree planted in his vineyard; and he came and sought fruit thereon, and found none" (Luke 13:6). Fig trees grow slowly, "taking several years to bear fruit. After the tree in the parable has grown to the point that it should have become a fruit-bearing tree, the owner of the vineyard gives it yet another three years to produce fruit, but it does not."[16] So the owner directs the tree to be cut down, but his servant asks for more time by saying, "Let it alone this year also" (Luke 13:8). The servant promises to continue nourishing the tree and appears to gain approval from his patient Lord.

The patience that the Lord showed for his barren fig tree symbolizes the patience Jesus has for each of us as He waits for our fruit to become manifest. It is this patience that James was referring to as he tried to get the early Saints to be patient for the Lord's Second Coming. He said, "Be patient therefore, brethren, unto the coming of the Lord. Behold, the husbandman waiteth for the precious fruit of the earth, and hath long patience for it" (James 5:7).

Those privileged to live in Jerusalem during the days of Jesus witnessed His tender patience. He taught them on the Mount, along the seashore, in their homes, and in the temple. He taught them and then patiently awaited their acceptance of His message. The Gospel of Matthew contains the tender feelings of a patient teacher who laments that His message was largely ignored. "O Jerusalem, Jerusalem, *thou that killest the prophets, and stonest them which are sent unto thee, how often would I have gathered thy children together,* even as a hen gathereth her chickens under *her* wings, and ye would not" (Matthew 23:37, emphasis added).

The Savior continually invites us to gather into His flock. With everlasting patience, He reaches out for "mine arm is lengthened out all the day long, saith the Lord God of Hosts" (2 Nephi 28:32).

Examples of Righteous Leaders

Jesus demonstrated and taught patience as He restored His gospel through a young fourteen-year-old boy. Following His appearance to Joseph Smith in the Sacred Grove, He had Joseph wait patiently for three long years before additional divine communication came. Then, Joseph waited patiently for another four years before being allowed to take possession of the gold plates and fulfill his assignment to translate that ancient record.

A few years later after the Church was established, Joseph led a large number of persecuted Saints to the banks of the Mississippi River where they turned swamps into the beautiful city of Nauvoo. Shortly after arriving, and while the city was still a swamp, these impoverished exiles were asked by the Lord to build a temple unto Him. However, the Lord showed patience because of the difficulty of their circumstances by granting them "sufficient time" to become settled. He said, "For this ordinance [baptism for the dead] belongeth to my house, and cannot be acceptable to me, only in the days of your poverty, wherein ye are not able to build a house unto me. But I command you, all ye my saints, to build a house unto me; and *I grant unto you a sufficient time* to build a house unto me; and during this time your baptisms shall be acceptable unto me" (D&C 124:30–31, emphasis added).

It is significant that when Jesus gave the Saints the assignment to build the temple, He allotted sufficient time to complete the task. This follows the pattern in the Old Testament, "when once the *longsuffering of God* waited in the days of Noah, while the ark was a preparing" (1 Peter 3:20, emphasis added). Jesus patiently took into account the difficulty of these tasks and the availability of resources. Ultimately, Noah built his ark and saved his family, and the Saints constructed their temple and received the promised blessings.

Summary of Examples

- A patient leader waits for things to take their normal course, as the Gods did during the Creation.
- A patient leader gives additional time if needed for full maturity to occur, as did the certain man with the fig tree.
- A patient leader factors in the ability and circumstances of his people when he gives them an assignment; then allows sufficient time to complete it, as Jesus did for the Saints to build the Nauvoo Temple, and for Noah to build the ark.

Questions for Personal Reflection

- How do you know when you have been patient long enough?
- How well are you delaying personal gratification by getting your education and other priorities before purchasing the niceties of life?
- Can you delay deadlines when you see your group is doing their best and still coming up short?
- Can you be patient while others learn from their mistakes?
- Have others in a checkout line been patient and pleasant by following your example?
- How calm are you when delayed by road construction or impacted by impatient drivers?

Attribute 13: Compassionate

Compassion: *A feeling of deep sympathy and sorrow for another who is stricken by misfortune, accompanied by a strong desire to alleviate the suffering.*

In many ways, the definition of compassion defines the whole mission of the Savior. He continually demonstrates deep sympathy and a desire to comfort those suffering by filling their souls with peace. The Gospel of Mark records that Jesus "had compassion upon all men" (Joseph Smith Translation, Mark 7:23). Jesus said to the Nephites, "Behold, my bowels are filled with compassion toward you" (3 Nephi 17:6). That compassion was manifest throughout His ministry.

"And Jesus went about all the cities and villages, teaching in their synagogues, and preaching the gospel of the kingdom, and healing every sickness and every disease among the people.

"But when he saw the multitudes, *he was moved with compassion on them,* because they fainted, and were scattered abroad, as sheep having no shepherd" (Matthew 9:35–36, emphasis added).

When Jesus learned about the beheading of John the Baptist, "he departed thence by ship into a desert place apart: and when the people had heard *thereof,* they followed him on foot out of the cities. And Jesus went forth, and saw a great multitude, and was *moved with compassion* toward them, and he healed their sick" (Matthew 14:13–14, emphasis added). Although He sought solitude and solace following the death of a great prophet and friend, He showed compassion toward those who sought it from Him. When Lazarus died, His compassion toward Mary led the Jews to marvel as they witnessed the depth of His tender feelings.

"Then when Mary was come where Jesus was, and saw him, she fell down at his feet, saying unto him, Lord, if thou hadst been here, my brother had not died.

"When Jesus therefore saw her weeping, and the Jews also weeping which came with her, he groaned in the spirit, and was troubled,

"And said, Where have ye laid him? They said unto him, Lord, come and see.

"Jesus wept.

"Then said the Jews, *Behold how he loved him!*" (John 11:32–36, emphasis added).

This compassion was not limited to those close to Him. It reached out to all because of the depth of His love. To the woman taken in adultery, He said, "Neither do I condemn thee" (John 8:11). To the Canaanite woman, He healed her daughter even though His mission was only to the house of Israel (Matthew 15:22–28). To His Apostles who were with Him in Gethsemane, He showed compassion even though they could "not watch with Him one hour."[17] He said with understanding, "the spirit indeed is willing, but the flesh is weak" (Matthew 26:40–41). To the soldiers who crucified Him and treated Him cruelly, He showed compassion and prayed, "Father, forgive them; for they know not what they do" (Luke 23:34).

Jesus began His triumphal entry from Bethphage, a hamlet between Jericho and Jerusalem. As He approached Jerusalem with a "very great multitude" (Matthew 21:8), "he beheld the city, and *wept over it*" (Luke 19:41, emphasis added). Luke tells us He knew that much anguish lay ahead for His beloved city and people. He lamented: "For the days shall come upon thee, that thine enemies shall cast a trench about thee, and compass thee round, and keep thee in on every side, And shall lay thee even with the ground, and thy children within thee; and they shall not leave in thee one stone upon another" (Luke 19:43–44).

In three of the parables of Jesus, there is a strong message of having compassion for other men. Each parable teaches the effects one compassionate person can have on others. In the parable of the good Samaritan, the Samaritan was shown to have compassion toward a wounded traveler. "The Greek word translated *compassion* . . . is the same word used to describe the feelings of the king in the parable of the unmerciful servant and the father in the parable of the prodigal son. It is the word used to refer to divine or godly compassion. The Samaritan felt deeply in behalf of the wounded man, desiring from the depths of his heart to help him."[18]

In the parable of the prodigal son, one son took his inheritance to enjoy a life of unrestrained pleasure. When he realized his mistake, he decided to return home to his father, willing to accept the role of a servant. So "he arose, and came to his father. But when he was yet a great way off, his father saw him, and *had compassion,* and ran and fell on his neck, and kissed him" (Luke 15:20, emphasis added). The father could have responded much differently, but his heart was filled with compassion which guided his actions. Now that his son was home and humbled, the father again had an opportunity to influence him to a life of righteousness. Had the father acted poorly, he may have lost his opportunity to save his son forever.

The father's heart that was so full of compassion toward one son would not be less compassionate towards his other son. When that son who had tried to remain obedient expressed concern for his father's actions towards his wayward brother, this compassionate father tenderly explained, "Son, thou are ever with me, and all that I have is thine" (Luke 15:31). What more could he offer him?

In the parable of the unmerciful servant, the servant is brought before a certain king because of the large debt he owed him. The servant pleaded for mercy and the king granted it, for he "was moved with compassion and loosed him, and forgave him the debt" (Matthew 18:27). This servant then failed to show that same compassion toward one who was indebted to him. As a result, he lost the blessings of the compassion shown him by the king.

These three parables show that compassion is a needed attribute of a leader. Compassion led the Samaritan to step in and lead a difficult situation to a better place. Compassion also led the father of the prodigal son and the king of the unmerciful servant to improve the circumstances of others. In each situation, the leader had a strong desire to alleviate suffering and acted on that desire.

Examples of Righteous Leaders

One of the great examples of Christlike compassion comes from Emma Smith, wife of the Prophet Joseph Smith. Emma endured as much of the trials faced by the early Saints as anyone. Her life was a reflection of the Lord's admonition to her husband, "For of him unto whom much is given much is required" (D&C 82:3). She was given many blessings by being married to a prophet who ushered in the dispensation of the fullness of times. However, those blessings brought responsibilities and trials and this elect woman showed great compassion as she tried to meet her own needs and the needs of so many others. For example, "she once stayed dutifully by the bedside of her ailing mother–in–law, Lucy, for five nights straight and never left her side until she became quite ill herself."[19]

Emma took into her home countless friends, strangers, travelers, and homeless people. Often these guests occupied every available bed leaving Joseph and Emma to sleep on the floor. In Kirtland, Ohio, Emma greeted with hospitality the many saints arriving from various parts of the country. She cared for the aged, disabled, and poor whose numbers seemed to be ever increasing. In Commerce, Illinois, while the Saints were building Nauvoo, a great number of people became ill with malaria. Joseph and Emma housed as many as their cabin could accommodate while they slept in a tent in their own yard. Even when Joseph was traveling, Emma continued by herself to care for those in need. For example, once when Joseph was in Washington, D. C., Emma took in 13 Saints and cared for them herself.[20]

Perhaps the greatest expression of compassion came after Joseph's martyrdom. Emma married a second husband named Lewis Bidamon who fathered a son by a young woman while still married to Emma. With compassion, Emma brought the child into her own home to raise at the request of the child's mother. Emma later gave the mother employment so she could be near her son. Emma died when the boy was only 12 years of age. Prior to her death, Emma encouraged Bidamon to marry the young woman so the boy would be raised in a stable family situation.[21] Yes, Emma had been given much and had endured much, but she gave so very much by her compassionate service to those who had so little.

Summary of Examples

- A compassionate leader is compassionate to all people without regard to why they are troubled, as Jesus was to the

Canaanite woman and to the Nephites who survived great destruction.

- A compassionate leader is not afraid to be compassionate, loving, or sorrowful, as demonstrated by Jesus when Lazarus died.
- A compassionate leader is compassionate to his friends but also to those who have made wrong choices, as Jesus was to the woman taken in adultery, and the citizens of Jerusalem.
- A compassionate leader has an understanding heart as to the frailties of mortal man, as demonstrated by the prodigal's father or the Savior's reaction to the slumbering Apostles in Gethsemane.
- A compassionate leader is compassionate even when in need of compassion herself, as was Emma Smith.

Questions for Personal Reflection

- Can you be compassionate while needing compassion yourself?
- Can you be compassionate toward a competitor who stumbles?
- Can you recognize that when someone has hurt you, they too are an imperfect child of God who needs to overcome their own weaknesses?
- How do you react to those who have committed serious sins either against you, a loved one, or a total stranger?
- How do you feel towards youth who seem more successful than your children?
- How compassionate are you towards a subordinate who makes a mistake that causes you to look bad?

Attribute 14: Kind

Kind: *Sympathetic, considerate, or helpful.*

Jesus demonstrated a sympathetic nature throughout His mortal ministry as He helped the blind, the deaf, the maimed, the lost, and the proud. In a much bigger sense, His sympathetic love for the lost and fallen of the whole human family led Him to provide the greatest help of all, the Atonement. This was the greatest expression of kindness possible, for He helped all mankind by providing a way to everlasting happiness.

The prophet Nephi learned through revelation that the Savior would atone for our sins by suffering on our behalf. Nephi then helped his people understand the character of Christ so they could have faith in Him. He taught that the Savior's "loving kindness" toward mankind led Him to suffer on our behalf. He said, "And the world, because of their iniquity, shall judge him to be a thing of naught; wherefore they scourge him, and he suffereth it; and they smite him, and he suffereth it. Yea, they spit upon him, and he suffereth it, because of his *loving kindness* and his long–suffering toward the children of men" (1 Nephi 19:9, emphasis added).

The "loving kindness" that led Jesus to atone for our sins also allows Him to be merciful toward us. Following His Crucifixion, the risen Lord visited the Nephites and renewed His promise given anciently that, "with *everlasting kindness* will I have mercy on thee, saith the Lord thy Redeemer . . . . For the mountains shall depart and the hills be removed, but *my kindness shall not depart from thee"* (3 Nephi 22:8–10, emphasis added). His kindness, His everlasting kindness, flows from the greatest of all unto the least of all. It was present in the Council in Heaven and continues through our judgment and resurrection. And, it will last through all eternity in the mansions He has prepared for us.

Elder Orson F. Whitney has given us a glimpse into the nature of the Savior from his personal experience. Below is an excerpt of that experience which is related in its entirety at the beginning of this book.

He records: "I shall never forget the *kind and gentle manner* in which He stooped and raised me up and embraced me. It was so vivid, so real that I felt the very warmth of His bosom against which I rested. Then He said: 'No, my son; these have finished their work, and they may go with me; but you must stay and finish yours.' Still I clung to Him. Gazing up into His face—for He was taller than I—I besought Him most earnestly: 'Well, promise me that I will come to You at the last.' He smiled sweetly and tenderly and replied: 'That will depend entirely upon yourself.' I awoke with a sob in my throat, and it was morning."[22]

Despite the pleadings from a faithful follower, Jesus did not alter His rules of personal accountability. He taught Elder Whitney important doctrine that he had not understood but did so in a spirit of kindness and love. Jesus did not offer rebuke or belittlement, he simply taught Elder Whitney what he needed to do to return to His presence. The kindness in which the message was given endeared him even more to his beloved Savior.

Examples of Righteous Leaders

President Gordon B. Hinckley has encouraged us, "May God help us to be a little kinder, showing forth greater forbearance, to be more forgiving, more willing to walk the second mile, to reach down and lift up those who may have sinned but have brought forth the fruits of repentance, to lay aside old grudges and nurture them no more."[23] Similarly, C. S. Lewis observed, "the Christian, trying to treat every one kindly, finds himself liking more and more people as he goes on— including people he could not even have imagined himself liking at the beginning."[24]

Mother Teresa said, "Spread love everywhere you go: First of all in your own home . . . let no one ever come to you without leaving better and happier. Be the living expression of God's kindness; kindness in your face, kindness in your eyes, kindness in your smile."[25] Mother Teresa taught kindness and lived kindness. She lifted the hearts of those who knew so little of kindness. She led by doing, and she led by being, the very expression of the loving kindness that was demonstrated by the Savior.

Kindness has been shown to soothe many wounds and bring a truce in many battles. David M. Sorensen, a retired counselor at Brigham Young University said, "I have seen troubled, contentious marriages 'turn on a dime' after both parties signed a contractual agreement to be kind to one another."[26] Such is the power of kindness. It can turn combatants back into the people they once were when a loving bride and groom fell in love and could see nothing but the best in each other. Oh, how kindness could spread like this among family members, neighbors, communities, states, and nations if people would only follow and emulate the Prince of Peace!

Summary of Examples

- The kind leader suffers embarrassment, fatigue, and ridicule because of his people, and still leads them, as does Jesus.
- The kind leader remains kind and committed to the end, as Jesus does with "everlasting kindness."
- The kind leader has a kind demeanor and mannerisms, as Elder Whitney described Jesus.
- The kind leader does not rebuke people for being naïve, as demonstrated by Jesus to Elder Whitney when explaining that he could not yet come with Him.
- The kind leader enforces the rules in a kind yet firm manner, as Jesus did with Elder Whitney.
- The kind leader, such as a mother and father or a wife and husband, can redefine and recreate relationships by using kindness, as taught by David M. Sorensen.

Questions for Personal Reflection

- How would other people rate your ability to be kind?
- Are you equally kind to those with little experience and ability as those who are very accomplished?
- How do you treat someone who received a choice opportunity that you would have liked to receive?
- Can you compete while maintaining civility?

- How kind are you to your family or associates after a hard day at work?
- Can you say something kind about each person in your community?

Attribute 15: Humble

Humble: *Not proud, haughty, arrogant or assertive. Expressing in a spirit of deference or submission. Unpretentious.*

Many people tend to misunderstand the notion of being humble by associating it with weakness. When properly understood, it is a trait of considerable strength. As stated in the definition above, the word "humble" is defined as, "not proud . . . not arrogant," and having "a spirit of deference."[27] Nowhere in scripture is the slightest hint that Jesus was proud and arrogant. Yet there are many references to His "spirit of deference."

While still in His youth, the Savior declared, "I must be about my Father's business." (Luke 2:49) It was a theme that defined His entire life. As He served, He continually gave deference to His Father by saying, "My Father . . . is greater than all" (John 10:29) and, "My Father is greater than I" (John 14:28). These statements, and many more like them, show one who is humble, directing all attention to His leader without any show of pride and arrogance. Yet, "He was of noble stature and of majestic mien [appearance, demeanor]."[28] He had the ability to balance the two apparent opposing traits of confidence and humility.

In the parable of the Pharisee and the Publican, the Savior taught about these two opposing traits as He contrasted different types of leaders. In the parable, "two men went up into the temple to pray; the one a Pharisee, and the other a publican" (Luke 18:10). In his prayer, the Pharisee extols his virtues and his righteousness while the Publican asks God to be merciful to him "a sinner." It is clear the Pharisee is self-centered as he uses the personal pronoun "I" five times.[29] He relies on his own abilities while the Publican relies on God. The Lord concludes the parable, "for every one that exalteth himself shall be abased; and he that humbleth himself shall be exalted" (Luke 18:14). Some may wonder if it is possible to balance confidence and humility in the kingdoms of the world. The answer is a clear "yes!" Many have done so and their influence has been powerful, for they have shown that both attributes can coexist and contribute to great leadership.

Examples of Righteous Leaders

John the Baptist was given one of the most important missions delegated to mortal man. It was his opportunity to prepare the way for the coming of the Son of God. While only eight days old, he was ordained by an angel to "overthrow the kingdom of the Jews and to prepare a people for the Lord" (Bible Dictionary, "John the Baptist"). He was a vigorous preacher and had many disciples, including at least two, and probably more, of the original Twelve Apostles. Then, "He watched, without feelings of jealousy, the waning of his own influence and the growth of the influence of Jesus" (Bible Dictionary, "John the Baptist"). As John the Baptist humbled himself before Jesus, Jesus raised him up and proclaimed, "Among them that are born of women there hath not risen a greater than John the Baptist" (Matthew 11:11).

Jesus taught, "Whosoever therefore shall humble himself as this little child, the same is greatest in the kingdom of heaven" (Matthew 18:4). John the Baptist exemplified this doctrine when he proclaimed, "There cometh one mightier than I after me, the latchet of whose shoes I am not worthy to stoop down and unloose" (Mark 1:7). John humbled himself before Jesus, and Jesus raised John as a great leader in three dispensations of the gospel. "He was the last of the prophets under the law of Moses, he was the first of the New Testament prophets, and he brought the Aaronic Priesthood to the dispensation of the fulness of times" (Bible Dictionary, "John the Baptist").

Half a world away and a few hundred years earlier, another group of leaders taught humility. Jacob taught his fellow Nephites, "Think of your brethren like unto yourselves" (Jacob 2:17). Alma taught, "for the preacher was no better than the hearer, neither was the teacher any better than the learner; and thus they were all equal" (Alma 1:26). This doctrine of equality can help leaders keep grounded for "Ye shall not esteem one flesh above another, or one man shall not think himself above another" (Mosiah 23:7). This same caution was given to the Latter-day Saints when Jesus said, "Let no man think he is ruler" (D&C 58:20). James taught, "God resisteth the proud, but giveth grace unto the humble" (James 4:6). Leadership requires strength, but as that strength is tempered by humility, then the influence of the leader grows exponentially.

President Brigham Young became a great leader, whom some likened to a modern Moses, for the way he led thousands of refugees into the unknown regions of the American Mountain West. Yet this great leader demonstrated a humble spirit toward his own leader, Joseph Smith. Bishop Richard Edgley said the following of Brigham: "A story is told of an encounter between the Prophet Joseph Smith and Brigham Young. In the presence of a rather large group of brethren, the Prophet severely chastised Brother Brigham for some failing in his duty. Everyone, I suppose somewhat stunned, waited to see what Brigham's response would be. After all, Brigham, who later became known as the Lion of the Lord, was no shrinking violet by any means. Brigham slowly rose to his feet, and in words that truly reflected his character and his humility, he simply bowed his head and said, 'Joseph, what do you want me to do?' The story goes that sobbing, Joseph ran from the podium, threw his arms around Brigham, and said in effect, 'You passed, Brother Brigham, you passed.'"[30]

Great leaders need to be great followers, and Brigham Young demonstrated that he was both. This helps keep themselves and the organization in balance and models the behavior the leader would like to see in his or her followers. Elder Dieter F. Uchtdorf gave this wise counsel regarding humility: "Humility does not mean convincing ourselves that we are worthless, meaningless, or of little value. Nor does it mean denying or withholding the talents God has given us. We don't discover humility by thinking less of ourselves; we discover humility by thinking less *about* ourselves. It comes as we go about our work with an attitude of serving God and our fellowman."[31]

Leaders who can truly think less about themselves and more about others will provide an environment where everyone can grow into more capable people, and organizations with capable people can accomplish great things. The concept of humility was captured well when the English author John Ruskin said, "The first test of a great man is his humility. I don't mean by humility, doubt of his power. But really great men have a curious feeling that the greatness is not of them, but through them. And they see something divine in every other man and are endlessly, foolishly, incredibly merciful."[32]

This expression describes the leadership of Jesus, one who lets the greatness of His leader flow through Him as He serves others. As taught throughout the scriptures, Jesus did not seek His own glory or His own will. His only desire was to be a conduit for His Father's power to be used in blessing the lives of His Father's children. We likewise can become a conduit for their power. As the Son became like the Father, so we can become like the Son. We can accelerate our development as we use the seven–step process discussed in chapter 4 to acquire the leadership attributes of Jesus.

Summary of Examples

- It takes wisdom and insight to discern who are the humble, as Jesus taught in the parable of the Pharisee and the Publican.
- It takes humility to acknowledge that your leader is better than yourself, as did Jesus.
- It takes humility to defer recognition and acclaim to your leader rather than keeping it for yourself, as demonstrated by John the Baptist and Jesus.
- It takes humility to think of your brother as yourself, as taught by Jacob.
- It takes humility for one with great leadership ability to also be a great follower, as Brigham Young was to Joseph Smith.

Questions for Personal Reflection

- Can you let others shine rather than always taking the spotlight?
- Do you assume your point of view is the best one or can you consider the views of others?
- How well do you handle correction?
- Do you apologize when you are wrong?
- Do you avoid blaming others for your own mistakes?
- Are you willing to serve in obscure positions or locations?

• Do you allow subordinates to get credit for notable successes?

---

1. George A. Smith, "My Journal," The Instructor 81 (1946); 82 (1947), abridged from holograph in LDS Church Archives. Grammar has been standardized. Cited in John Henry Evans, *Joseph Smith, an American Prophet*, New York: MacMillan Co., 1946, 9.
2. Gordon B. Hinckley, *Standing for Something*, 101.
3. Becky Reeve, *The Spirit Knows No Handicap*, preface.
4. Anthony J. D'Angelo, *The College Blue Book*.
5. Albert Camus, in John Bartlett, comp., *Familiar Quotations*, 17th ed. (2002), 790. Cited in Dieter F. Uchtdorf, "The Infinite Power of Hope," *Ensign*, November 2008.
6. Joseph Fielding Smith, *Life of Joseph F. Smith*, 131-33, emphasis added.
7. "Worth While," in *The Best-Loved Poems of the American People*, sel. Hazel Felleman (1936), 144.
8. Willard Sterne Randall, *George Washington A Life*, 450-51.
9. Orson F. Whitney, "The Divinity of Jesus Christ," *Improvement Era*, January 1926, 224–25.
10. Orson F. Whitney, "The Divinity of Jesus Christ," *Improvement Era*, January 1926, 224–25.
11. Parley P. Pratt, *Autobiography of Parley P. Pratt*, edited by his son, Parley P. Pratt, 179.
12. Pratt, 180.
13. Jay A. and Donald W. Parry, *Understanding the Parables of Jesus Christ*, 116.
14. Dallin H. Oaks, "Joseph, the Man and the Prophet," *Ensign*, May 1996.
15. Letter from Joseph Smith to Emma Smith, June 6, 1832, Greenville, Indiana; Chicago Historical Society, Chicago, Illinois. (See *Teachings of Presidents of the Church: Joseph Smith*, 238-47.)
16. Jay A. and Donald W. Parry, *Understanding the Parables of Jesus Christ*, 131.
17. Orson F. Whitney, "The Divinity of Jesus Christ," *Improvement Era*, January 1926, 224–25.

18. Jay A. and Donald W. Parry, *Understanding the Parables of Jesus Christ,* 108.

19. Barbara B. Smith, Blyth Darlyn Thatcher, *Heroines of the Restoration*, Bookcraft (1997), p.27.

20. Barbara B. Smith, Blyth Darlyn Thatcher, *Heroines of the Restoration*, Bookcraft (1997), p.27.

21. Barbara B. Smith, Blyth Darlyn Thatcher, *Heroines of the Restoration*, Bookcraft (1997), p.27.

22. Orson F. Whitney, "The Divinity of Jesus Christ," *Improvement Era*, Jan. 1926, 224–25.

23. Gordon B. Hinckley. "Forgiveness," *Ensign*, November 2005.

24. C. S. Lewis, *Mere Christianity*, 117.

25. Templeton, John. *Worldwide Laws of Life: 200 Eternal Spiritual Principles* (1998), 448.

26. Told to the author by Elder Spencer J. Condie from his personal knowledge.

27. Merriam-Webster's Collegiate Dictionary, "Humble."

28. Orson F. Whitney, "The Divinity of Jesus Christ," *Improvement Era*, January 1926, 224–25.

29. Jay A. and Donald W. Parry, *Understanding the Parables of Jesus Christ,* 178.

30. Richard C. Edgley, "The Empowerment of Humility," *Ensign*, November 2003 (see Truman G. Madsen, "Hugh B. Brown—Youthful Veteran," *New Era*, Apr. 1976, 16.

31. Dieter F. Uchtdorf, "Pride and the Priesthood," *Ensign*, November 2010, emphasis added.

32. *The Works of John Ruskin*, ed. E. T. Cook and Alexander Wedderburn, 39 vols. (1903–12), 5:331. Cited in Marlin K. Jensen, "To Walk Humbly with Thy God," *Ensign*, May 2001.

CHAPTER 7

HIS ABILITY

Attribute 16: Confident

Confident: *Having or showing assurance and self-reliance, full of conviction, freedom from uncertainty. Confidence stresses faith in oneself and one's powers without any suggestion of conceit or arrogance.*

During the Council in Heaven when our Heavenly Father's plan for the salvation of His children was presented, it was made known a savior was needed to atone for the sins of man. If we understand the attribute of confidence properly, we can picture in our mind's eye Jesus confidently stepping forward and saying, "Here am I, send me" (Abraham 3:27). Confidence is defined as having faith in oneself "without any suggestion of conceit or arrogance."[1] As such, it seems likely that Jesus stood erect and strong, "full of conviction, certain, [and had] freedom from uncertainty."[2] He simply knew He could do what needed to be done.

During His mortal ministry, Jesus declared, "I am able to do mine own work" (2 Nephi 27:21). He also said, "My wisdom is greater than the cunning of the devil" (3 Nephi 21:10). These were not arrogant boastings but were an expression of confidence so His followers could have faith in His ability. Without this confidence, few would follow Him, for as Paul taught, "For if the trumpet give an *uncertain* sound, who shall prepare himself to the battle?" (1Corinthians14:8, emphasis added).

The confident, certain sound in the Savior's voice must have been persuasive as He said to Peter and Andrew, "Follow me, and I will make you fishers of men," for "they straightway left their nets, and followed him." Jesus then "saw other two brethren, James the son of

Zebedee, and John his brother, in a ship with Zebedee their father, mending their nets; and he called them. And they immediately left the ship and their father, and followed him" (Matthew 4:18–22). These four men and a multitude of others like them heard in His voice, confidence, strength, conviction, and certitude. As a result, they set aside their lives to follow Him.

Examples of Righteous Leaders

The story of David and Goliath is often used to encourage one who is facing enormous challenges. We are told we can face the Goliaths in our lives if we have faith like David. However, David had more than faith, for faith has a twin, and that twin is confidence. David had faith to act because he trusted God but he also had confidence from his own experiences. When David was making his case before Saul that he should be allowed to fight Goliath, he told Saul:

"Thy servant kept his father's sheep, and there came a lion, and a bear, and took a lamb out of the flock:

"And I went out after him, and smote him, and delivered it out of his mouth: and when he arose against me, I caught him by his beard, and smote him, and slew him.

"Thy servant slew both the lion and the bear: and this uncircumcised Philistine shall be as one of them, seeing he hath defied the armies of the living God.

"David said moreover, The Lord that delivered me out of the paw of the lion, and out of the paw of the bear, he will deliver me out of the hand of this Philistine. And Saul said unto David, Go, and the Lord be with thee" (1 Samuel 17:34–37).

David, following the pattern of Jesus, stepped forward with confidence and in essence said, "Here am I, send me." As he stepped forward, all the armies of Israel saw the emergence of their future king, for he demonstrated attributes of true leadership that soon turned observers into supporters.

The Prophet Joseph Smith was widely regarded as a confident and strong man. From his youth, he demonstrated unusual confidence as he solemnly bore witness of his visions from God and the mission He had for him to complete. The conviction he felt was so strong that he attracted the admiration of not just his followers, but also many others. Of the work for which he finally gave his life, he boldly stated: "The Standard of Truth has been erected; no unhallowed hand can stop the work from progressing; persecutions may rage, mobs may combine, armies may assemble, calumny may defame, but the truth of God will go forth boldly, nobly, and independent, till it has penetrated every continent, visited every clime, swept every country, and sounded in every ear, till the purposes of God shall be accomplished, and the Great Jehovah shall say the work is done."[3]

The confidence he demonstrated in statements such as this gave strength to his followers who were persecuted for their belief. They could not have endured such persecution had the trumpet sounded with an uncertain sound.

Summary of Examples

- It takes confidence and being full of conviction to do difficult tasks while being so visible, as Jesus did in carrying out the Atonement.
- It takes confidence to believe you can accomplish your chosen work, as Jesus did when He said, "I am able to do mine own work" (2 Nephi 27:21).
- It takes confidence to believe you are wise enough to conquer your enemies, as Jesus did when He said, "My wisdom is greater than the cunning of the devil" (3 Nephi 21:10).
- It takes confidence to ask people to follow your lead, especially if doing so changes their lives, as Jesus did with Peter, Andrew, James, and John.
- It takes confidence to face and defeat major opponents or obstacles, as David did with Goliath.
- It takes confidence to boldly proclaim you will carry God's message to "every country" and sound "in every ear," as Joseph Smith did to the young restored Church.

Questions for Personal Reflection

- Are you confident enough to step forward and lead an emotionally charged situation to a peaceful resolution?
- Are you confident enough that you can have your fame, fortune, prestige, positions, and power removed and still maintain your stability of character and a sense of well–being?
- Are you confident enough that you do not need to live vicariously through the lives of others? For example, some have an unhealthy obsession for their children to succeed or their favorite ball team to win to compensate for their own feelings of inadequacy.
- Can you remain confident even when someone outshines you at something?
- Are you confident enough that you do not need a high position to validate your self–worth?
- Are you confident enough to acknowledge to your leader the noteworthy accomplishments of a subordinate?
- Are you confident enough to accept a suggestion or an evaluation of your performance from a subordinate?
- How many of the people you surround yourself with are more capable than yourself?

Attribute 17: Courageous

Courageous: *Mental or moral strength to venture, persevere, and withstand danger, fear, or difficulty. Not deterred by danger or pain.*

In difficult circumstances, courageous leaders move forward undeterred and say, "Follow me." During the Council in Heaven, Jesus was the first to step forward and volunteer to accept the most important and difficult responsibility within the plan of salvation, the Atonement. For upon it the future happiness of all God's children rested. The scriptures record, "And the Lord said: Whom shall I send? And one answered like unto the Son of Man: Here am I, send me. And another answered and said: Here am I, send me. And the Lord said: I will send the first" (Abraham 3:27), for the second "sought to destroy the agency of man" (Moses 4:3).

In asking to be sent, the Savior clearly knew He would be ransomed for the sins of all mankind. However, His courage and deep love for His Father and each of us kept Him from being deterred. This courageous step forward, coupled with His alignment to the will of the Father, led most of Heavenly Father's children to place their eternal future in His mighty hands.

Little is known of the first 30 years of the Savior's life. Most likely it was a normal life with normal challenges and normal opportunities. That all changed as He returned to the place of His youth and to the people who knew him as the carpenter's son. One can only imagine what was going through His mind and heart as He walked toward Nazareth. Knowing that now was the time to formally begin His mission designed in the Council in Heaven. Those who saw Jesus enter the city may have noticed His courage and humble dignity but were unaware of who He would soon proclaim to be. Perhaps they watched as He ascended the steps into the synagogue where He had always been welcomed in His youth. Those sentiments of being welcome soon changed. Luke records that moment as follows:

"And he came to Nazareth, where he had been brought up: and, as his custom was, he went into the synagogue on the sabbath day, and stood up for to read.

"And there was delivered unto him the book of the prophet Esaias. And when he had opened the book, he found the place where it was written,

"The Spirit of the Lord *is* upon me, because he hath anointed me to preach the gospel to the poor; he hath sent me to heal the broken-hearted, to preach deliverance to the captives, and recovering of sight to the blind, to set at liberty them that are bruised.

"And he closed the book, and he gave *it* again to the minister, and sat down. And the eyes of all them that were in the synagogue were fastened on him.

"And he began to say unto them, *This day is this scripture fulfilled in your ears*" (Luke 4:16–21, emphasis added).

Jesus had courageously announced that He was indeed the Promised Messiah, the literal Son of God. Those, who moments before accepted Him as one of their own, would now seek His life.

"And all they in the synagogue, when they heard these things, were *filled with wrath,*

"*And rose up, and thrust him out of the city, and led him unto the brow of the hill whereon their city was built, that they might cast him down headlong.*

"But he passing through the midst of them went his way" (Luke 4:28–30, emphasis added).

These former friends and other evil men sought Jesus's life for the next three years. However, Jesus was undeterred and courageously moved forward and healed those with spiritual and physical infirmities. He also exposed the wickedness of these evil men. Jesus said to His disciples, "The world cannot hate you; but me it hateth, because I testify of it, that the works thereof are evil" (John 7:7). Though the people hated Him and "were offended at him" (Mark 6:3), He continued to fulfill His mission with courage and confidence.

Jesus manifested courage many times throughout His life. It was His courage that allowed Him to withstand the attacks from opponents and the betrayals and denials from His associates. It was courage that allowed Him to again declare He was the son of God in the face of being stoned (John 10:31–32). It was His courage and the power of His presence that caused the soldiers who came for Him in Gethsemane to fall to the ground.

"Jesus therefore, knowing all things that should come upon him, went forth, and said unto them, Whom seek ye?

"They answered him, Jesus of Nazareth. Jesus saith unto them, I am *he.* And Judas also, which betrayed him, stood with them.

"As soon then as he had said unto them, I am *he, they went backward, and fell to the ground"* (John 18:4–6, emphasis added).

Clearly, His greatest acts of courage occurred in Gethsemane and Calvary. Yes, it was His mission to be ransomed for all mankind. And yes, He had additional strength by being the Only Begotten Son of God, yet He dwelt in a tabernacle of clay. He was subject to all the pains and weaknesses of mortality including the ability to feel anguish over what He knew was coming, but He was undeterred. The courage He demonstrated gives us strength as we courageously fulfill our own missions. Although our suffering pales in comparison, our courage can emulate His.

Between Gethsemane and Calvary, there was the palace and the trial. When Jesus was brought before Pilate, He knew He could make a successful defense for He had the intellect to do so. Instead, He courageously stated His mission. When Pilate asked, "Art thou a king then?" Jesus answered, "Thou sayest that I am a king. *To this end was I born, and for this cause came I into the world,* that I should bear witness unto the truth" (John 18:37, emphasis added). When the questioning continued, He restrained Himself from defending himself, for the testimony He came to give had been given.

"And when he was accused of the chief priests and elders, *he answered nothing.*

"Then said Pilate unto him, Hearest thou not how many things they witness against thee?

"And he *answered him to never a word;* insomuch that the governor marvelled greatly" (Matthew 27:12–14, emphasis added).

Even with His life hanging in the balance, Jesus did not cower or wilt. He stood courageously in silent strength, His very presence proclaiming His majesty.

Examples of Righteous Leaders

There are many leaders throughout the scriptures who also demonstrated great courage as they led and influenced tens of thousands. For example, David going before Goliath saved Israel; Moses going before Pharaoh freed captive Israel; Queen Esther going before King Ahasuerus saved the Jews from death; Daniel being thrust into the lions' den led King Darius, King of Persia, to declare "Unto all people, nations, and languages, that dwell in all the earth . . . the God of Daniel . . . *is* the living God" (Daniel 6:25–26).

Likewise, Shadrach, Meshach, and Abed–nego were thrust into the fiery furnace which led King Nebuchadnezzar to decree, "That every people, nation, and language, which speak any thing amiss against the God of Shadrach, Meshach, and Abed–nego, shall be cut in pieces, and their houses shall be made a dunghill: because there is no other God that can deliver after this sort" (Daniel 3:29). In the Americas, Abinadi going before King Noah led to an increase in righteousness among the people. Ammon and his brethren courageously traveled throughout the dangerous Lamanite lands and boldly preached the Gospel of Christ. As a result, they converted King Lamoni and thousands of their former enemies.

It took courage for Lehi to listen to the prophets in Jerusalem and pray to know if their warnings about the destruction of Jerusalem were true. It took courage for him to tell his family that they were going to leave friends, business colleagues, neighbors, property, and all wealth behind and travel into the wilderness, never to return. It took courage for Nephi to build a ship and lead his family on a voyage over the "great deep" (2 Nephi 4:20) to an unknown place. It took courage for Captain Moroni to raise the title of liberty. It took courage for Lachoneus, governor of the Nephites, to stand firm against overwhelming forces. The scriptures record that he "could not be frightened by the demands and the threatening" of his enemies (3 Nephi 3:12).

Few women are named in the scriptures and when they are, their story is especially meaningful. Consider the story of Abish, a Lamanite woman who entered a dangerous and emotionally charged situation and lead it to a better outcome. This situation began when the Nephite Ammon was found preaching the gospel to the Lamanite King Lamoni who had been an enemy of the Nephites all his days. Lamoni listened to Ammon and allowed his heart to be softened so the Holy Ghost could rest upon him. Under the influence of the Holy Ghost, Lamoni slumbered for "two days and two nights" (Alma 19:1) while going through a spiritual renovation.

When Lamoni awoke, Ammon continued to minister to him, the queen, and all their household. The Holy Ghost rested upon each of them and they all fell as though asleep, being filled with great joy. Abish, who had been converted many years earlier, "knew that it was the power of God; and supposing that this opportunity, by making known unto the people what had happened among them, that by beholding this scene it would cause them to believe in the power of God, therefore she ran forth from house to house, making it known unto the people" (Alma 19:17). However, as these Lamanites gathered, they saw the Nephite Ammon near their king and queen and were struck with fear which soon turned to anger.

Abish, seeing that the contention began to be "exceedingly sharp among them" (Alma 19:28) went forward and took the queen's hand and helped her arise. Then King Lamoni arose and declared to all who were gathered that "their hearts had been changed; that they had no more desire to do evil" (Alma 19:33). This conversion was a remarkable event for Lamoni and his people. The influence of this event was magnified many times because one woman courageously took the lead and initiated action. She helped lead many people to Christ and to the new life He could offer them.

Courage has been displayed often over the centuries and occupies almost every page of early Church history. It took courage for Joseph Smith to proclaim he had seen a vision and courage to never deny it. It took courage for Brigham Young to lead thousands over the frozen Mississippi into the wintery prairies of the Midwest. It took courage for him to say, "This is the right place, drive on."[4] It then took courage for the pioneers to drive on, and it took courage for them to stay in that "right place."

Summary of Examples

- It takes courage to step forward and volunteer for a worthy cause even though it may bring personal suffering, as Jesus did regarding the Atonement.
- It takes courage to declare who you are and what you stand for, as Jesus did in declaring He was the Son of God.
- It takes courage to stand for truth and be persecuted for it, as Jesus did when the Jews attempted to throw Him headlong down the hill, or when He appeared before Pilate; when Lehi took his family into the wilderness; when Abinadi stood before king Noah; or when Joseph Smith proclaimed he had seen a vision.
- It takes courage to not fight back, as demonstrated by Jesus when He remained silent before Pilate.
- It takes courage to stand for truth against those who are in power, as Jesus did when He stood before Pilate; or when David, Moses, Queen Esther, Daniel, Shadrach, Meshach, Abed–nego, and Abinadi stood against powerful men and led countless souls to freedom, peace, and righteousness.
- It takes courage to stand for truth when people are complacent, as Moroni did with the Title of Liberty.
- It takes courage to embrace the enemy, especially when the enemy is right, as the Lamanite woman Abish did when supporting the message of the Nephite Ammon.
- It takes courage to do the right thing when doing so leads to persecution and trials; as was experienced by Jesus, Lehi, Abinadi, Joseph Smith, and Brigham Young.

Questions for Personal Reflection

- When was the last time you stood up for someone who was being criticized?
- Will you intervene when someone is being attacked, either physically or verbally?

- Have you led family members through their trials by courageously facing your own?
- How often do you have the courage to speak the truth to those in power?
- Have you lost opportunities by standing firm to your values?
- What are you doing to lead others in fighting against the ills of society?

Attribute 18: Durable

Durable: *Able to exist for a long time without significant deterioration. Able to withstand wear, pressure, or damage; hard-wearing.*

Leaders who are durable are those who can withstand the wear and pressures of their own lives and still have the strength to lead and serve others. For example, at the beginning of His ministry, Jesus fasted 40 days and 40 nights. This endeavor was to prepare Him spiritually but likely weakened Him physically as well. Toward the end of that fast, in His "hungered" and weakened condition, the "tempter" (Matthew 4:3) came to destroy Him. It was then that Jesus demonstrated His durability by remaining strong while withstanding that assault. He had sufficient strength to cast out and conquer His adversary. He withstood the urges to turn inward and address His own personal needs and instead turned outward to serve others. Specifically, after casting out Satan, Jesus became concerned for His friend John the Baptist who was languishing in prison. To strengthen and comfort John, the Savior "sent angels" (Joseph Smith Translation, Matthew 4:11) to minister to him and fortify his durability.

This ability to strengthen and care for others, while being subpar yourself, is a hallmark of durable leaders. It is difficult to lift and encourage others if all your strength is spent on your own needs. As Proverbs says, "If thou faint in the day of adversity, thy strength *is* small" (Proverbs 24:10). Leadership is hard work and it involves fighting battles for your cause whether ideological, political, or social. It involves absorbing blows directed at you and your people. One who wilts from such adversity does not have the durability to make lasting change.

Jesus never wilted, even during the emotional and physical trials associated with the Atonement and Crucifixion. He endured much for the benefit of His people, for He loved them and wanted to lead them to a better place. Isaiah teaches us of the enduring nature of Christ in these words (later re-quoted by Jacob), "I gave my back to the smiter, and my cheeks to them that plucked off the hair. I hid not my face from shame and spitting" (2 Nephi 7:6).

Nephi also speaks of the durability and enduring nature of Jesus when he said, "And the world, because of their iniquity, shall judge him to be a thing of naught; wherefore they scourge him, and he suffereth it; and they smite him, and he suffereth it. Yea, they spit upon him, and he suffereth it, because of his loving kindness and his long-suffering toward the children of men" (1 Nephi 19:9).

Jacob continued, "for behold, he suffereth the pains of all men, yea, the pains of every living creature, both men, women, and children, who belong to the family of Adam" (2 Nephi 9:21). The prophet Mosiah said that Jesus "suffereth himself to be mocked, and scourged, and cast out, and disowned by his people" (Mosiah 15:5). Later, the Prophet Alma added, "And he shall go forth, suffering pains and afflictions and temptations of every kind; and this that the word might be fulfilled which saith he will take upon him the pains and the sicknesses of his people" (Alma 7:11). These prophets describe Jesus as a durable leader, one who is strong enough to do what is needed for the sake of His people. They also teach the life of a leader is not always an easy and peaceful life, but rather a life fully devoted to lifting others.

Examples of Righteous Leaders

Each of these prophets just referenced—Nephi, Jacob, Mosiah, and Alma—not only spoke of the durability of Jesus, they also demonstrated it in their own ministries. For example, during one of Alma's missionary journeys to the city of Ammonihah he showed his own durability, for they "reviled him, and spit upon him, and caused that he should be cast out of their city" (Alma 8:13). He left, "being weighed down with sorrow, wading through much tribulation and anguish of soul, because of the wickedness of the people" (Alma 8:14).

Ammon, a fellow missionary with Alma, recorded similar experiences: "And we have entered into their houses and taught them, and we have taught them in their streets; yea, and we have taught them upon their hills; and we have also entered into their temples and their synagogues and taught them; and we have been cast out, and mocked, and spit upon, and smote upon our cheeks; and we have been stoned, and taken and bound with strong cords, and cast into prison" (Alma 26:29).

The durableness of Alma and Ammon kept them from succumbing to their trials so they could continue their mission to bring souls to Christ. They learned more fully from their suffering the love Jesus has for His people—for love comes from suffering, and suffering comes from love.

The scriptures record that Ammon and his associates were durable leaders. They endured hardships for fourteen years as they labored to teach the gospel to the Lamanites. Speaking of them, Alma records "they had many afflictions; they did suffer much, both in body and in mind, such as hunger, thirst and fatigue, and also much labor in the spirit" (Alma 17:5). Alma's record describes "their sufferings in the land, their sorrows, and their afflictions, and their incomprehensible joy" (Alma 28:8). This is not a description of comfort that some people associate with leadership. It is the life of struggle to lift people to a better place.

The Prophet Joseph Smith understood the role of a leader is not always a life of comfort. On one occasion he confessed, "Notwithstanding my weaknesses, I am under the necessity of bearing the infirmities of others, who when they get into difficulty, hang on to me tenaciously to get them out, and wish me to cover their faults."[5] Joseph suffered as other men did, but as their leader, he carried an additional burden. This additional leadership burden requires durability to withstand the additional weight of carrying others until they can carry themselves.

President Dallin H. Oaks said: "The Church leaders I know are durable people. They made their way successfully in a world of unrestrained criticism before they received their current callings. They have no personal need for protection; they seek no personal immunities from criticism—constructive or destructive. They only seek to declare what they understand to be the word of the Lord to his people."[6]

Leaders who are durable still need to be cautious. President Henry B. Eyring gave this warning to leaders, "The wolf who would kill the sheep will surely tear at the shepherd. So, we must watch over ourselves as well as others."[7] Joseph must have felt the fangs of that wolf as he and his associates suffered in the damp unheated cellar of the Liberty Jail in Missouri. Here again, Joseph proved his durability. He wrote in a letter to Emma, "I bear with fortitude all my oppressions, so do those that are with me, not one of us has flinched yet."[8] Without such durability in a leader, the opposition could stop all forward progress and scatter the entire flock.

Summary of Examples

- It takes durability to withstand attacks, especially when in a weakened condition, as Jesus did following His forty–day fast and as Joseph Smith in the Liberty Jail.
- It takes durability to endure your own personal trials while lifting others through theirs, as did Jesus following His forty-day fast and temptation; as did Ammon when wading through afflictions to teach the Lamanites; as did Joseph Smith during his captivity in the Liberty Jail; as do parents with their children.
- It takes durability to suffer because of your service to others, as Jesus did because of us in Gethsemane and as Ammon did because of the Lamanites.
- It takes durability to give your whole energy to teach your people in every location possible while enduring physical and emotional affliction, as did Alma among the Nephites and Ammon among the Lamanites.

Questions for Personal Reflection

- Are you strong enough to endure the constant leveling that comes from those trying to pull you down, yet still have desires to lift and love them?
- Are you able to endure and flourish amid criticism for doing what you truly believe is right?
- Are you able to live according to high moral values for a lifetime when so many forces work against you?

- Are you willing to endure the personal, financial, and emotional sacrifice needed to parent children for decades because of your love and desire for their personal growth?

Attribute 19: Capable

Capable: *Having physical or mental attributes required for performance or accomplishment. The ability, fitness, or quality necessary to do or achieve a specified thing.*

Each of the 75 leadership attributes discussed in this book speak to the capability of Jesus. For example, He is knowledgeable, accountable, diligent, optimistic, inclusive, compassionate, persuasive, loved, trusted, and united. He succors the weak, gives clear direction, mentors, disciplines with kindness, forgives, and accepts people's best. He defines objectives, initiates action, counsels together, and steps in as needed.

The attributes discussed in this book form a partial description of His capability. There are undoubtedly more attributes than those identified, and the level of attainment of each one is more than we can understand. To these 75 attributes, we add His infinite knowledge, wisdom, and experience to get a glimpse of His overall capability. Perhaps Jesus gave us the best understanding of His capability when He said, "I am able to do mine own work" (2 Nephi 27:21). He gave further understanding when He said, "My wisdom is greater than the cunning of the devil" (3 Nephi 21:10), adding that He "retain[ed] all power, even to the destroying of Satan and His works at the end of the world" (D&C 19:3). He is the greatest of all leaders because He has the most capability of all the offspring of God, and He uses that capability in perfect righteousness.

When we consider the magnitude and scope of Jesus's work, we can better understand His capability. Especially when He explained that His work was not too heavy for Him to help us. To this end, He gave us an invitation with an associated affirmation:

"Come unto me, all *ye* that labour and are heavy laden, and I will give you rest.

"Take my yoke upon you, and learn of me; for I am meek and lowly in heart: and ye shall find rest unto your souls.

"For *my yoke is easy, and my burden is light"* (Matthew 11:28–30, emphasis added).

People are more likely to follow a leader who has the capability to bear his or her own responsibilities while still having the ability to help them with theirs. Leaders who always seem to be burdened or overly busy do not generate much confidence in them. And those who lack capability are often unsure of the path to follow. That uncertainty weakens the will of those who follow. As the Apostle Paul taught, "For if the trumpet give an *uncertain sound*, who shall prepare himself to the battle?" (1 Corinthians 14:8, emphasis added). With Jesus, He gives a certain and consistent sound as we move through our personal battles of life.

Perhaps there are times when each of us feel the adversary is too powerful or that mortality is too arduous. Joseph of old may have had those thoughts as he was sold into Egypt. These are times that our faith and determination can be strengthened by a capable leader. Elder Mark E. Petersen explained that the Lord has the capability to turn challenges into blessings. He taught, "The Lord often turns adverse circumstances to His advantage. It has been true down through the ages. Even persecution has stimulated His work,"[9] for as Jesus said, "the master will not suffer his house to be broken up" (D&C 104:86). As it was with Joseph, so it can be with us. The Savior has the capability to turn our individual and collective difficulties into blessings.

One of the first times people noticed the capability of Jesus was in the temple at the age of twelve. He was "sitting in the midst of the doctors, both hearing them, and asking them questions. And all that heard him were astonished at his understanding and answers" (Luke 2:46–47). Luke further records that "Jesus increased in wisdom and stature, and in favour with God and man" (Luke 2:52). In this verse, "stature" seems to reflect His standing in the eyes of the learned men because of His wisdom, and therefore He increased in favor with His fellow man. In other words, they respected and admired Him for His capability and began to hold Him in high esteem until He declared Himself the literal son of God.

Following His declaration, the powerful and learned men of the day tried to discredit Jesus by testing His capability through intellectual sparring. One such example is recorded by Matthew.

"And when he was come into the temple, the chief priests and the elders of the people came unto him as he was teaching, and said, By what authority doest thou these things? and who gave thee this authority?

"And Jesus answered and said unto them, I also will ask you one thing, which if ye tell me, I in like wise will tell you by what authority I do these things.

"The baptism of John, whence was it? from heaven, or of men? And they reasoned with themselves, saying, If we shall say, From heaven; he will say unto us, Why did ye not then believe him?

"But if we shall say, Of men; we fear the people; for all hold John as a prophet.

"And they answered Jesus, and said, We cannot tell. And he said unto them, Neither tell I you by what authority I do these things" (Matthew 21:23–27).

These learned men tried repeatedly to trap Jesus, but due to His capability, He emerged as the wisest of all. Often, those wishing to lead will have their capability challenged. If they stand up to scrutiny, they usually will attract followers.

Throughout His three–year ministry, Jesus allowed His capabilities to be manifest enough to attract followers but hidden enough to not overpower them. For example, He had the power to completely overthrow all Roman rule and cast off the wicked Jewish leaders. Yet He showed restraint because His mission was not for that purpose. His mission was to lead Heavenly Father's children back home in the manner determined in the Council in Heaven.

Examples of Righteous Leaders

Practically everyone in the scriptures was a man or a woman of great capability. They seemed to have had some natural ability that the Lord then magnified into tremendously capable people. Some of these people have been so capable and their influence so widely felt that their names frequently come to our minds even now, centuries later. One of the most notable is Moses, the Great Lawgiver. Not only was he capable as a Prince of Egypt, but with God's help, he led hundreds of thousands of undisciplined and disobedient former slaves out of bondage. Moses then governed them in the inhospitable wilderness for four decades. The laws he established were followed by millions of people for thousands of years.

Any mention of Moses automatically brings up the name of Joshua who was capable enough to step into the almost immortal shoes of Moses. Joshua was able to lead the whole host of Israel who had been loyal to Moses across the river Jordan into the Promised Land. Joshua led the Israelites against the well–fortified city of Jericho in one of the most miraculous battles in history. He led them many times against seasoned armies in their quest to establish a new home.

Many years later, David emerged as a capable leader of Israel. His capability was first displayed publicly when he courageously stepped in front of the armies of Israel as their representative before Goliath. The capability and bravery he demonstrated that day to all Israel significantly contributed to his rise to the throne. Later, David's son Solomon was so capable that his wisdom and knowledge were admired among many nations. His reputation has spanned thousands of years and the respect for his capability continues to this day.

More examples of capable leaders are found in the Book of Mormon. Who can overlook the capability of young Nephi? He had enough ability to build a seaworthy ship that could cross the great deep. Yes, Nephi was instructed by revelation how to build the ship, but it was his capable hands that allowed his hammer and saw to construct it. Consider Captain Moroni who was so capable that he altered the management of war among the Nephites and prepared them in a way never before known (Alma 49:11). Consider young Mormon who had such capability at the age of 15 that he was appointed to lead a Nephite army of 42,000 men. Yes, he was "large in stature" (Mormon 2:1) but the people must have seen something of greatness in him. And consider the capability of his son, Moroni, who finished his father's work and delivered it into the hands of a boy prophet some 1,400 years hence.

Summary of Examples

• It takes capability to have confidence, as Jesus demonstrated

126

when He said, "I am able to do mine own work" (2 Nephi 27:21).

- It takes capability to do your own work and still be able to help others, as Jesus did when He said, "my burden is light" (Matthew 11:28–30).
- It takes capability to give confident and certain directions like the sound of a "certain" trumpet, as does Jesus.
- It takes capability to turn challenges into opportunities, as Jesus did with Joseph of old.
- It takes capability to associate with other capable people, as Jesus did in conversing with the learned men of Jerusalem.
- It takes capability to avoid traps set by opponents, as Jesus did with the chief priests.
- It takes capability to bring order to unruly people, as Moses did with the freed children of Israel.
- It takes capability to fill the shoes of a capable person, as Joshua did in replacing Moses.
- It takes capability to conquer enemies, as David did with Goliath.
- It takes capability to attract widespread respect, as Solomon did because of his wisdom.
- It takes capability to alter the established ways of management, as Captain Moroni did in defending the Nephites.

Questions for Personal Reflection

- Do others follow you because of your capability rather than because you have the most domineering or charismatic personality?
- Do you properly balance the effort you put into your own growth with the effort you put into building others?
- Are you relying primarily on capability you developed in your youth, or are you continuing to develop greater capability?
- What are you doing to build spiritual, intellectual, physical, emotional, and social skills?

- Are you leading yourself by developing personal capability rather than being overly engaged in leisure activities?
- Are you leading others by being capable enough to contribute to a discussion on a wide variety of secular topics?

Attribute 20: Knowledgeable

Knowledgeable: *Knowing something with familiarity gained through experience or association. Facts or ideas acquired by study, investigation, observation, or experience.*

Jesus was clearly the most knowledgeable of all God's children, but it is unknown how much of His premortal knowledge carried forward during His mortal life. He did say, "my Father hath taught me" (John 8:28), but not much more is known about His learning process. It was evident, however, that He was very knowledgeable and wise. We know that at an early age when Jesus taught in the temple, "all that heard him were astonished at his understanding and answers" (Luke 2:47). Isaiah said Jesus had "the spirit of wisdom and understanding, the spirit of counsel and might, the spirit of knowledge and . . . of quick understanding" (Isaiah 11:2–3).

Throughout His ministry, Jesus taught both from His own personal knowledge where He was the source of doctrine, and from the scriptures where they were the source of doctrine. Using both sources helped establish His credibility as someone worth following. Below are a few examples where Jesus displayed His knowledge of the scriptures by frequently quoting from them:

- *Have ye not read what David did,* when he was an hungred, and they that were with him (Matthew 12:3, emphasis added*).*
- *Have ye not read in the law,* how that on the sabbath days the priests in the temple profane the sabbath, and are blameless? (Matthew 12:5, emphasis added).
- *Ye* hypocrites, *well did Esaias prophesy* of you, saying, This people draweth nigh unto me with their mouth, and honoureth me with *their* lips; but their heart is far from me (Matthew 15:7–8, emphasis added).
- All this was done, that it *might be fulfilled which was spoken by the prophet,* saying, Tell ye the daughter of Sion, Behold, thy King cometh unto thee, meek, and sitting upon an ass, and a colt the foal of an ass (Matthew 21:4–5, emphasis added).

- Jesus saith unto them, *Did ye never read in the scriptures,* The stone which the builders rejected, the same is become the head of the corner: this is the Lord's doing, and it is marvellous in our eyes? (Matthew 21:42, emphasis added).

- Jesus answered and said unto them, *Ye do err, not knowing the scriptures,* nor the power of God. For in the resurrection they neither marry, nor are given in marriage, but are as the angels of God in heaven (Matthew 22:29–30, emphasis added).

- *For Moses said,* Honour thy father and thy mother; and, Whoso curseth father or mother, let him die the death (Mark 7:10, emphasis added).

- And said unto them, *It is written,* My house shall be called the house of prayer; but ye have made it a den of thieves (Matthew 21:13, emphasis added).

The Savior's knowledge of the scriptures enabled Him to teach with power and authority. Numerous times He lent authority to His teachings with the prelude, "It is written." In fact, He resisted Satan's temptation in the desert by saying, "It is written, Man shall not live by bread alone" (Matthew 4:4) and "It is written again, Thou shalt not tempt the Lord thy God" (Matthew 4:7). And then, "It is written, Thou shalt worship the Lord thy God, and him only shalt thou serve" (Matthew 4:10). This identical expression, "It is written," is also recorded in Matthew 11:9–11; Matthew 21:13; Mark 7:6; Mark 9:12; Mark 11:17; Luke 24:46; John 8:17, John 10:34; and John 12:14.

These examples reflect the knowledge Jesus had of the scriptures. This knowledge and His wise use of it, allowed Jesus to circulate among the learned men of His day. His familiarity with this group is evident by the phraseology He uses with them. For example, a "certain lawyer" asked, "Master, what shall I do to inherit eternal life?" (Luke 10:25). Jesus replied, "What is written in the law? *how readest thou*?" (Luke 10:26, emphasis added). From His choice of words, one can picture a group of learned men sitting around a room warmed by the evening fire burning in the background. While discussing their various points of view on a particular topic, one scholar turns to another and says, "this is how I read it, how readest thou?" Clearly, Jesus would have been a prominent participant in any such discussion due to His vast knowledge of the scriptures.

Examples of Righteous Leaders

The scriptures contain many accounts of those who were knowledgeable and who valued learning. For example, King Benjamin taught his sons "that they should be taught in all the language of his fathers, that thereby they might become men of understanding" (Mosiah 1:2). Ammon was referred to as "being wise, yet harmless" (Alma 18:22). In the Old Testament, Solomon was widely known for his wisdom and knowledge. The record states:

"And God gave Solomon wisdom and understanding exceeding much, and largeness of heart, even as the sand that *is* on the sea shore.

"And Solomon's wisdom excelled the wisdom of all the children of the east country, and all the wisdom of Egypt.

"For he was wiser than all men; than Ethan the Ezrahite, and Heman, and Chalcol, and Darda, the sons of Mahol: and his fame was in all nations round about.

"And he spake three thousand proverbs: and his songs were a thousand and five.

"And he spake of trees, from the cedar tree that *is* in Lebanon even unto the hyssop that springeth out of the wall: he spake also of beasts, and of fowl, and of creeping things, and of fishes.

"And there came of all people to hear the wisdom of Solomon, from all kings of the earth, which had heard of his wisdom" (1 Kings 4:29–34).

The admiration and confidence people had for Solomon was due in large part to his knowledge and wisdom. This gave him tremendous influence to lead others. Much of Solomon's knowledge seemed to be secular in nature but it was critically important. Jesus taught this principle to the early elders of the restored Church when He said, "Seek ye diligently and teach one another words of wisdom; yea, seek ye out of the best books words of wisdom; seek learning, even by study and also by faith" (D&C 88:118). Also, He admonished them to "obtain a knowledge of history, and of countries, and of kingdoms, of laws of God and man" (D&C 93:53). With this increased knowledge, they would have greater influence to improve society and make a greater contribution in forwarding His kingdom.

In the parable of the foolish rich man, Jesus tells of a man who was foolish because he spent his whole life obtaining possessions that he could not carry beyond the grave. The parable states that he "layeth up treasure for himself, and is not rich toward God" (Luke 12:21). Clearly, Solomon could have been the object of this parable for he amassed riches far above other men. He also amassed great knowledge, wisdom, and understanding that made him "rich toward God." Elder Bruce R. McConkie described those with this type of riches as, "Rich in the currency negotiable in the courts above; rich in eternal things; rich in the knowledge of the truth, in the possession of the characteristics and attributes of Deity, in all of the things which will continue to be enjoyed in eternity."[10]

Those who invest their efforts in acquiring knowledge and wisdom enlarge their souls and enhance their enjoyment in this life and throughout eternity. They also put themselves in a better position to lead others because of their increased capability.

Summary of Examples

- It takes knowledge to converse with learned men, as Jesus did in the temple.
- It takes knowledge to quote from respected works to strengthen your position, as Jesus did as He quoted from the scriptures.
- It takes knowledge to train others to be knowledgeable, as King Benjamin did in teaching his sons.
- It takes knowledge to be respected, as was Solomon by kings and commoners.
- It takes knowledge to know what type of knowledge to obtain, as we learn from the foolish rich man.

Questions for Personal Reflection

- Do you allow new knowledge to supersede old outdated knowledge?
- How are you getting more knowledge so that you can speak with more influence?
- Are you the most knowledgeable in each meeting so you can have the most influence?
- How well do you answer gospel questions by quoting from scripture?
- What secular topics have you studied in the last twelve months?
- Are you knowledgeable enough to help guide a wide range of situations or decisions?

Attribute 21: Accountable

Accountable: *Willingness to accept responsibility.*

If being accountable is defined as a "willingness to accept responsibility,"[11] then certainly Jesus demonstrated this attribute in the Council in Heaven when the great plan of salvation was presented. He voluntarily stepped forward to accept responsibility when He said, "Here am I, send me" (Abraham 3:27), "thy will be done, and the glory be thine forever" (Moses 4:2). Jesus was selected and remained accountable for this responsibility until it was finished.

During His mortal ministry, Jesus taught two parables with the theme of personal accountability. The first is the parable of the lost coin where a woman was responsible for "ten pieces of silver" (Luke 15:8–10). She lost one of those pieces and the parable tells how she earnestly tried three different methods of searching for it. She first lit a candle, and then swept the house and finally sought diligently until she found it. She did all in her power to be accountable for that which was lost.

The second example Jesus taught is the parable of the talents where "a man traveling into a far country . . . called his own servants, and delivered unto them his goods. And unto one he gave five talents, to another two, and to another one; to every man according to his several ability" (Matthew 25:14–15). The Lord of the servants returned after a long time and "reckoneth with them" (Matthew 25:19). He asked for an accounting from each one and rewarded them based on their diligence and accomplishment. So, it is with each who has been entrusted by their leader to perform his or her work. An accounting is required, diligence is expected, and future opportunities are based on past performance.

During the final hours of His life, Jesus demonstrated personal accountability. While hanging on the cross, He "saw his mother, and the disciple standing by, whom he loved, he saith unto his mother, Woman, behold thy son! Then saith he to the disciple, Behold thy mother! And from that hour that disciple took her unto his own *home*" (John 19:26–27). In this hour of grief and heavy burden, He remained accountable for His mother's well-being and planned for her continual care. Moments later, as His mortal life drew to a close, once again He demonstrated His accountability by saying, "Father, it is finished, thy will is done" (Joseph Smith Translation, Matthew 27:54). In this final utterance, as the brief chapter of His mortal life closed, He gave a final accounting of the responsibility He accepted. Now, He had fully completed all that had been required of His holy hands.

Examples of Righteous Leaders

Through the Prophet Joseph Smith, Jesus teaches us more about accountability when he said, "it is required of the Lord, at the hand of every steward, to *render an account of his stewardship,* both in time and in eternity. For he who is faithful and wise in time is accounted worthy to inherit the mansions prepared for him of my Father" (D&C 72:3–4, emphasis added). The Book of Mormon leader King Benjamin demonstrated this well. Shortly before his death, he gathered all his people to give such an accounting. He knew of the warnings from Isaiah who centuries earlier cautioned about the influence of wicked leaders. Isaiah said, "For the leaders of this people cause them to err; and they that are led of them are destroyed" (2 Nephi 19:16). King Benjamin did not want that same fate for those he led. Below is a partial record of the accounting he made.

"I say unto you that as I have been suffered to spend my days in your service, even up to this time, and have not sought gold nor silver nor any manner of riches of you;

"Neither have I suffered that ye should be confined in dungeons, nor that ye should make slaves one of another, nor that ye should murder, or plunder, or steal, or commit adultery; nor even have I suffered that ye should commit any manner of wickedness, and have taught you that ye should keep the commandments of the Lord, in all things which he hath commanded you—

"And even I, myself, have labored with mine own hands that I might serve you, and that ye should not be laden with taxes, and that there should nothing come upon you which was grievous to be borne—and of all these things which I have spoken, ye yourselves are witnesses this day.

"Yet, my brethren, I have not done these things that I might boast, neither do I tell these things that thereby I might accuse you; but *I tell you these things that ye may know that I can answer a clear conscience before God this day*" (Mosiah 2:10–15, emphasis added).

King Benjamin was a perfect example of a leader who focused more on accountability than personal comfort. He wore out his life trying to lead his people to become better and do better than they had done before. He remained accountable for them through the end of his days.

Summary of Examples

- It takes accountability to ensure you have provided for those who are in your care, as Jesus did for His mother.
- It takes accountability to do all in your power to fulfill your responsibility, as did the woman who lost the coin.
- It takes accountability to diligently follow instructions and increase the assets of those who have given you that responsibility, as taught by the parable of the talents.
- It takes accountability to complete your assignment and report back to your leader, as Jesus did when He said, "Father, it is finished, thy will is done" (Joseph Smith Translation, Matthew 27:54).
- It takes accountability to give an accounting to the people you lead, as King Benjamin did in his final address.

Questions for Personal Reflection

- Can you look at those you lead as people you need to serve and make them successful, rather than seeing them as people who need to serve you and make you successful?
- If you hurt or offended someone, will you apologize and take steps to repair the damage rather than ignoring the situation?
- Can you accept accountability for your own actions rather than blaming others?

- If someone you are mentoring is unsuccessful or makes a mistake, can you take accountability for not preparing them better?
- How well are you improving the lives of others by bearing their burdens, even when not given an assignment to do so?

Attribute 22: Has Integrity

Integrity: *Firm adherence to a code of moral values. An unimpaired condition, undivided, completeness, soundness.*

The word *integrity* is often used to describe a person of unquestioned honesty whose character is complete, sound, and unimpaired. Integrity is also used to describe a ship whose hull is constructed so solidly that there is no fear of it sinking. It is complete, sound, and unimpaired. When one thinks of the Savior, it would be hard to question His integrity for He was complete, sound, and unimpaired. It was these qualities, along with His firm adherence to His Father's plan, which influenced most of the hosts of heaven to choose Him as their leader. They trusted in His integrity to accomplish the Atonement and Resurrection on their behalf.

During mortality, Jesus continued to demonstrate His integrity by living a perfect life. He never wavered from a "code of moral values" nor from fulfilling His mission exactly as He had been directed. He "suffer[ed] temptations, and pain of body, hunger, thirst, and fatigue, even more than man can suffer, except it be unto death" (Mosiah 3:7), yet His character remained intact. His integrity was manifest through His 40 days and 40 nights of fasting, and again as He was tempted by the adversary. It remained intact when He was baited by wicked men. Even during the trials of Gethsemane and Calvary, His integrity never weakened, and He remained true to His divine commission.

Jesus taught both by example and by instruction. For example, He taught His disciples of the need for integrity when He said, "No man can serve two masters: for either he will hate the one, and love the other; or else he will hold to the one, and despise the other. Ye cannot serve God and mammon" (Matthew 6:24). This dividedness is the antithesis of integrity and is perhaps better illustrated by the words attributed to Jesus in the Gospel of Thomas, an apocryphal Christian text. In that account, "Jesus said, 'It is impossible for a man to mount two horses [or] to stretch two bows. And it is impossible for a servant to serve two masters—otherwise he will honor the one and contemn the other.'"[12]

Following His Resurrection, Jesus told His disciples that He would send them forth following the same pattern used by His Father. He said, "as my Father hath sent me, even so send I you" (John 20:21). In this one phrase, Jesus reaffirmed His integrity to act in exactly the same manner as His Father had done. This was a theme repeated throughout His entire life—acknowledging that He came to do His Father's work, in His Father's way, with perfect integrity, nothing varying.

Now, Jesus invites us to live our lives following the pattern He set which is the pattern His Father set. He taught, "Therefore I would that ye should be perfect even as I, or your Father who is in heaven is perfect" (3 Nephi 12:48). Perfection is defined as "entire development; the state of being complete so that nothing requisite is wanting."[13] Integrity is also defined as completeness. Leaders who have strong integrity have developed a completeness of attributes that are so interwoven that their character would never be compromised. These leaders are men and women so sound that they form an unshakable foundation upon which families, organizations, communities, and other entities can be built.

Examples of Righteous Leaders

Another dimension of integrity is defined as a "firm adherence to a code of moral values." The Prophet Abinadi exemplified this unwavering integrity when he was sentenced to death because of his firm adherence to the code of moral values he taught to King Noah. He was offered his life if he would recant his words, but Abinadi responded with this courageous declaration: "Now Abinadi said unto him: I say unto you, I will not recall the words which I have spoken unto you concerning this people, for they are true; and that ye may know of their surety I have suffered myself that I have fallen into your hands. Yea, and I will suffer even until death, and I will not recall my words, and they shall stand as a testimony against you. And if ye slay me ye will shed innocent blood, and this shall also stand as a testimony against you at the last day" (Mosiah 17:9–10).

Abinadi suffered death by fire but his character remained

"undivided." He had maintained his integrity to the very end. He followed the resolute decree of Job who said, "Till I die I will not remove mine integrity from me" (Job 27:5). Abinadi's testimony and integrity influenced his contemporaries and generations after him to remain complete, sound, and unimpaired to the very end.

President Karl G. Maeser, the first principal of Brigham Young Academy, gave a memorable response to the meaning of the word *honor,* but it applies to its synonym, *integrity.* He said: "I have been asked what I mean by word of honor. I will tell you. Place me behind prison walls—walls of stone ever so high, ever so thick, reaching ever so far into the ground—there is a possibility that in some way or another I may be able to escape; but stand me on the floor and draw a chalk line around me and have me give my word of honor never to cross it. Can I get out of that circle? No, never! I'd die first!"[14]

He, like other great leaders, understood that integrity is the attribute that holds all other attributes together into one perfectly complete soul. And when integrity is gone, tragic consequences soon follow. President Russell M. Nelson taught about integrity by using one of Shakespeare's characters, Tarquinius from the poem *Lucrece.* President Nelson said, "During a moment of mental weakness, Tarquinius contemplated the conquest of a woman in lust. He temporarily repaired that flaw in his own thinking when he declared:

> What win I, if I gain the thing I seek?
> A dream, a breath, a froth of fleeting joy.
> Who buys a minute's mirth to wail a week?
> Or sells eternity to get a toy?
> For one sweet grape who will the vine destroy?
> (Act 1, lines 211–15.)

> 'Pawning his honor to obtain his lust,' however, Tarquinius rejected wisdom (act 1, line 156). As a result, he lost his integrity, then his life."[15]

Oh, that he would have followed the example of Joseph who fled from the reaching arms of Potiphar's wife.

Summary of Examples

- It takes integrity to remain unimpaired while going through your own trials so you can help others with their trials, as Jesus did in Gethsemane and Calvary.
- It takes integrity to refrain from activities that divide your soul by serving two masters, as taught by Jesus.
- It takes integrity for a leader to emulate his leader, as Jesus did in sending forth His disciples as His Father sent Him.
- It takes integrity to maintain your character despite severe trials, as did Jesus, Job, and Abinadi.
- It takes integrity to give your word and never give in, as taught by President Maeser.
- It takes integrity to maintain your character despite temptation, as Joseph did in fleeing from Potiphar's wife.

Questions for Personal Reflection

- Are you strengthening your integrity by correcting fatal flaws in your character? If these flaws are exposed to intense pressure, could they cause your downfall?
- Are you strengthening your integrity by keeping your word?
- Are you strengthening your integrity by living the same set of values when you are alone or with friends as when you are with your parents?
- When was the last time you acted with integrity when you easily could have acted otherwise?
- Are you overcoming any divided loyalty between an allegiance to God and the allure of carnal desires?
- Have you led others to do what is right by standing firm to your principles in the face of temptation?

Attribute 23: Diligent

Diligent: *Steady, earnest, and energetic effort. Having or showing care and conscientiousness in one's work or duties. Attentive and persistent.*

Our Savior has been "steady, attentive, [and] conscientious" in doing the will of the Father from the beginning. He diligently seeks after each lost sheep and persistently calls for them to return to the safety of His fold. He continues to extend comfort through our afflictions and never lessens the pace or loses interest in His mission to bring all mankind safely back home. And to each of those who minister on His behalf, He encourages them to maintain diligence with those who appear disinterested or unprepared for their message.

Jesus taught: "Nevertheless, ye shall not cast him out of your synagogues, or your places of worship, *for unto such shall ye continue to minister;* for ye know not but what they will return and repent, and come unto me with full purpose of heart, and I shall heal them; and ye shall be the means of bringing salvation unto them" (3 Nephi 18:32, emphasis added).

It is this type of diligence that causes a shepherd to leave ninety-nine sheep to rescue one that has strayed. It is this same diligence that caused Jesus to leave the newly trained Twelve Apostles, so He could continue His own work of ministering to others. Matthew records, "And it came to pass, when Jesus had made an end of commanding his twelve disciples, he departed thence to teach and to preach in their cities" (Matthew 11:1). He did not resort to a life of leisure now that others could do His work. Instead, He diligently went out among the people as well and ministered to them.

Shortly before His ordeal in the Garden of Gethsemane, the Savior met with His Apostles to partake of the feast of the Passover. He could have been at home with His mother and family. Instead, He diligently sought to prepare the Twelve before His departure. Here during the Last Supper, He strengthened them, encouraged them, and taught them. He taught them that "he that is chief" is "as he that doth serve"

(Luke 22:26). He taught them that when they are converted, they should strengthen their brethren (Luke 22:32). He taught them to "love one another" (John 13:34). The Savior taught them with all diligence; even to the end of His mortal life, because He knew they had so much to learn before He was gone.

Diligence is one of the themes of the parable of the wheat and the tares, and it is taught twice in that parable. The parable begins when an "enemy came and sowed tares among the wheat" while the "men slept" (Matthew 13:25). Had they been more diligent in looking after the field where a man had "sowed good seed," then the enemy could not have sowed tares. The second reference to diligence comes when the Savior teaches that the wheat now will have to grow alongside the tares until they both are fully ripe and harvested. The wheat will have to compete for available resources of sunlight, water, and nutrients through the entire growing season. This constant diligence is necessary for the wheat's survival. How fitting a comparison to each of us as we grow toward being harvested ourselves.

Diligence is also one of the themes of the parable of the importunate widow and unjust judge. In this parable, the widow diligently seeks the judge's help in avenging her of her adversary. The judge is slow and resistant to help because he is not a man of God. He finally concedes by saying, "Yet because this widow troubleth me, I will avenge her, lest by her *continual coming* she weary me" (Luke 18:5, emphasis added). Her diligence paid off and she got the help she needed. Jesus then uses this parable to teach another leadership principle. He contrasts the slow response of this unrighteous judge with the speedy response of a righteous leader. He explained that God would "avenge his own elect, which cry day and night unto him . . . [and] will avenge them *speedily*" (Luke 18:7–8, emphasis added). This is the type of attentive response one would expect from a diligent shepherd.

Jesus used this parable of the importunate widow to teach the early Latter-day Saints to be diligent in seeking redress for the crimes committed against them.

"Thus will I liken the children of Zion.

"Let them importune at the feet of the judge;

"And if he heed them not, let them importune at the feet of the governor;

"And if the governor heed them not, let them importune at the feet of the president;

"And if the president heed them not, then will the Lord arise and come forth out of his hiding place, and in his fury vex the nation" (D&C 101:85–89).

History records that the Prophet Joseph did lead the Saints diligently in their importuning, but in their case, the judge did not intercede. Countless attempts were made to governmental agencies for protection, compensation, and fair treatment but each went unanswered. So as promised, the Lord did arise and came forth out of His hiding place to vex the nation. Soon the nation was in Civil War followed by financial collapse, "Dust Bowl" droughts, disease, and natural calamities that ravaged the land and its people.

Examples of Righteous Leaders

The scriptures contain many examples of leaders who diligently labored for those they led. Consider the Jaredite prophet Ether who "did cry from the morning, even until the going down of the sun, exhorting the people to believe in God unto repentance lest they should be destroyed" (Ether 12:3). Mosiah records a similar example regarding the prophet Alma. "And now all these things did Alma and his fellow laborers do who were over the church, walking in all diligence, teaching the word of God in all things, suffering all manner of afflictions, being persecuted by all those who did not belong to the church of God. And they did admonish their brethren . . . every one by the word of God" (Mosiah 26:38–39).

Captain Moroni's diligence kept his people safe, despite constant attacks by their enemies. Alma records: "And now it came to pass that Moroni *did not stop making preparations for war, or to defend his people* against the Lamanites; for he caused that his armies should commence in the commencement of the twentieth year of the reign of the judges, that they should commence in digging up heaps of earth round about all the cities, throughout all the land which was possessed by the Nephites" (Alma 50:1, emphasis added).

Many years later, Samuel the Lamanite recounted to the Nephites the success his brethren were having in establishing righteousness among the Lamanites, for "they are striving with *unwearied diligence* that they may bring the remainder of their brethren to the knowledge of the truth; therefore there are many who do add to their numbers daily" (Helaman 15:6, emphasis added). Samuel and his associates knew that getting people to change takes hard, consistent work, as though they were pushing a stone up the mountain. Any break in their effort would allow the stone to reverse direction and roll back down the hill.

The Prophet Joseph Smith demonstrated diligence as he translated the Book of Mormon. It was one of the most important tasks in all history, and Joseph put his full effort into its completion. Of this effort, President Thomas S. Monson said: "Following the visits of the angel Moroni to young Joseph and his acquisition of the plates, Joseph commenced the difficult assignment of translation. One can but imagine the dedication, the devotion, and the labor required to translate in fewer than 90 days this record of over 500 pages covering a period of 2,600 years."[16]

Joseph's diligence in translating these records is significant by itself, but it was only the beginning. The continued expression of his diligence was repeated over and over throughout his life. In doing so, he inspired countless others to join with him in his cause, acting in full diligence.

Summary of Examples

- It takes diligence for a leader to never give up on his people, as demonstrated by Jesus when He taught, "for unto such shall ye continue to minister" (3 Nephi 18:32).
- It takes diligent attentiveness to care about detail as small as 1%, as did the shepherd in going after the lost sheep.
- It takes diligence to continue your own labors even though

you have enlisted others to your cause, as Jesus did after calling the Twelve Apostles.

- It takes diligence to always be alert for your enemies who endeavor to impede your work, as taught by Jesus in the parable of the wheat and the tares.
- It takes diligence to remain strong in a competitive world, as did the wheat among the tares.
- It takes diligence to earnestly seek help from those who can provide it, as did the importunate widow.
- It takes diligence to seek day and night for the welfare of your people, as did Ether who "did cry from the morning, even until the going down of the sun" (Ether 12:3).
- It takes diligence to serve your people through great affliction and effort, as did Alma as he preached among the unrighteous.
- It takes diligence to keep your people safe, as Captain Moroni did by never stopping the preparations for defense against the Lamanites.
- It takes diligence to continue laboring even after having great success, as did the Lamanites who strived "with *unwearied diligence* that they may bring the *remainder* of their brethren to the knowledge of the truth" (Helaman 15:6, emphasis added).
- It takes diligence to stay focused on an important and substantial task, as Joseph did in translating the Book of Mormon.

Questions for Personal Reflection

- How would you compare your level of diligence now as when you first started your current assignment?
- Are you making a difference by diligently fighting against drugs, crime, pornography, illiteracy, corruption, poverty, and the other ills of society?
- What are you doing to become more like the Savior?
- Are you continuing to improve yourself or have you started to coast to the finish line?

- How many more people have you added this year to the circle of your influence?
- Are you actively helping those in need regardless of whether you have been assigned or they have asked for it?
- Do you fulfill your responsibilities with energy and excitement, or are you lethargically plodding along?

Attribute 24: Perceptive

Perceptive: *Having or showing keenness of understanding, or intuition. Sympathetic understanding or insight. A capacity for comprehension. Discernment.*

Following the feeding of the five thousand, many who were in that group sought after Jesus. They traveled to Capernaum on the northern shore of the Sea of Galilee and found Him in a synagogue. As they approached Him, He perceptively identified their true intentions and their level of understanding so He could tailor His message accordingly. He said, "Verily, verily, I say unto you, Ye seek me, not because ye saw the miracles, *but because ye did eat of the loaves, and were filled*"(John 6:26, emphasis added). He then proceeded to teach them that the loaves of bread He provided had nourished their body, but His words would nourish their soul.

John records: "Jesus said unto them, I am the bread of life: he that cometh to me shall never hunger; and he that believeth on me shall never thirst" (John 6:35). "The Jews then murmured at him, because he said, I am the bread which came down from heaven. And they said, Is not this Jesus, the son of Joseph, whose father and mother we know? how is it then that he saith, I came down from heaven?" (John 6:41–42). "When Jesus knew in himself that his disciples murmured at it, he said unto them, Doth this offend you?" (John 6:61).

The Savior followed this declaration by saying, "But there are some of you that believe not. For Jesus knew from the beginning who they were that believed not, and who should betray him" (John 6:64). With this understanding, He then could focus His influence where it would bring about the most good.

In the Gospel of Luke, we read an account of men who brought to Jesus a man confined to bed with palsy. These men "went upon the housetop, and let him down through the tiling with his couch in the midst before Jesus. And when he saw their faith, he said unto him, Man, thy sins are forgiven thee" (Luke 5:19–20). The scribes who witnessed this miracle felt Jesus had spoken blasphemy, for "Who can forgive sins, but God alone" (Luke 5:21). "But when Jesus perceived their thoughts, he answering said unto them, What reason ye in your hearts? Whether is easier, to say, Thy sins be forgiven thee; or to say, Rise up and walk?" (Luke 5:23). By being perceptive, Jesus was able to respond to criticism and take the opportunity to teach. Undoubtedly, some of His perceptiveness was due to His divinity, but some also could have come through the traditional means of association and observation.

The Savior also demonstrated perceptiveness among the Nephites as He again tailored His message to the specific needs and circumstances of those He taught. As He addressed them following His Resurrection, He repeatedly made comments like, "I know your thoughts" (3 Nephi 28:6), and "I perceive that ye are weak" (3 Nephi 17:2). He also said, "I perceive that ye desire that I should show unto you what I have done unto your brethren at Jerusalem, for I see that your faith is sufficient that I should heal you" (3 Nephi 17:8). With this insight, He adjusted His ministering to best serve them. This is a pattern repeated over and over as Jesus leads with perceptiveness that is aided by His divinity and expanded by His familiarity and observations of those He leads.

Examples of Righteous Leaders

Following the death of Nephi, his brother Jacob assumed the leadership role of the Nephites and used his perceptiveness to help guide his people away from sin. He perceived that they were in a state of moral decline and used all his influence to reverse that decline. Jacob said to them, "I can tell you concerning your thoughts, how that ye are beginning to labor in sin" (Jacob 2:5). He said that he perceived their thoughts "by the help of the all-powerful Creator of heaven and earth" (Jacob 2:5) and could help prevent them from doing great iniquity. Jacob labored all his days to lead his people toward a life of righteousness, to help them become better and do better than they hitherto had done. Jacob, like Jesus, was aided in his leadership by a perceptiveness that comes from familiarity, proximity, love, and by simply paying attention.

In addition to being aware of the needs of followers, perceptive leaders also can be aware of traps laid by opponents. As Amulek preached repentance to wicked men in Ammonihah, he was able to "know of their designs" for "he perceived their thoughts" and side-stepped their traps (Alma 10:17). Another example is when Ammon was brought before King Lamoni for questioning. He had been so valiant in protecting the King's flocks that the King felt he was the Great Spirit. Therefore, the King feared him so much he could not speak. Ammon "perceived the thoughts of the king" and was able to tailor his teaching to the needs of the king. As a result, thousands were led to the path of happiness (Alma 18:16).

The prophet Nehemiah also perceived the traps laid by opponents. He had been given authority to rebuild the walls of Jerusalem and labored with his people to do so. However, several rulers who lived near Jerusalem opposed this effort and sought to stop it. Four times they called for Nehemiah to leave the protection of the city and meet with them to resolve their conflict "but Nehemiah *knew that their intent was to do him harm.* Each time they approached him, he responded with the same answer: 'I am doing a great work, so that I cannot come down.'"[17] Because of this perception, he avoided the traps that would surely have halted their efforts to rebuild the protective walls of their city.

Parents who are perceptive can better influence their children. For example, the scriptures record that Alma had three boys, Helaman, Shiblon, and Corianton (Alma 49:30). Like any loving father, he diligently tried to teach them the correct way to live. His record states that he perceived the things each of his sons needed to hear and what issues they struggled with. With this insight, he tailored his teaching for each son. To Helaman, he taught him to "Counsel with the Lord in all thy doings" (Alma 37:37). To Shiblon, he taught him to "Use boldness, but not overbearance; and also see that ye bridle all your passions" (Alma 38:12). To Corianton, he warned, "ye cannot hide your crimes from God" (Alma 39:8). Each of these three sons was different, and Alma adjusted his leadership and parenting based on what he perceived their needs to be.

Perceptive leaders who know the hearts of their people can fortify them in times of trouble. Captain Moroni was a bold and diligent military leader and led many successful campaigns. On one occasion, his armies faced a terrible foe and victory seemed uncertain. The record states: "And it came to pass that when the men of Moroni saw the fierceness and the anger of the Lamanites, they were about to shrink and flee from them. And Moroni, *perceiving their intent,* sent forth and inspired their hearts with these thoughts—yea, the thoughts of their lands, their liberty, yea, their freedom from bondage. And it came to pass that they turned upon the Lamanites, and they cried with one voice unto the Lord their God, for their liberty and their freedom from bondage. And they began to stand against the Lamanites with power" (Alma 43:48–50, emphasis added).

Being perceptive requires paying attention and maintaining close association. Absentee leaders are often ineffective because they are not close enough to their people to understand or to be understood. Perceptiveness is an attribute that can be acquired by familiarity, proximity, love, and by simply paying attention.

Summary of Examples

- It takes perceptiveness to understand the heart and intent of people, as Jesus did at Capernaum.
- It takes perceptiveness to recognize a person who is close to falling, as did Jacob who perceived his people were "beginning to labor in sin" and Captain Moroni who perceived his warriors were close to retreat.
- It takes perceptiveness to see traps laid by enemies, as did Amulek with the wicked men in Ammonihah and Nehemiah whose neighbors did not want the protective walls of Jerusalem to be rebuilt.
- It takes perceptiveness to know how best to teach a person, as did Ammon with King Lamoni.
- It takes perceptiveness to know the needs of each of your children, as did Alma with his three sons.

Questions for Personal Reflection

- Can you look beyond someone's polished persona to discover his or her true inner character?
- Which of your friends do you perceive as true friends and which may be impersonators?
- Have you led someone to the truth by perceiving the real reasons he or she may be reluctant to embrace the gospel?
- Can you perceive the capabilities of those you lead even if they are not self–promoters?
- Can you look off into the horizon and perceive opportunities that may arise?
- Thinking back on someone you observed misbehaving, what do you perceive was the root cause of his or her actions?

---

1. Merriam-Webster's Collegiate Dictionary, "Confidence."
2. Merriam-Webster's Collegiate Dictionary, "Confidence."
3. Joseph Smith, "The Wentworth Letter," *History of the Church*, 4:540.
4. B. H. Roberts, *A Comprehensive History of the Church*, 3:224.
5. Joseph Smith, *History of the Church*, 5:516.
6. Dallin H. Oaks, "Criticism," *Ensign*, February 1987.
7. Henry B. Eyring, "Watch with Me," *Ensign*, May 2001.
8. Joseph Smith, Letter, Liberty, MO, to Emma Smith, Quincy, IL, 4 April 1839; handwriting of JS; three pages; JS papers, Beinecke Rare Book and Manuscript Library, New Haven, CT. Cited in *Teachings of Presidents of the Church: Joseph Smith*, 242.
9. Mark E. Petersen, *Joseph of Egypt*, 28.
10. Bruce R. McConkie, *Doctrinal New Testament Commentary*, 1:474.
11. Merriam-Webster's Collegiate Dictionary, "Accountable."
12. Fitzmyer, *The Gospel According to Luke*, 1106, Cited in Jay A. and Donald W. Parry, *Understanding the Parables of Jesus Christ*, 150.
13. Cambridge Dictionary, Merriam-Webster's Collegiate Dictionary, "Perfection."

14. Emerson Roy West, "Vital Quotations," Salt Lake City: Bookcraft (1968), 167.

15. Russell M. Nelson, Brigham Young University devotional on 23 February 1993. Cited in Russell M. Nelson, "Integrity of Heart," *Ensign*, August 1995.

16. Thomas S. Monson, "The Prophet Joseph Smith: Teacher by Example," *Ensign*, November 2005.

17. Dieter F. Uchtdorf, "We Are Doing a Great Work and Cannot Come Down," *Ensign*, May 2009; emphasis added.

CHAPTER 8

HE GOVERNS HIMSELF

Attribute 25: Disciplined

Disciplined: *Consistent self–government through self–control, obedience, and self–restraint.*

In Proverbs we learn that "*He that is* slow to anger *is* better than the mighty; and he that ruleth his spirit than he that taketh a city*" (Proverbs 16:32). In other words, being disciplined is a valued and necessary attribute of leadership. Jesus is the perfect example of being disciplined for He was born to be the unblemished lamb that would be offered as a sacrifice to the laws of justice. Every thought, every action, even the intent of His heart needed to be perfectly controlled to be worthy to fulfill His divine mission. His self–control or discipline would be tested almost daily throughout His mortal life. One of the most quoted examples is when He responded to the temptations of the adversary by saying, "Get thee behind me, Satan" (Luke 4:8).

The Savior's discipline, however, was manifest even in small, insignificant matters. For example, on one occasion a man said unto him, "Master, speak to my brother, that he divide the inheritance with me" (Luke 12:13). As Jay and Donald Parry explained, "The speaker obviously was referring to his older brother. According to Jewish tradition and law, the oldest son in a family received a double portion of the inheritance. With that extra portion, he was obligated to care for members of the family who were unable to care for themselves. . . . The man who interrupted Jesus appears to have wanted Jesus to convince his brother that he should vary from tradition and law and divide the inheritance fifty–fifty."[1] However, "Jesus always refused to become involved in matters of civil law, and this case was no exception. 'Man,' Jesus answered, 'who made me a judge or a divider over you?'"[2] It is tempting for one who is looked to as a capable person to overextend the reach of his or her authority. Jesus resisted this temptation and showed strong discipline by restraining Himself in these matters of civil law and letting them be handled by those who had that responsibility.

Jesus again showed restraint when He stood before Herod who "questioned with him in many words; but he answered him nothing" (Luke 23:9). Later, when Jesus was before Pilate, we read:

"And Pilate asked him, Art thou the King of the Jews? And he answering said unto him, Thou sayest *it.*

"And the chief priests accused him of many things: but he answered nothing.

"And Pilate asked him again, saying, Answerest thou nothing? behold how many things they witness against thee.

"But Jesus yet answered nothing; so that Pilate marveled" (Mark 15:2–5, emphasis added).

Speaking to the Nephites following His Resurrection, Jesus showed restraint when He said:

"And not at any time hath the Father given me commandment that I should tell it unto your brethren at Jerusalem.

"Neither at any time hath the Father given me commandment that I should tell unto them concerning the other tribes of the house of Israel, whom the Father hath led away out of the land.

"This much did the Father command me, that I should tell unto them" (3 Nephi 15:14–16).

Perhaps the greatest examples of discipline occurred in Gethsemane and Calvary. In the garden, when the weight of all mankind was on His shoulders, Jesus pleaded, "O my Father, if it be possible, let this cup pass from me: *nevertheless not as I will,* but as thou *wilt"* (Matthew 26:39, emphasis added). He willingly restrained His own emotions and desires so He could accomplish His divine mission and the will of His Father.

The same discipline is evident when Jesus hung in agony at Golgotha. Surely, His impulses would have been to end the pain and humiliation, instead, He reached out to others in need. For example, He spoke with compassion to one of the "malefactors" (Luke 23:32) who hung also and promised that He would be with him in "paradise" (Luke 23:43). He spoke with loving concern to His mother when He referred to the disciple who would now take care of her, "Woman, behold thy son!" (John 19:26). He spoke with understanding when He said of the soldiers, "Father, forgive them; for they know not what they do" (Luke 23:34).

Throughout this ordeal, Jesus had the power to lay down His life whenever He wanted, but He maintained control despite the extreme pain until He could rightly say, "It is finished" (John 19:30). Having set the example of discipline, Jesus now invites us to do the same with these words, "Whosoever will come after me, *let him deny himself*, and take up his cross, and follow me" (Mark 8:34, emphasis added). Those who do follow Him are called His disciples because they have discipline.

President James E. Faust taught: "The word for *disciple* and the word for *discipline* both come from the same Latin root—*discipulus*, which means pupil. It emphasizes practice or exercise. Self-discipline and self-control are consistent and permanent characteristics of the followers of Jesus, as exemplified by Peter, James, and John, who indeed 'forsook all, and followed him.'"[3]

President Faust taught in essence that Jesus is the teacher and disciples are His pupils. They learn through practice and exercise to control themselves, rather than to be controlled. It is tempting for some teachers and some leaders to use external measures of control, but the Savior's approach is to develop control or discipline from within.

Examples of Righteous Leaders

President David O. McKay often taught of the need for discipline and self-control. He said: "It is as impossible to think of moral manhood apart from self-control as to separate sunlight from the day. Self-control means the government and regulation of all our natural appetites, desires, passions, and affections; and there is nothing that gives a man such strength of character as the sense of self-conquest, the realization that he can make his appetites and passions serve him and that he is not a servant to them. This virtue includes temperance, abstinence, bravery, fortitude, hopefulness, sobriety, chastity, independence, tolerance, patience, submission, continence, purity."[4]

The great philosopher Plato echoed this sentiment when he said, "The first and the best victory is to conquer self; to be conquered by self is, of all things, the most shameful and vile."[5] Leaders who demonstrate control or discipline over themselves will be given increasing responsibility in whatever endeavor they pursue.

Summary of Examples

- It takes discipline to resist overextending yourself and being pulled into topics or situations where you do not belong, as demonstrated by Jesus in staying out of civil matters.
- It takes discipline not to divulge more than authorized by your leader, or by good judgment, as demonstrated by Jesus who refrained from telling the Jews about the Nephites.
- It takes discipline to resist temptation with boldness and strength, as Jesus did when He said, "Get thee behind me, Satan" (Luke 4:8).
- It takes discipline to remain silent when necessary, as Jesus did before Pilate.
- It takes discipline to do unpleasant and painful assignments, as Jesus did in Gethsemane and Calvary.
- It takes discipline to demonstrate and develop discipline in your followers, as Jesus does with His disciples.

Questions for Personal Reflection

- Can you lead volatile situations to stable outcomes by keeping calm when everyone else around you seem to be losing their temper?
- Can you respond to false accusations or other personal attacks with controlled dignity?
- Do you maintain discipline by keeping confidences in all circumstances?

- How well do you lead yourself by controlling your thoughts, feelings, and actions so that you can acquire the attributes of Christ?
- How well do you lead your organization in focusing on the tasks that are the most important?

Attribute 26: Maintains Confidentiality

Confidential: *Limiting disclosure to persons authorized to have or use the information.*

Jesus practiced confidentiality when teaching His disciples by sharing information that would help them while withholding that which may hurt or condemn them. In addition, He could have easily overpowered His contemporaries with His vast knowledge and intellectual superiority, yet He withheld information because of His sensitivity for them and because He had no desire to elevate Himself in their eyes. Therefore, He chose to keep some information confidential. As Proverbs records, "A prudent man concealeth knowledge" (Proverbs 12:23).

The Gospel of Matthew records one of the choicest teaching experiences that the Savior's disciples would enjoy. Matthew states, "The same day went Jesus out of the house, and sat by the sea side. And great multitudes were gathered together unto him, so that he went into a ship, and sat, and the whole multitude stood on the shore" (Matthew 13:1–2). He then gives them seven wonderful parables:

1. The sower
2. The wheat and the tares
3. The grain of mustard seed
4. The leaven
5. The treasure hid in the field
6. The pearl of great price
7. The net cast into the sea

As Jesus continued to teach the multitude, the account states:

"And the disciples came, and said unto him, Why speakest thou unto them in parables?

"He answered and said unto them, Because *it is given unto you to know the mysteries of the kingdom of heaven, but to them it is not given.*

"For whosoever hath, to him shall be given, and he shall have more abundance: but whosoever hath not, from him shall be taken away even that he hath.

"Therefore speak I to them in parables: because they seeing see not; and hearing they hear not, neither do they understand" (Matthew 13:10–13, emphasis added).

Jesus taught His disciples that He withheld information from those who would not understand His teachings. He also stated they had been privileged to see and hear things He had withheld even from past prophets and righteous men. "For verily I say unto you, That many prophets and righteous *men* have desired to see *those things* which ye see, and have not seen *them*; and to hear *those things* which ye hear, and have not heard *them*"(Matthew 13:17, emphasis added).

In His wisdom, the Savior withholds information from both the spiritually young as well as those more spiritually mature, based on their level of understanding and their need and desire for additional knowledge. Additional knowledge requires additional responsibility so He waits patiently until the student is prepared and circumstances warrant.

Examples of Righteous Leaders

The scriptures tell of one prophet who had developed so much faith and had prepared himself so well that he both saw and heard great things that were kept confidential from other prophets. In his record, Ether records that the Lord revealed himself to the brother of Jared and showed him many great and wonderful things. However, the brother of Jared was instructed to keep this sacred experience confidential *before* he was allowed to experience it. Following his vision, he again was cautioned to share it with no one until the proper time. He was told:

"Behold, *thou shalt not suffer these things which ye have seen and heard to go forth unto the world,* until the time cometh that I shall glorify my name in the flesh; wherefore, ye shall treasure up the things which ye have seen and heard, and show it to no man (Ether 3:21, emphasis added).

"And when the Lord had said these words, he showed unto the

brother of Jared all the inhabitants of the earth which had been, and also all that would be; and he withheld them not from his sight, even unto the ends of the earth (Ether 3:25).

"And the Lord said unto him: Write these things and seal them up; and I will show them in mine own due time unto the children of men (Ether 3:27).

"For the Lord said unto me: *They shall not go forth unto the Gentiles* until the day that they shall repent of their iniquity, and become clean before the Lord" (Ether 4:6, emphasis added).

During the last recorded sermon of Nephi, he taught his people with all diligence for he wanted to influence them towards righteousness. Near the end of that sermon, as he was talking of "the doctrine of Christ," he interrupts himself by saying, "And now I, Nephi, cannot say more; the Spirit stoppeth mine utterance" (2 Nephi 32:7). One can only wonder what more Nephi could have taught his people, but he was instructed to keep confidential that which he was about to reveal. And the ever–obedient Nephi remained obedient to the end.

Six hundred years later, another Nephi had a similar directive. He was a first–hand witness to the risen Lord and recorded much from that sacred experience. He was instructed by the Lord to "Write the things which ye have seen and heard, save it be those which are forbidden" (3 Nephi 27:23). Here again, there were beautiful things both seen and heard which were to be kept confidential.

Many centuries later, the Prophet Joseph Smith was also instructed to keep certain information confidential. In March 1831, the Lord revealed much to Joseph and then commanded him to withhold it for a time. "And now I say unto you, *keep these things from going abroad* unto the world until it is expedient in me, that ye may accomplish this work in the eyes of the people, and in the eyes of your enemies, that they may not know your works until ye have accomplished the thing which I have commanded you" (D&C 45:72, emphasis added).

Also, on the banks of Fishing River during Zion's Camp, the Lord revealed through the Prophet Joseph Smith that some of what had been revealed should be kept confidential for a while. "And let all my people who dwell in the regions round about be very faithful, and prayerful, and humble before me, and *reveal not the things which I have revealed unto them, until it is wisdom in me that they should be revealed*" (D&C 105:23, emphasis added).

More recently, Camilla Kimball, wife of President Spencer W. Kimball, once addressed maintaining confidentiality. She wrote: "A wife should avoid problems with confidentiality. My husband and I were married in 1917, and in all those years I haven't sat beside him in a sacrament meeting a dozen times. His place has always been on the stand, and when our children were little, it wasn't easy to wrestle with them alone. A woman must be severely self–disciplined when her husband is in leadership positions. She must realize that there are many areas he is not free to discuss with her. I have always been glad that when a friend in curiosity would ask me about selections of officers to be made or personalities or problems of any kind, I could honestly say, 'I know nothing about it. I can tell you when I read it in the newspaper or hear it from the pulpit.' I know that sometimes capable and worthy men have been passed by because they had wives who were not cooperative. I try not to know of any confidential matters, but there is rarely any problem because Spencer is so careful that often I am the last to know something. Out of an abundance of caution, Spencer does not even tell me things that are not confidential. It is probably easier for him not to try to remember which things are public information and which are not."[6]

Camilla Kimball knew what all leaders need to know; confidentiality breeds trust and curtails speculation.

Summary of Examples

- Honorable leaders maintain confidentiality as they withhold information that would be misunderstood or would be harmful, as Jesus did with the parables.
- Honorable leaders give information that will be helpful to one who is ready but then commands them to keep it confidential from others who are not ready, as Jesus did with the brother of Jared.
- Honorable leaders maintain confidentiality by not revealing

they have confidential information, as demonstrated by Jesus throughout His life.

- Honorable leaders maintain confidentiality even among trusted associates, as did President Kimball with his wife Camilla.

Questions for Personal Reflection

- Do you avoid teasing others by advertising you have confidential information that would be interesting for them to receive?
- Do you refrain from sharing confidential information prematurely?
- Do you refrain from spreading unflattering information about others?
- How many people trust your confidentiality enough to share with you their private concerns and aspirations?
- How well do you avoid sharing precious experiences that should not be shared, or as the scriptures warn to avoid "casting your pearls before swine" (Matthew 7:6)?
- Do you have the wisdom to know when and with whom to share confidential information, while withholding it from the wrong people?

Attribute 27: Frugal

Frugal: *Economical in use or expenditure; prudently saving or sparing; not wasteful.*

On one occasion as Jesus and His disciples sat upon a mountain preparing for the Passover, Jesus "lifted up his eyes, and saw a great company come unto him [and] he saith unto Philip, Whence shall we buy bread, that these may eat? (John 6:5). John's account states that Jesus knew what He was going to do, but He wanted to test him. Philip replied, "Two hundred pennyworth of bread is not sufficient for them" (John 6:7). Andrew also commented, "There is a lad here, which hath five barley loaves, and two small fishes: but what are they among so many?" (John 6:9). Jesus then asked that they have the men, which numbered 5,000, sit on the grass in preparation for another miracle.

"And Jesus took the loaves; and when he had *given thanks,* he distributed to the disciples, and the disciples to them that were set down; and likewise of the fishes as much as they would.

"When they were filled, he said unto his disciples, Gather up the fragments that remain, that *nothing be lost.*

"Therefore they gathered them together, and filled twelve baskets with the fragments of the five barley loaves, which remained over and above unto them that had eaten.

"Then those men, when they had seen the miracle that Jesus did, said, This is of a truth that prophet that should come into the world" (John 6:11–14, emphasis added).

The focus of this story has been and should be the great miracle of expanding so little food into so much food. The main lesson is that Jesus of Nazareth is indeed a prophet of God. In addition, there are at least two more lessons the Savior taught. The first lesson is that He gave thanks for the blessing of the food they were receiving. The second lesson is His demonstration of frugality as they "Gather up the fragments that remain, that nothing be lost." The fragments of this precious food, which filled twelve baskets, were blessings from God and surely would be used to bless additional lives. This ability to bless more lives with the resources we have received is at the core of frugality. The old adage, "waste not, want not" has guided many people to be wise stewards of the blessings received from God. "For the earth is full, and there is enough and to spare" (D&C 104:17) if we but use our influence for wise distribution and consumption of those resources.

Examples of Righteous Leaders

The great colonizer Brigham Young taught that the wise use of resources would give the Saints greater power, influence, and blessings. He said: "It is to our advantage to take good care of the blessings God bestows upon us; if we pursue the opposite course, we cut off the power and glory God designs we should inherit. It is through our own carefulness, frugality, and judgment which God has given us, that we are enabled to preserve our grain, our flocks and herds, wives and children, houses and lands, and increase them around us, continually gaining power and influence for ourselves as individuals and for the Kingdom of God as a whole."[7]

This counsel to be frugal is echoed by President J. Reuben Clark who said, "Live within your means. Get out of debt. Keep out of debt. Lay by for a rainy day which has always come and will come again. Practice and increase your habits of thrift, industry, economy, and frugality."[8] In short, being frugal demonstrates the discipline and wisdom that Jesus exemplified. It utilizes available resources for the growth and stability of people and organizations.

Summary of Examples

- A frugal leader makes full use of his resources to further his cause, as Jesus did with the surplus loaves and fishes.
- A frugal leader uses his resources to increase his power and influence for good, as taught by Brigham Young.
- A frugal leader avoids debt to the extent possible, as taught by President J. Reuben Clark.

Questions for Personal Reflection

- Are you content with what you have without always wishing for that which you do not have?
- Are you influencing your associates not to feel pressured to continually obtain the best, newest, trendiest, costliest, or showiest items?
- Are you following frugality with a wise budget so that your income is used properly?
- Are you setting a good example by avoiding debt to the extent possible?
- How do you utilize your surpluses? Do you use your personal resources to increase your influence for good and help others as situations arise?
- Are you as frugal on a business trip with company funds as you are on a vacation with personal funds?

Attribute 28: Consistent

Consistent: *Free from variation or contradiction. Constantly adhering to the same principles, course.*

Jesus declared to the Nephites, "I change not" (3 Nephi 24:6) for "I am the same yesterday, today, and forever" (2 Nephi 27:23). He explained to the Latter-day Saints, "For God doth not walk in crooked paths, neither doth he turn to the right hand nor to the left, neither doth he vary from that which he hath said, therefore his paths are straight" (D&C 3:2). Jesus is the perfect example of consistency in His character, in His message, and in His treatment of others.

In both Jerusalem and the Americas, Jesus appointed twelve Apostles to ensure consistency in the words He spoke, for He knew there would be those who would alter them for their own purposes. The Apostle Paul taught that Jesus "gave some, apostles; and some, prophets; . . . For the perfecting of the saints . . . Till we all come in the unity of the faith . . . That we *henceforth* be no more children, tossed to and fro, and carried about with every wind of doctrine, by the sleight of men, *and* cunning craftiness, whereby they lie in wait to deceive" (Ephesians 4:11–14).

In the morning of the second day of the Savior's visit to the Nephites, a great multitude assembled at the temple. The newly called Twelve Apostles sought to prepare the minds and hearts of the multitude for another visitation. The scriptures record, "And when they had ministered those same words which Jesus had spoken— *nothing varying from the words which Jesus had spoken*—behold, they knelt again and prayed to the Father in the name of Jesus" (3 Nephi19:8, emphasis added). These Apostles were consistent in both the manner and content of their ministering as exemplified by Jesus. The words they spoke are the words Jesus has always spoken, for He said, "my words shall hiss forth unto the ends of the earth, *for a standard unto my people,* which are of the house of Israel" (2 Nephi 29:2, emphasis added). These words are applied consistently to all people regardless of when or where they lived.

Jesus taught: "Know ye not that the testimony of two nations is a witness unto you that I am God, that I remember one nation like unto another? Wherefore, *I speak the same words unto one nation like unto another.* And when the two nations shall run together the testimony of the two nations shall run together also" (2 Nephi 29:8, emphasis added).

These *same words* that Jesus spoke never changed, whether He was speaking to different nations or to believers and non-believers. Yes, He hid some truths from the non-believers by speaking in parables, but His underlying message never changed even when it was unpopular. For example, when Jesus taught in Capernaum that He was "the living bread which came down from heaven" (John 6:51), "many of his disciples went back, and walked no more with him" (John 6:66). They viewed His message as "an hard saying" (John 6:60). Though the Savior lost followers, He remained consistent with His message and never altered its tone or content to gain popularity. This is further attested to when He said, "The world cannot hate you; but me it hateth, because I testify of it, that the works thereof are evil" (John 7:7). Though unpopular, Jesus consistently spoke out against evil and the consequences of sin.

The Apostle Peter taught that "God is no respecter of persons" (Acts 10:34). He is consistent in His actions towards one person as He is towards another. When Jesus taught the parable of the prodigal son, many people understood the obvious message of forgiveness that is central to the story. As in all parables, there are other significant messages as well. In this parable, we also learn something about the consistency of character. We are told about three main people—the prodigal son, the faithful son, and the father. Regarding the father, it is his character that is on display. As one commentator wrote, "The attitude of the father toward his sons is not determined by their character, but his."[9] This noble father demonstrated consistency as he responded to two sons with very different personalities, situations, and needs. With each son, he was consistent in his love, understanding, persuasion, forgiveness, civility, and celebration.

Examples of Righteous Leaders

President David O. McKay demonstrated consistency both at home and at work. For example, Robert and Edward McKay, two of President McKay's sons were once asked, "Was it really the case that he never raised his voice in his home or that he never shouted or said something a little bit angry?" These sons simply attested, "It was."[10] This behavior was consistent in two ways. First, President McKay was consistent throughout his son's lives, and second, he was consistent in living the principles at home that he taught from the pulpit.

Another example of President McKay's consistency was expressed by his long–time secretary who said she never saw him depressed or strike out at someone. She said she "saw people come in an endless stream who were both depressed and sometimes angry, but when they left his presence they had been changed."[11] By living and demonstrating Christlike attributes such as love, patience, and consistency, President McKay used his influence to help people be better and do better. This influence came from his example as much as it was from his preaching.

Summary of Examples

- A consistent leader lives the same yesterday, today, and forever by unchanging principles of righteousness, as does Jesus.
- A consistent leader ensures followers are consistent as they share his message and manage his work, as Jesus did with His Apostles.
- A consistent leader remains true to his or her core values and message even if unpopular, as Jesus did when He declared He was the literal Son of God.
- A consistent leader treats each person consistently regardless of rank, influence, good deeds, or bad deeds, as demonstrated by Jesus and the prodigal son's father.
- Consistent leaders do not allow the actions or emotions of others to draw them into degrading behavior, as demonstrated by President McKay.

Questions for Personal Reflection

- When you encounter a new situation, do you stop and ask yourself, "What is the principle that should guide my actions?"
- Are you consistently avoiding hypocrisy by living the same principles of the gospel at home, work, or school that you espouse at Church?
- Are you consistently the same person when mingling among the so-called elite as with the humble and disadvantaged?
- How well do you lead your associates in living gospel principles even while having fun?
- Do you administer correction consistently without being influenced by favoritism?
- How well are you influencing others by consistently following the Golden Rule and treating others as you would want to be treated?

Attribute 29: Endures to the End

Endure: Suffer (something painful or difficult) patiently.
End: *The point at which something ceases: conclusion.*

When Jesus declared, "I am Alpha and Omega, the beginning and the end, the first and the last" (Revelation 22:13), He established the parameter of His time frame "to bring to pass the immortality and eternal life of man" (Moses 1:39). He is declaring that as our leader, He started with this effort and He "endureth forever" (Moroni 7:47). He also said, "I, the Lord . . . will be their king, and I will be a light unto them *forever*" (2 Nephi 10:14, emphasis added). Jesus assures us that He will be in it for the long haul or until it can be said, "It is finished; it is finished! The Lamb of God hath overcome" (D&C 88:106).

In the parable of the lost sheep, Jesus teaches that the shepherd cares for his sheep and never gives up on them. "What man of you, having an hundred sheep, if he lose one of them, doth not leave the ninety and nine in the wilderness, and go after that which is lost, *until he find it?*" (Luke 15:4, emphasis added). There was no provision for a premature withdrawal of his responsibility for his sheep. So it is with the Master, He endures to the end until all His followers are found and safely gathered in. He said: "For unto such shall ye continue to minister; for ye know not but what they will return and repent, and come unto me with full purpose of heart, and I shall heal them; and ye shall be the means of bringing salvation unto them" (3 Nephi 18:32). "And if it so be that you should labor all your days in crying repentance unto this people, and bring, save it be one soul unto me, how great shall be your joy with him in the kingdom of my Father!" (D&C 18:15).

Jesus taught His disciples that He had been given a work to do and would not move on until it was done. He said, "I must work the works of him that sent me, while I am with you; the time cometh when I shall have finished my work, then I go unto the Father" (Joseph Smith Translation, John 9:4). During His final hours of finishing that work, Jesus gathered His Apostles together in the upper room to instruct and strengthen them, for "he loved them *unto the end*" (John 13:1, emphasis added). When all had been done that He was sent to do,

Jesus was able to report back, "Father, it is finished, *thy will is done*" (Joseph Smith Translation, Matthew 27:50, emphasis added).

Jesus taught, "But he that shall endure to the end, the same shall be saved" (Matthew 24:13). The Apostle Paul exemplified this doctrine as he endured many trials for the sake of Christ until the end of his mortal journey. Then he said what all followers of Christ hope to say, "I have fought a good fight, I have finished my course, I have kept the faith" (2 Timothy 4:7).

Examples of Righteous Leaders

After Alma heard the final words of the prophet Abinadi, he departed into the wilderness and began teaching the words he had been taught. He then proceeded to baptize those willing to enter into a covenant with the Lord. The record states, "Alma took Helam, he being one of the first, and went and stood forth in the water . . . and he said: Helam, I baptize thee, having authority from the Almighty God, as a testimony that *ye have entered into a covenant to serve him until you are dead as to the mortal body*" (Mosiah 18:12–13, emphasis added). In this baptism, Alma impressed upon Helam that the covenant he was making was to serve his entire life, even until the very end.

The scriptures record many examples of those who endured faithfully to the end. They also record the sad accounts of those who did not. For example, King Saul fell because he did not endure to the end, did not pass his test, did not wait in patience, and did not follow Samuel the prophet's counsel (1 Samuel 13:13–14).

In more modern times, there is the account of Jesse Gause who was called to the First Presidency. "However, when he failed to continue in a manner consistent with this appointment, the call was subsequently transferred to Frederick G. Williams" (D&C 81 section heading). Another example is James Covill who "received the word with gladness, but straightway Satan tempted him, and the fear of persecution and the cares of the world caused him to reject the word" (D&C 40:2).

These accounts of those who do not endure to the end are painful to review because their outcome could be our outcome if we do not "learn to be more wise than [they] have been" (Mormon 9:31). As President Brigham Young said, "The men and women, who desire to obtain seats in the celestial kingdom, will find that they must battle every day [for this sacred goal]."[12] So it is with anything we must endure. We need to be diligent in following the course that leads to our objective.

This enduring is a continual effort from which we can never relax. However, it does not need to be unpleasant. Elder Dieter F. Uchtdorf gave this encouraging counsel: "Therefore, enduring to the end is not just a matter of passively tolerating life's difficult circumstances or "hanging in there." Ours is an active religion, helping God's children along the strait and narrow path to develop their full potential during this life and return to Him one day. Viewed from this perspective, enduring to the end is exalting and glorious, not grim and gloomy. This is a joyful religion, one of hope, strength, and deliverance. 'Adam fell that men might be; and men are, that they might have joy'" (2 Nephi 2:25).[13]

Leaders must endure to the end if they expect their followers to endure to the end. A coach who heads to the locker room when his or her team is down by 30 points cannot expect the players to stay on the court. Leadership is about improving people and situations, it is about moving forward more than it is about arriving at an artificial destination. The work of the Savior is not yet complete so neither is ours. And this journey can be so much more effective if it is driven by a heart full of joy for the opportunity to progress.

Summary of Examples

- Honorable leaders endure to the end by staying with an assignment until it is finished, as Jesus does until He can say, "It is finished; it is finished! The Lamb of God hath overcome" (D&C 88:106).
- Honorable leaders endure to the end by not giving up on their people, as Jesus taught about continuing to minister even to a single individual or a lost sheep.

- Honorable leaders have endured to the end when they can say like Paul, "I have finished my course, I have kept the faith" (2 Timothy 4:7).
- Honorable leaders who do not endure might be removed from their positions, as was Saul, Jesse Gause, and James Covill.
- Honorable leaders strengthen others during difficult times by not just enduring to the end, but by working in strength and with cheerfulness, as taught by Dieter F. Uchtdorf.

Questions for Personal Reflection

- Is your quest to acquire the attributes of Christ a lifelong endeavor, or is it for short–term purposes?
- Are you enduring to the end by continuing to teach and mentor someone who appears to be making little progress?
- How many lifelong friendships are you continuing to foster?
- Do you fully complete a task or assignment, or is "good enough, good enough?"
- Are you continuing to progress as you age, or are you coasting to the finish line?

Attribute 30: Prioritizes

Priority: *Something given or meriting attention before competing alternatives.*

Jesus succinctly taught His disciples of the need to prioritize and how to prioritize. In doing so, He set a foundational principle that we can use to make many of the decisions we face each day of our lives. He taught, "Wherefore, seek not the things of this world but seek ye first to build up the kingdom of God, and to establish his righteousness" (Joseph Smith Translation, Matthew 6:33). There are two elements to this commission: building the Lord's organization and building His people. Both simply have priority over other things.

Jesus set the example of prioritization by preparing himself spiritually before ministering to the people. Undoubtedly, the scriptures do not record each time He did this, but they do record a few examples that were indicative of others. For example, at the beginning of His formal three-year ministry, He fasted 40 days to prepare Himself for that ministry. Before calling the Twelve Apostles, He prepared himself spiritually as He "went out into a mountain to pray, and continued all night in prayer to God" (Luke 6:12). Later, before walking on the water to His disciples, He "went up into a mountain apart to pray" (Matthew 14:23).

This spiritual preparation is a form of prioritizing. It is a realization that some things are a prerequisite before other things can be done. Also, it is an acknowledgment that some things are more important than others. This was a lesson Jesus taught His close friend Martha when she chose to focus on serving Him rather than learning from Him, as Mary was doing. The Savior taught her that "Mary hath *chosen that good part"* (Luke 10:38–42, emphasis added). Martha was doing a good work but her priority was not Jesus's priority.

Jesus taught this same message of prioritizing to another group of people when He said, "Woe unto you, scribes and Pharisees, hypocrites! for ye pay tithe of mint and anise and cummin, and *have omitted the weightier matters* of the law, judgment, mercy, and faith: these ought ye to have done, and not to leave the other undone"

(Matthew 23:23, emphasis added). When Jesus is approached by a Canaanite woman whose "daughter is grievously vexed with a devil," He revealed that His ministry had a priority, for He said, "I am not sent but unto the lost sheep of the house of Israel" (Matthew 15:24). Ultimately, Jesus healed her daughter because of her faith and persistence. However, He clearly stated that His priority at that point was to minister to the house of Israel.

Another example of prioritizing comes just before Jesus's Crucifixion when it would be understandable for Him to spend time with His family. However, He knew His priority was to prepare and strengthen the Twelve Apostles so they could continue His work after His death. During the Last Supper, the Savior prepared them by instituting the sacrament, washing their feet, teaching that those called to high positions are servants to all, warning Peter that Satan would seek his destruction, and finally, by commanding them to love one another. With all His priorities now set in order, our Savior turned aside to complete that which only He could do, His Atonement and Resurrection.

Examples of Righteous Leaders

Nehemiah is an example of a leader who stayed fixed on the priorities at hand even during great diversionary pressure. Nehemiah had been given authority to rebuild the walls of Jerusalem and labored with his people to do so. Several rulers who lived near Jerusalem opposed this effort and sought to stop it. Four times they called for Nehemiah to leave the protection of the city and meet with them to resolve their conflict, "but Nehemiah knew that their intent was to do him harm. Each time that they approached him, he responded with the same answer: *I am doing a great work*, so that I cannot come down.'"[14] The priority was to build the city walls so they would have protection. Had Nehemiah not focused on this top priority, his endeavor likely would have failed.

The prophet Nephi also led his people by following sound priorities. Upon arriving in the Promised Land, Nephi separated his people from the others so they could live in righteousness. He also established a solid agricultural based society. He states, "we did sow seed, and we did reap again in abundance. And we began to raise flocks, and herds, and animals of every kind" (2 Nephi 5:11). Because of this prioritized preparation, they lived a stable and comfortable life. Contrast this to the manner of preparation of his brother Laman, whose people appeared to live for generations mainly upon stolen food and wild game.

Years later, Alma demonstrated that his leadership also was based on priorities. At one point during his tenure as chief judge, he felt the people had become so wicked that it threatened the very fabric of their society. As Alma considered this situation, he determined that his top priority was to use his personal influence to help people repent. Therefore, he resigned his civic position so he could give his full effort to building righteousness among the people (Alma 4:20). Alma believed "the preaching of the word had a great tendency to lead the people to do that which was just—yea, it had had more powerful effect upon the minds of the people than the sword, or anything else, which had happened unto them" (Alma 31:5). Alma preached the word of God with all diligence which changed many lives and brought peace again to the land. A peace that would not have been possible had he not addressed the heart of the problems they were experiencing.

Several years later, the Nephites again needed to repent and another leader emerged who also understood priorities. This leader was Captain Moroni who wrote those priorities on a banner called the title of liberty. He had it raised from every tower in the land to remind the people of their priorities which were God, religion, freedom, peace, their wives and children (Alma 46:12). He equipped his army with the best armor and sent spies to gather information. He protected the cities with great fortifications which he continually strengthened.

At one point, after Captain Moroni and his armies had fought nobly and had many victories he faced an unexpected enemy, his own government. Because of corruption in the government, his resources were dwindling and his ability to maintain his armies was severely weakened. Even though the opposing Lamanite armies continued to attack, Moroni felt it was a higher priority to reestablish a solid government that could provide the support his armies desperately needed. So, he took many his warriors and pulled down the corruption, fortified his armies, and eventually established peace the remainder of his days (Alma 62:11). The outcome, however, would have been much different had he not taken care of his priorities.

Volumes could be written about how the Lord prioritized the events of the Restoration of the gospel and how He guided the life of the Prophet Joseph accordingly. However, one example is illustrative of this prioritization. The angel Moroni led Joseph to the ancient records of his people and directed him to translate them. At that time, this assignment was his first priority. The Savior reaffirmed this with these words, "And you have a gift to translate the plates; and this is the first gift that I bestowed upon you; and I have commanded that you should pretend to no other gift until my purpose is fulfilled in this; for *I will grant unto you no other gift until it is finished*" (D&C 5:4, emphasis added). Priorities are often established because as with building blocks, some need to be placed first to form a foundation for other blocks to be placed on them. This was surely the case with translating these records.

Mahatma Gandhi once said, "There is more to life than increasing its speed."[15] There is a need to choose wisely among the many choices that are placed before us. Our choices determine our happiness and influence with others. Elder Dieter F. Uchtdorf counseled: "It is possible to take even good things to excess. One example can be seen in a father or grandfather who spends hours upon hours searching for his ancestors or creating a blog while neglecting or avoiding quality or meaningful time with his own children and grandchildren. Another example could be a gardener who spends his days pulling weeds from the soil while ignoring the spiritual weeds that threaten to choke his soul."[16]

There are many good things that can occupy our time, but a wise person will prioritize them so the most important activities get the most attention. Making a life-long commitment to acquiring the attributes of Jesus is a top priority, for it will produce wonderful fruits in this life and build a firm foundation for the eternities. Using the seven-step process discussed in chapter 4 will aid in acquiring these attributes so we can have greater influence for good.

Summary of Examples

- Honorable leaders prioritize by establishing a personal set of core values, as taught by Jesus to first seek the kingdom of God.
- Honorable leaders prioritize by preparing themselves first, as Jesus did when He fasted and prayed before ministering to others.
- Honorable leaders prioritize by choosing the best choices based on sound core values, as Mary did when she chose to listen when Jesus taught.
- Honorable leaders prioritize when they choose first to help people in need, as Jesus did in healing the daughter of the Canaanite woman.
- Honorable leaders prioritize by not being distracted, as demonstrated by Nehemiah who refused to meet with neighboring rulers; and Joseph Smith who focused on translating the plates.
- Honorable leaders prioritize by building a stable foundation for their lives, as Nephi did in having his people till the ground and plant seeds for future sustenance.
- Honorable leaders prioritize by focusing on teaching pure doctrine, as Alma did when he left his judgment seat to preach the word of God.
- Honorable leaders prioritize by removing impediments if they are halting forward progress, as Captain Moroni did when he redirected his fight from the Lamanites to corruption within the Nephite government.
- Honorable leaders prioritize as they balance their time between self–rejuvenation and work, as taught by Mahatma Gandhi.
- Honorable leaders prioritize as they minimize time spent on good things so they can maximize time spent on doing great things, as taught by Dieter F. Uchtdorf.

Questions for Personal Reflection

- Are you changing your very nature to be more like the Savior and be less influenced by natural man tendencies?
- Do you prioritize by balancing your life between spiritual, intellectual, physical, social, and emotional needs? What are you doing to lead others to do the same?
- How many of your decisions are based on what is right, rather than on what you prefer, or what would bring you the most gain?
- Is one of your top priorities the development and well–being of those you lead?
- How often do you set aside your busy schedule to respond to a call for assistance?

Attribute 31: Plans Ahead

Plan: *A detailed formulation of a program of action. A method for achieving an end.*

In the book of Abraham, an account is given of the creation of the world. It is an abbreviated account but there are enough details to show that planning and preparation went into the creation. "And the Gods prepared the waters . . . And the Gods prepared the earth . . . And the Gods organized the earth" (Abraham 4:21–25). This creation occurred in two well-planned phases, the first a spiritual creation followed by a physical creation (D&C 29:32). President Boyd K. Packer taught that this creation was planned with a purpose. "The beauty and precision of the universe, the endless variety of plant and animal life, all testify of a plan, and of a Creator . . . . The plan is not based on chance, nor on accident. It is based on purpose, on agency, on choice. It accords with laws which were in force long before the plan was ever laid down. All of it has order; all of it was planned for us."[17]

During His mortal mission, Jesus taught His disciples the need to plan ahead. In the parable of the unrighteous steward, the steward made a mistake that cost him his job. Before being fired, he cunningly made a deal with those to whom his boss was in debt. Thereby, when he became unemployed, he had others who would assist him. As he explained, "when I am put out of the stewardship, they may receive me into their houses" (Luke 16:4). The parable explains that the wicked prepare for their futures but the "children of light" do not. Elder James E. Talmage taught of this parable, "Take a lesson from even the dishonest and the evil; if they are so prudent as to provide for the only future they think of, how much more should you, who believe in an eternal future, provide therefore!"[18]

Perhaps a more familiar parable on planning ahead is the parable of the ten virgins. In this parable, ten virgins "went forth to meet the bridegroom. And five of them were wise, and five were foolish. They that were foolish took their lamps, and took no oil with them" (Matthew 25:1–3). These five foolish virgins had not planned ahead and lost a significant opportunity because they were unprepared.

During the Savior's final week, He demonstrated how to plan ahead for significant events. The first event occurred on the fifth day before the Passover in preparation for His triumphal entry into Jerusalem. The Gospel of Mark records:

"He sendeth forth two of his disciples,

"And saith unto them, Go your way into the village over against you: and as soon as ye be entered into it, ye shall find a colt tied, whereon never man sat; loose him, and bring *him*.

"And if any man say unto you, Why do ye this? say ye that the Lord hath need of him; and straightway he will send him hither.

"And they went their way, and found the colt tied by the door without in a place where two ways met; and they loose him. And certain of them that stood there said unto them, What do ye, loosing the colt? And they said unto them even as Jesus had commanded: and they let them go.

"And they brought the colt to Jesus, and cast their garments on him; and he sat upon him" (Mark 11:1–7).

Now that the preparations were complete as He planned, the Savior entered His beloved city.

"And many spread their garments in the way: and others cut down branches off the trees, and strawed *them* in the way.

"And they that went before, and they that followed, cried, saying, Hosanna; Blessed *is* he that cometh in the name of the Lord:

"Blessed *be* the kingdom of our father David, that cometh in the name of the Lord: Hosanna in the highest" (Mark 11:8–10).

The second example of planning ahead is when Jesus prepared to cleanse the temple. This cleansing was not some random overreaction or irrational emotional outburst. Rather, it was a pre–planned lesson He needed to teach. The scriptures point out that Jesus clearly slept on His decision before carrying out His plans.

"And Jesus entered into Jerusalem, and into the temple: and when he had looked round about upon all things, and now the eventide was come, he went out unto Bethany with the twelve.

"And *on the morrow*, when they were come from Bethany . . . they come to Jerusalem: and Jesus went into the temple, and began to cast out them that sold and bought in the temple, and overthrew the tables of the moneychangers, and the seats of them that sold doves; And would not suffer that any man should carry *any* vessel through the temple.

"And he taught, saying unto them, Is it not written, My house shall be called of all nations the house of prayer? but ye have made it a den of thieves" (Mark 11:11–17, emphasis added).

The final example is the planning and preparation for the Feast of the Passover, or the Last Supper. Luke records:

"And he sent Peter and John, saying, *Go and prepare* us the passover, that we may eat. And they said unto him, Where wilt thou that we prepare?

"And he said unto them, Behold, when ye are entered into the city, there shall a man meet you, bearing a pitcher of water; follow him into the house where he entereth in.

"And ye shall say unto the goodman of the house, The Master saith unto thee, Where is the guestchamber, where I shall eat the passover with my disciples?

"And he shall shew you a large upper room furnished: there make ready" (Luke 22:8–12, emphasis added).

Jesus taught His disciples that planning and advance preparation is needed to ensure important events occur properly to produce the intended results. Each of these events was critically significant and their success could not be left to chance.

Examples of Righteous Leaders

Few leaders have been thrust into service as was Joseph of old. He was brought "hastily out of the dungeon" (Genesis 41:14) and barely had time to shave and change his clothes before he entered Pharaoh's chambers. A few minutes later he was "set . . . over all the land of Egypt" (Genesis 41:41). His assignment, given by Pharaoh himself, was to lead Egypt through seven years of plenty so they could survive the seven years of famine that God revealed would then follow. This task required careful planning and diligent execution, and Joseph led the way.

Although the Old Testament does not give many details of

Joseph's efforts, it seems reasonable to assume these plans called for getting the support of the people, the creation of storage facilities, the collection and protection of the food, and developing procedures governing its wise distribution. The initial plans called for Joseph to collect "the fifth part of the land of Egypt in the seven plenteous years" (Genesis 41:34). Therefore Joseph, at the age of thirty, "went throughout all the land of Egypt . . . And he gathered up all the food of the seven years, which were in the land of Egypt, and laid up the food in the cities: the food of the field, which *was* round about every city, laid he up in the same" (Genesis 41:46–48). The success of his efforts is evident for he "gathered corn as the sand of the sea, very much, until he left numbering, for it *was* without number" (Genesis 41:49). This success came because a visionary leader looked over the horizon, knowing what lay on the other side, and developed a plan to get his people prepared.

Capable leaders throughout the Book of Mormon also guided and protected their people by their advance planning. For example, Alma prepared his people for battle and "sent spies that he might know of their plans and their plots, whereby he might guard himself against them, that he might preserve his people from being destroyed" (Alma 2:21). In another example many years later, the Nephites were attacked by armies of robbers determined to destroy them. However, the Nephites prevailed "for it was impossible for the robbers to lay siege sufficiently long to have any effect upon the Nephites, because of their much provision which they had laid up in store" (3 Nephi 4:18). The advance planning by their leaders led to their survival.

Perhaps the most detailed account of advance planning by a leader is the account of Captain Moroni. The record states that he "altered the management of affairs among the Nephites" (Alma 49:11) to give them the advantage. For, "he thought it no sin that he should defend them by stratagem" (Alma 43:30). He prepared his armies with armor and weapons superior to his opponents (Alma 43:19). He prepared "the minds of the people" (Alma 48:7) and he strengthened their weakest fortifications (Alma 48:9). In short, "they were prepared . . . in a manner which never had been known among the children of Lehi"

(Alma 49:8). Most importantly, "Moroni did not stop making preparations for war" (Alma 50:1).

Wisdom would suggest that those who most enjoy the sunny days are the ones who are prepared for the gathering storm. In May 2011, such a storm hit the United States causing the worst tornado damage in history. Below is an account published in the Church News of how advance planning minimized suffering.

"Last fall, Elder [Walter F.] Gonzalez of the Presidency of the Seventy asked our stakes in the Southeast to schedule a day of service in the spring.

"He [Stake President Harmon] explained that his stake and others had months ago made plans for that day of service to be April 30. As a result of that advance planning, dozens of bales of clothing from the Church's Humanitarian Services department arrived in Birmingham a few days before the storms hit.

"The result was that just three days after the storms we distributed that clothing to those who now needed it," he said. "We hadn't anticipated the disaster, but through the Lord's guidance and following the direction of His servants, the clothing was already here."[19]

Leaders who plan ahead and focus on the needs of others can be a great blessing to their people. They can have them ready to weather the storms of life or take advantage of unforeseen opportunities.

Summary of Examples

- Honorable leaders plan ahead by providing for their future, as taught in the parable of the unrighteous steward.
- Honorable leaders plan ahead by ensuring that they and their people are fully prepared with necessary provisions, as taught by the ten virgins.
- Honorable leaders plan ahead by giving specific instructions in preparing for important events so success is not left to chance, as Jesus demonstrated with His triumphal entry, and the Last Supper.
- Honorable leaders plan ahead by carefully considering bold

actions before carrying them out, as Jesus did before cleansing the temple.

- Honorable leaders plan ahead by preparing for attacks from their enemies by keeping a close eye on them and by having sufficient defenses, as Alma did against the Lamanites.
- Honorable leaders never stop planning ahead, as demonstrated by Captain Moroni who "did not stop making preparations" (Alma 50:1).

Questions for Personal Reflection

- What is your plan for acquiring the leadership attributes of Jesus? Are you tracking your progress on this plan?
- What plan do you have for leading others to Christ?
- What is your plan to increase your capability, your skills, and your knowledge?
- What have you done to prepare yourself to influence others you meet throughout the day?
- Are you leading your organization based on a well–thought–out plan?
- Are you making a difference by helping your community plan for future growth, services, and activities?

Attribute 32: Prepares Himself

Prepare: *To make ready beforehand for some purpose, use, or activity. To put in a proper state of mind.*

Jesus told the brother of Jared, "I am he who was prepared from the foundation of the world to redeem my people" (Ether 3:14). We do not fully understand what those preparations included but we do know that during His mortal mission, Jesus continued to prepare Himself before various situations in His ministry. For example, at the age of thirty, He prepared for His forthcoming ministry by fasting 40 days. Then, shortly after that fast, He engaged in a full night of prayer in preparation for calling His Twelve Apostles.

"And it came to pass in those days, that he went out into a mountain to pray, and continued *all night in prayer* to God.

"And when it was day, he called *unto him* his disciples: and of them he chose twelve, whom also he named apostles" (Luke 6:12–13, emphasis added).

Part of His preparation was to prepare to teach His followers in their language and according to their understanding. The parables He used were crafted to liken spiritual truths to the students' surroundings such as mustard seeds, fig trees, oil lamps, bridegrooms, wheat and tares, sowing seeds in unprepared soil, or becoming "fishers of men" (Matthew 4:19). He also prepared Himself to teach from the scriptures used by the learned men of Judea. His ability to quote from these scriptures helped establish His credibility and authenticity.

Before teaching His disciples the Sermon on the Mount, Jesus first "went up into a mountain: and *when he was set,* his disciples came unto him: And he opened his mouth, and taught them" (Matthew 5:1–2, emphasis added). He first prepared himself, and then He taught. The Gospel of Mark records an account of Jesus taking time for His spiritual renewal and preparation. "And in the morning, rising up a great while before day, he went out, and departed into a solitary place, and there prayed" (Mark 1:35). Surely, this was not an isolated event but a lifelong practice that kept Him continually prepared to do His Father's will.

In the parable of the leaven, we can see a correlation between the effect leaven has on bread and the effect a prepared leader can have on his or her people. In that parable, leaven was added to "three measures of meal" (Matthew 13:33) which is about 50 pounds. This would produce enough bread to feed more than a 100 people.[20] The point Jesus made was that a little influence can produce dramatic results. And so it is with leaders. When they have prepared themselves to become someone people will follow, then they can use their influence to help others to rise. They can infuse life into their communities, families, and organizations. In short, they can be the leaven in the proverbial bread.

Examples of Righteous Leaders

The scriptures contain many examples of righteous individuals who prepared themselves to lead people to a better life. For example, Nephi's brother Jacob first got directions from his leader before teaching his people. "Wherefore I, Jacob, gave unto them these words as I taught them in the temple, having first obtained mine errand from the Lord" (Jacob 1:17). Alma "fasted and prayed many days" (Alma 5:46) as he prepared to teach his people. The sons of Mosiah prepared themselves to be men of wisdom and knowledge. Then they could lift their brethren for "they had waxed strong in the knowledge of the truth; for they were men of a sound understanding and they had searched the scriptures diligently, that they might know the word of God" (Alma 17:2).

In the early days of the Restoration, Sister Eliza R. Snow who served as the second Relief Society general president, counseled the women of the Church to prepare themselves for the great responsibilities the Lord had in store for them. She said, "We know the Lord has laid high responsibilities upon us . . . and the greatest good we can do to ourselves and each other is to refine and cultivate ourselves in everything that is good and ennobling to qualify us for those responsibilities."[21]

Sister Eliza R. Snow mentored many women and helped them

prepare for greater roles of influence. One of these women was Emmeline B. Wells who later become the fifth Relief Society general president at the age of 82. Emmeline began her personal preparation at a young age as she sat under the branches of a favored old tree, dreaming of becoming someone of great influence. She recorded that she sat "with proud ambition burning in my soul, ambition to be great and known to fame, when a gentle whisper came. . . . 'There is no excellence without labor.'"[22]

Emmeline B. Wells immediately embarked on a life of labor, a life of learning, of serving others, of growing from new and demanding experiences. She studied at the New Salem Academy, a private high school in her native Massachusetts. She studied at the feet of the Prophet Joseph Smith in Nauvoo. She visited Washington D.C. many times appearing before congressional committees and nurturing many lifelong relationships with other women of national prominence. She became a leading national voice and influence in securing the right for women to vote in Utah. Throughout her long life of 94 years, she continued to prepare herself for some future role where her influence could improve lives.

In more modern times, President Gordon B. Hinckley desired to offer a prayer for the youth of the Church in an upcoming worldwide broadcast. In that meeting, he explained how he prepared himself for that prayer. He said, "I want you to know that I have been on my knees asking the Lord to bless me with the power and the capacity and the language to reach into your hearts."[23] His desire was to help the youth rise above the carnal world so they could become better and do better than they have done. President Hinckley put in the preparation necessary to influence them.

Summary of Examples

- Honorable leaders prepare themselves before significant events, as Jesus did before calling the Twelve Apostles.
- Honorable leaders prepare themselves by developing a plan to teach their people, as Jesus did in preparing parables that would convey the proper meaning to His disciples.

- Honorable leaders prepare themselves by becoming knowledgeable and capable, as Jesus did in learning the scriptures and the sons of Mosiah did in becoming "men of a sound understanding."
- Honorable leaders prepare themselves prior to going before their followers, as Jesus did before the "Sermon on the Mount."
- Honorable leaders prepare themselves by rejuvenating himself, as Jesus did by going in the mornings to a solitary place to pray.
- Honorable leaders prepare themselves for future unknown responsibilities by working to refine and cultivate their personal attributes, as taught by Eliza R. Snow.
- Honorable leaders prepare themselves by getting strength and wisdom from their own leader, as President Hinckley did before leading the worldwide youth in prayer.

Questions for Personal Reflection

- Are you able to lead others because you are becoming someone they want to follow?
- How well are you developing yourself in a balanced approach, giving due attention to the spiritual, intellectual, physical, social, and emotional aspects of your life?
- What can you do to lead others to follow the seven–step process outlined in this book to acquire the leadership attributes of Jesus?
- Are you improving your personality?
- Are you ready to offer meaningful counsel to one who asks for your advice?

Attribute 33: Rejuvenates Himself

Rejuvenate: *To restore to an original or new state. To make youthful again. Give new vigor to.*

Our mortal bodies are prone to a weariness of mind and body and have natural limitations. To counteract fatigue, periodic rejuvenation is needed to maintain strength, energy, and a desire to keep working. During His mortal ministry, Jesus engaged in self–rejuvenation by taking time for Himself. He separated from others where He could refresh His mind and body by worshiping, pondering, and praying alone. In the New Testament, Mark records, "And in the morning, rising up a great while before day, he went out, and departed into a *solitary place,* and there prayed" (Mark 1:35, emphasis added). Matthew also records, "And when he had sent the multitudes away, he went up into a *mountain apart* to pray: and when the evening was come, he was there alone" (Matthew 14:23, emphasis added).

In addition to taking care of His own needs, Jesus also ensured that His disciples rejuvenated themselves by resting and having some leisure time. "And he said unto them, Come ye yourselves apart into a desert place, and *rest a while:* for there were many coming and going, and *they had no leisure so much as to eat"* (Mark 6:31, emphasis added). It is not possible to serve others continually without first taking care of yourself. Mortal minds and bodies need rest and rejuvenation. The Lord expects us to work hard for that is how we grow, but there are natural limitations. He counseled the Prophet Joseph Smith "Do not run faster or labor more than you have strength and means provided" (D&C 10:4). This is consistent with the counsel King Benjamin gave his people when he said, "see that all these things are done in wisdom and order; for it is not requisite that a man should run faster than he has strength" (Mosiah 4:27).

Examples of Righteous Leaders

As valuable as the counsel is to not run faster than we have strength, there are times when life just weighs us down with heavy burdens and responsibilities. The Prophet Joseph Smith knew his full share of burdens. An early church member shared a story of when Joseph was observed with his head down. The man said to him, 'Brother Joseph, why don't you hold your head up and talk to us like a man?' The Prophet's response was, 'Look at those heads of grain.' The man looked out at the field of ripened wheat and saw that the heaviest sheaves, the ones full of grain, were bent down. The Prophet was implying that his mind was heavy laden."[24] Had Joseph not found a way to continually rejuvenate himself, he would not have had the strength to finish his mission. He saw this need for rejuvenation in himself and in his associates.

In a private moment, the Prophet Joseph counseled his secretary, Robert B. Thompson, to take care of himself. He told him, "Robert, you have been so faithful and relentless in this work, you need to relax." This charge may have been followed with suggestions of how he could relax but Robert's response was simply, "I can't do it." Joseph pressed further, "You must do it, if you don't do it, you will die." His urging went unheeded, and two weeks later, the Prophet Joseph spoke at Robert's funeral.[25]

One of the most quoted comments made by Joseph deals with the need to "unstring your bow" for "He did not want it strung up all the time."[26] He understood that people must periodically release the pressures of mortality or they could lose the will and strength to persevere. Joseph also taught that such unstringing should be short–lived, for "When a man is reigned up continually by excitement, he becomes strong and gains power and knowledge; but when he relaxes for a season he loses much of his power and knowledge."[27] To achieve this proper balance, Joseph rejuvenated himself through occasional short bursts of relaxing activities.

In reviewing the life of the Prophet Joseph, one can picture him rolling around with the young children, laughing and being carefree. "It was not uncommon to see him involved in sports activities with the young and vigorous men of a community. He is known to have wrestled, pulled sticks, engaged in snowball fights, played ball, slid on the ice with his children, played marbles, shot at a mark, and fished."[28]

He also loved a social atmosphere of dining, music, and engaging conversation.

Brigham Young also understood the absolute necessity of recreational activities and used them often to rejuvenate the Saints. He had a motto that divided the twenty–four hours of a day into "eight hours work, eight hours sleep, and eight hours recreation."[29] This recreation was to achieve a balance in life by doing voluntary activities to rebuild oneself, but never idleness. He believed his children should "dance, study music, read novels and do anything else that will tend to expand their frames, add fire to their spirits, improve their minds, and make them feel free and untrammelled in body and mind."[30] Brigham had employed this same philosophy from the very first day of the exodus out of Nauvoo as the Saints walked into the frozen prairies of the Midwest.

"Capt. Pitt and his band left Nauvoo on the same day with Brigham Young, Feb. 15, 1847, crossing the Mississippi on the ice and with him journeyed that day to the 'Camp of Israel' which waited for the leader on 'Sugar Creek.' And at night the weather was bitterly cold, the trumpet by the order of Brigham Young called the camp out to a concert in the open air, and the Nauvoo Brass Band performed its best selections, after which the pilgrims joined in the dance and the music was as joyous as at a merrymaking."[31]

In the years that followed their arrival in the Salt Lake Valley, Brigham Young continued to lead the Saints in rejuvenating their spirits by organizing picnics and other social events. One such event was a celebration in 1860 at Silver Lake in Big Cottonwood Canyon. An invited guest wrote of his experience in an article for the *New York Herald.* An excerpt is as follows:

"As the sun peeped out from behind heavy clouds, the hearts of the faithful were cheered, and the subject of conversation everywhere was the dance. The word was soon given and the three boweries were soon occupied with young and old, ready to spring away on the light fantastic toe. Each bowery was forty by twenty–four feet, and in that space were packed six sets of cotillions from about 10 a.m. till between the small hours of the following morning, with only very short intervals of rest for the musicians. Notwithstanding the occasional showers the merry dance continued.

"The floor was cleared of the anxious youngsters, and the Prophet, with his two eldest sons and his sons–in–law, with their wives, filled the first set. The musicians had orders for something lively, and off they went in right good earnest. Brigham Young is particularly gay in the dance, and evidently thinks, when at it, that he may amuse himself and everybody else as well as he can. I felt satisfied, while I stood gazing on the man whom some intensely hate and others intensely love, that he had the affections of the people and his joy seemed to gratify them more than their own enjoyment. Every eye was upon him and following him round and round, and every little piece of his amuse- ment was solid enjoyment to them. Strange world, strange folk!"[32]

Brigham Young continued to use his influence to rejuvenate the poor and downtrodden. At a gathering in Brigham City, the following is recorded: "Then Brother Brigham said to President Snow, 'You send the teachers and brethren out and bring in the aged, the lame and blind and all your poor and let them have a good dinner and then give them a free ticket to the theatre that comes on to–night and then do this once every year in this city and our Heavenly Father will smile upon you and your city and bless you forever.'"[33]

Brother Brigham, the great leader who led tens of thousands of homeless pioneers to create a great civilization in the Mountain West, understood the need for periodic rejuvenation. And he used his influence to maintain a healthy balance in the minds and bodies of those who followed him in that great endeavor.

Summary of Examples

- An honorable leader rejuvenates herself by getting away to a solitary place, as did Jesus.
- An honorable leader rejuvenates herself by enjoying leisure time and relaxation, as demonstrated by Jesus.
- An honorable leader assists his people in rejuvenating themselves, as Jesus did with His disciples.
- An honorable leader rejuvenates himself by pacing his life and

not running faster than he has strength, as taught by King Benjamin and Joseph Smith.

Questions for Personal Reflection

- How well are you taking care of your own needs in addition to caring for others?
- Do you achieve the right amount of rejuvenation each day so when evening comes, you are still pleasant with others?
- Do you have a clear conscience so you can enjoy meditating in a solitary place without needing to distract your mind?
- Do you take time to look at your life from the perspective of being a coach to yourself? Do you follow the counsel of that coach?
- Are you balanced enough to have activities outside of a Church setting where you can find rejuvenation such as reading, socializing, golfing, four-wheeling, hiking, or belonging to a bowling league or tennis club?
- Do you start each day ready to contribute to situations by being fully rested and having exercised and eaten properly?

Attribute 34: Grows Personally

Grow: *Develop to maturity. Become greater or larger; expand, increase in size or substance.*

It is unknown how much of His premortal knowledge Jesus carried into mortality. He was a perfect being before Bethlehem, but clearly, He grew and developed during His mortal experience from His youth through adulthood. We know that at the age of twelve, His parents "found him in the temple, sitting in the midst of the doctors, both hearing them, and asking them questions" (Luke 2:46). It may be inferred that this was a growing experience for Jesus as He *listened* and *learned* from the doctors. Still, "all that heard him were astonished at his understanding and answers" (Luke 2:47). We know from Luke that "Jesus increased in wisdom and stature, and in favour with God and man" (Luke 2:52). The Apostle Paul recorded that Jesus, "Though he were a Son, yet learned he obedience by the things which he suffered" (Hebrews 5:8).

The experiences Jesus had during His mortal life, including the Atonement, helped Him grow to the point He could lift and succor all humanity. Paul explains, "For in that he himself hath suffered being tempted, he is able to succour them that are tempted" (Hebrews 2:18). Alma recorded this same doctrine: "And he will take upon him death, that he may loose the bands of death which bind his people; and he will take upon him their infirmities, that his bowels may be filled with mercy, according to the flesh, *that he may know according to the flesh how to succor his people according to their infirmities*" (Alma 7:12, emphasis added).

Jesus has given all men counsel to continually grow and develop their minds, talents, and spirit. He teaches us to "seek not for riches but for wisdom, and behold, the mysteries of God shall be unfolded unto you" (D&C 6:7). He encourages us to "seek ye out of the best books words of wisdom; seek learning, even by study and also by faith" (D&C 88:118). He teaches us to "treasure up in your minds continually the words of life" (D&C 84:85).

In the parable of the foolish rich man, Jesus teaches us the type of personal growth that we should pursue. The central figure in this parable is a rich man who spends his life accumulating possessions so great that he needs to build greater barns to store them. However, Jesus points out the man "is not rich toward God" (Luke 12:21). Those who are "rich toward God" are "rich in the knowledge of the truth . . . in the possession of the characteristics and attributes of Deity."[34] These are the true riches because what we become is all that we take into eternity. We leave behind on this side of the veil all those items stored in our barns.

Examples of Righteous Leaders

Nephi was a great prophet and leader of his people and established their society "after the manner of happiness" (2 Nephi 5:27). However, before he became a great prophet, Nephi needed to grow himself into a person that others would follow. His leadership attributes matured on each of the return missions to Jerusalem as he obtained the plates of brass and wives for him and his brethren. However, it was the personal knowledge he received from God that allowed him to become a spokesman for God. This knowledge came because he wanted to know for himself the same knowledge his father learned through revelation. He explained, "I, Nephi, *was desirous also that I might see, and hear, and know of these things,* by the power of the Holy Ghost, which is the gift of God unto all those who *diligently seek him*" (1 Nephi 10:17, emphasis added). Because of Nephi's personal growth, the Lord was able to use him to lead His people.

If a leader wants to influence others to greatness, he or she needs to be a person worth emulating. Leaders need to grow in knowledge, wisdom, and experience so they can be authentic as they encourage others to be the best and do the best they can. President Thomas S. Monson taught, "In the private sanctuary of one's own conscience lies that spirit, that determination to cast off the old person and to measure up to the stature of true potential."[35] As people mature, they often see a need to "cast off the old person" and to grow into a new person. With many people, this desire comes multiple times in their life as they learn that life is about *becoming* rather than *obtaining.*

Summary of Examples

- Honorable leaders continually grow by learning from their life experiences, as demonstrated by Jesus.
- Honorable leaders continually grow by studying words of wisdom out of the best books, as taught by Jesus.
- Honorable leaders continually grow by seeking to know for themselves rather than relying on others, as demonstrated by Nephi who wanted to experience what his father experienced.

Questions for Personal Reflection

- How have you improved your ability to be guided by personal revelation?
- Which strengths are you currently cultivating?
- Which weaknesses are you currently addressing?
- What professional certificate or advanced training can you attain that will increase your capability?
- What are you currently studying?
- Are you gaining the confidence to interject yourself in situations where you can lead others to a better outcome?

Attribute 35: Labors Also

Labor: *To strive to effect or achieve through effort. To exert one's powers of body or mind especially with painful or strenuous effort.*

Jesus led by doing. He took action and invited everyone to follow His example. "The *works that I do* in my Father's name, they bear witness of me" (John 10:25, emphasis added). These works included His miracles, His sermons, His one–on–one teaching, and His Atonement and Resurrection. They were actions He did Himself rather than delegate to others. People followed Jesus because of His preaching but also because of His labors. For example, when Jesus came to Galilee, "the Galileans received him, having seen all the things *that he did* at Jerusalem at the feast: for they also went unto the feast" (John 4:45, emphasis added).

Many Samaritans became followers of Jesus when they heard testimony from the woman at Jacob's well who proclaimed, "Come, see a man, which told me all things that ever I did: is not this the Christ?" (John 4:29). In addition, "a great multitude followed him, because they saw his miracles which he did on them that were diseased" (John 6:2). John records, "And there are also many other things which Jesus did, the which, if they should be written every one, I suppose that even the world itself could not contain the books that should be written" (John 21:25). John's expression is a tribute to a leader who labors. Jesus labors by Himself and He labors alongside His people, ever trying to bless them.

In Jesus, the people saw a man of action. For example, "Jesus went into the temple, and began to cast out them that sold and bought in the temple, and overthrew the tables of the moneychangers, and the seats of them that sold doves" (Mark 11:15). This was a deliberate, well–thought–out act designed to teach the sanctity of the temple. It was not an action He could delegate but one only He could perform.

Jesus taught that all men need to work and be involved. It is not good enough just to give directions and tell others what to do. Leaders themselves actually need to labor. He said, "Verily I say, men should be anxiously engaged in a good cause, and do many things of their own free will, and bring to pass much righteousness; For the power is in them" (D&C 58:27–28). The role of the leader is to help release this power within, both in themselves and in their people. It is a power to become, to do, and to produce.

In the parable of the barren fig tree, the Savior taught that each tree in His vineyard was expected to bring forth fruit. If there was no fruit then the tree simply "cumbereth" the ground (Luke 13:7). Some leaders may feel once they arrive at their high position, they no longer need to produce fruits, but rather they need to get others to produce the fruit. It is this life of perceived leisure that draws some into leadership positions.

Jesus uses the parable of the lost sheep to teach that leaders actually perform labors themselves. They do not delegate everything to other people. In this parable, the leader is represented as a shepherd, which suggests the higher level of love a leader should have for his people. This leader, or shepherd, goes out himself after a lost lamb. He does not assign a hireling or even an under–shepherd to go back out— he does it himself.

In the parable of the good Samaritan, Jesus gives an example of a person who labors to lead a situation to a better outcome. The Samaritan, who is traveling along a road, comes upon a man severely beaten and robbed. He "went to him, and bound up his wounds, pouring in oil and wine, and set him on his own beast, and brought him to an inn, and took care of him" (Luke 10:34). The next day, he gives money to the host for the man's continual care. Again, the main character of the parable is a man of action, one who influences others by performing labors himself.

Following the Lord's ascension into heaven, His Twelve Apostles carried on His work to preach the gospel and to bring as many into the fold of God as would hearken unto His message. These Apostles "went forth, and preached everywhere, *the Lord working with them*" (Mark 16:20, emphasis added). They were not left to work alone because Jesus remained involved. Even though His earthly mission was now over, and He was removed from daily physical contact, Jesus demonstrated true leadership by continuing to influence those who were following His lead.

One of the great doctrines taught in the scriptures is that Jesus will always labor on behalf of those who follow Him. Jacob taught: "O then, my beloved brethren, come unto the Lord, the Holy One. Remember that his paths are righteous. Behold, the way for man is narrow, but it lieth in a straight course before him, and the keeper of the gate is the Holy One of Israel; *and he employeth no servant there;* and there is none other way save it be by the gate; for he cannot be deceived, for the Lord God is his name" (2 Nephi 9:41, emphasis added).

As a perfect leader, Jesus delegates when appropriate, but He also knows when not to delegate, for there are some labors the leader needs to perform personally. As each of us moves forward in faith, growing from our own labors, we are strengthened by knowing our leader continually labors with us. We also are strengthened by knowing that our leader will be at the finish line waiting to receive us with open arms.

Examples of Righteous Leaders

One of the great statements on leadership is given by the Savior to the brother of Jared. Jesus said to him, "Go to work and build" (Ether 2:16). That is what leaders are to do—whether they are building ideas, products, or people—they work and they build. This charge for the brother of Jared was to build barges so the Lord could guide his family to a better land. Therefore, the brother of Jared did "Go to work and build." He did not build barges only, he built his family as he labored and led them, as Jesus led him.

Centuries later, Nephi also set an example of a leader who labors for his people. His brother gave a succinct summary of the relationship Nephi had with his people and the feelings they felt in return. Jacob said, "The people . . . loved Nephi exceedingly, he having been a great protector for them, having wielded the sword of Laban in their defence, and having labored in all his days for their welfare" (Jacob 1:10). When leaders labor, the influence they have with their people is magnified exponentially, and as they work together, tremendous transformative power can be generated.

King Benjamin was another leader who also labored. Mormon

spoke of him with these words, "king Benjamin, by laboring with all the might of his body and the faculty of his whole soul . . . did once more establish peace in the land" (Words of Mormon 1:18). In addition to laboring for the cause of peace, he labored for his own support. In his final address, as he gave an accounting to his people, he said, "I, myself, have labored with mine own hands that I might serve you, and that ye should not be laden with taxes, and that there should nothing come upon you which was grievous to be borne" (Mosiah 2:14). His son, King Mosiah, followed this same pattern, for he "himself, did till the earth, that thereby he might not become burdensome to his people, that he might do according to that which his father had done in all things" (Mosiah 6:7). These two great leaders, father and son, taught that leadership is not a life of privilege, but a life of service, a life of labor.

The prophet Jacob demonstrated his willingness to labor as he said, "we labored diligently among our people, that we might persuade them to come unto Christ" (Jacob 1:7). Alma said the same thing, "And now it came to pass that the sons of Alma did go forth among the people, to declare the word unto them. And Alma, also, himself, could not rest, and he also went forth" (Alma 43:1). One of the reasons these leaders gave so much of themselves is summarized in these words; "unto whom much is given much is required" (D&C 82:3).

Teancum, a great Book of Mormon military leader gives another example of how a leader labors also. On one occasion, Teancum decided he could shorten the war against the Lamanites by going directly after the opposing leader. The record states that "Teancum stole privily into the tent of the king, and put a javelin to his heart; and he did cause the death of the king immediately that he did not awake his servants" (Alma 51:34). This brave action likely saved the lives of many of his warriors and made them more determined to fight for him in the future. It was an action he could have assigned to one of his men. Instead, Teancum chose to lead out and set the example himself.

Leadership is often manifest by one person who sees a problem, identifies a solution, and then works tirelessly to rally others around his or her cause until the problem is resolved. Such was the case in

Nauvoo in 1841 with Mercy Fielding Thomson. She could see the exterior stone of the temple raising rapidly and the interior wood flooring was progressing well. The finish carpenters were getting ready for their work but there was an acute need for nails and glass. Wondering what to do, she records, "At one time after seeking diligently to know from the Lord *if there was anything I could do* for the building up of the Kingdom of God, a most pleasant sensation came over me with the following words, 'Try to get the sisters to subscribe one cent per week for the purpose of buying glass and nails for the Temple.'"[36]

Mercy followed that prompting and enlisted the support of her older sister Mary Fielding Smith, wife of Hyrum Smith, who was a member of the temple committee. In that role, he was responsible for finances and raising the necessary funds to complete the temple. He responded to this idea enthusiastically and "did all in his power to encourage and help by speaking to the sisters in private and public, promising them they should receive their blessings in that Temple." [1]

Mercy and Mary labored passionately and soon had 1,000 subscribers in the Nauvoo area and the pennies started to roll in. Later, on Christmas day in 1843, these sisters proposed to Hyrum the expansion of their effort to include the women in England. He again supported their efforts so they prepared a hasty letter as follows:

"Nauvoo, Dec. 25, 1843

"To the sisters of the Church of Jesus Christ

"in England, greetings:

"Dear Sisters: —This is to inform you that we have here entered into a small weekly subscription for the benefit of the Temple Funds. One thousand have already joined it, while many more are expected, by which we trust to help forward the great work very much. The amount is only one cent or a halfpenny per week.

"As brother Amos Fielding is waiting for this, I cannot enlarge more than say, that myself and sister Thompson are engaged in collecting the same.

"We remain,

"Your affectionate sisters in Christ

"Mary Smith

"M. R. Thompson"[37]

These two women, Mercy and Mary demonstrated true leadership. They did not act out of duty to some officially appointed position. They simply saw a need, took initiative, and led out. They used their influence to rally thousands, both in America and in England, to contribute 50,000 pennies. This collection, gathered over two to three years, weighed almost 350 pounds when complete and was kept hidden from the mobs until needed.

At one point, with the mob "threatening to rob and massacre the inhabitants of Nauvoo, [they] hid up the bag containing that money in a pile of bricks which Hyrum had intended for building had his life been spared."[38] Then, when the time came to purchase the nails and glass, the money was available and the temple was completed. The completion occurred in sufficient time so that 6,000 Saints, including Mercy and Mary, received their sacred temple ordinances before being driven across the frozen Mississippi River and onto the unknown Western plains.

Summary of Examples

- Honorable leaders labor also by doing the work their followers cannot, as Jesus did when He cleansed the temple and at the gate where "he employeth no servant there."
- Honorable leaders labor also when they are viewed as people of action, as was Jesus when He performed miracles and went out teaching among the people.
- Honorable leaders labor also by going out after those who are lost that only they can bring back, as taught by Jesus regarding the lost sheep.
- Honorable leaders labor also so they do not "cumber" the ground by taking up valuable resources without producing any fruit, as taught by Jesus regarding the barren fig tree.

- Honorable leaders labor also by providing for their own needs, as did King Benjamin and Mosiah.
- Honorable leaders labor also as they teach from a position of authority, as did Jacob and Alma.
- Honorable leaders labor also by taking their share of difficult assignments, as did Teancum in the war with the Lamanites.
- Honorable leaders see a need and find a way to solve it by starting with their own personal efforts, and then by inviting others to emulate their actions, as did Mercy Fielding Thomson and Mary Fielding Smith.

Questions for Personal Reflection

- How many of those you lead think you strike the right balance between laboring and delegating?
- Do you continually scan your surroundings looking for opportunities to use your influence to improve products, people, or circumstances?
- Do you help with family chores?
- Do you ask someone to go outside and get the mail when you are just as capable of doing it yourself?
- How well do you contribute your efforts to the community?

---

1. Jay A. and Donald W. Parry, *Understanding the Parables of Jesus Christ*, 121.
2. Parry, 121.
3. Faust, James E., "Discipleship," *Ensign*, November 2006.
4. David O. McKay, *Conference Report*, April 1968, "First Day—Morning Meeting," 8.
5. Plato, *Laws*, Book I, section 626E.
6. Camilla Eyring Kimball, *The Writings of Camilla Eyring Kimball*, edited by Edward L. Kimball, 110.
7. John A. Widtsoe, *Discourses of Brigham Young*, 291-92.
8. J. Reuben Clark, *Conference Report*, Oct. 1937, 107.
9. Arland J. Hultgren, *The Parables of Jesus*, 86.

10. Truman G. Madsen, *Presidents of the Church - David O. McKay*, Deseret Book (1991).

11. Truman G. Madsen, *Presidents of the Church - David O. McKay*, Deseret Book (1991).

12. John A. Widtsoe, *Discourses of Brigham Young*, 392.

13. Dieter F. Uchtdorf, "Have We Not Reason to Rejoice?," *Ensign*, November 2007.

14. Dieter F. Uchtdorf, "We are Doing a Great Work and Cannot Come Down," *Ensign*, May 2009; emphasis added.

15. Mahatma Gandhi, in Larry Chang, *Wisdom for the Soul* (2006), 356.

16. Dieter F. Uchtdorf, "We are Doing a Great Work and Cannot Come Down," *Ensign*, May 2009.

17. Boyd K. Packer, *Things of the Soul*, 50.

18. James E. Talmage, *Jesus the Christ*, 463-64.

19. "Tornado damage extensive: More than 3,000 volunteers get to work," *Church News*, May 14, 2011, 8.

20. Jay A. and Donald W. Parry, *Understanding the Parables of Jesus Christ*, 38.

21. *Relief Society Minute Book*, 27. Punctuation and spelling modernized.

22. "Midnight Soliloquy," *Woman's Exponent*, 15 Apr. 1880, 175-76.

23. Gordon B. Hinckley, "A Prophet's Counsel and Prayer for Youth," *Ensign*, January 2001.

24. This took place in 1841, at the home of the Henry Sherwoods in Nauvoo. (See recollection of Henrietta Cox in JI 27 (April 1, 1892): 203; Andrus, *They Knew*, 147.) Cited in Truman G. Madsen, *Joseph Smith the Prophet*, 31.

25. See diary of Oliver B. Huntington, 166. Cited in Truman G. Madsen, *Joseph Smith the Prophet*, 31.

26. See recollection of William M. Allred in JI 27 (August 1, 1892): 472. Cited in Truman G. Madsen, *Joseph Smith the Prophet*, 31.

27. HC 5:389.

28. Daniel H. Ludlow, *Encyclopedia of Mormonism* 4 vols.

29. Susa Young Gates, *Life Story of Brigham Young*, 251.

30. Gates, 252.

31. Gates, 253.
32. Gates, 258-59.
33. Gates, 260.
34. Bruce R. McConkie, *Doctrinal New Testament Commentary*, 1:474.
35. Thomas S. Monson, "Looking Back and Moving Forward," *Ensign*, May 2008.
36. Thompson, Mercy Fielding. Autobiographical sketch,1880. Church Archives; emphasis added. (See also *Hyrum Smith: A Life of Integrity*, Jeffrey S. O'Driscoll, "I Have a Big Soul," Salt Lake City: Deseret Book (2003)).
37. (Smith, *HC,* op. cit., VI, 143.
38. Don Cecil Corbett, *Mary Fielding Smith, Daughter of Britain: Portrait of Courage*, Deseret Book (1966), 155.

CHAPTER 9

HE LEADS OUT

Attribute 36: Defines Objectives

Objective: *Something toward which effort is directed: an aim, goal, or end of action.*

Jesus made it clear that His entire objective in life, His ultimate purpose and mission, was to do the will of the Father. Heavenly Father and Jesus defined their joint objective or mission statement by simply stating, "This is my work and my glory to bring to pass the immortality and eternal life of man" (Moses 1:39). It is the most perfect mission statement ever devised. The entire plan of salvation for billions of people spanning all eternity is summarized in this one concise sentence. In support of that overarching objective, the Savior issued another objective when He said, "The Father having raised me up . . . to bless you in turning away every one . . . from his iniquities" (3 Nephi 20:26). A more detailed explanation that clearly defines His objective follows:

"Behold I have given unto you my gospel, and this is the gospel which I have given unto you—that I came into the world to do the will of my Father, because my Father sent me.

"And my Father sent me that I might be lifted up upon the cross; and after that I had been lifted up upon the cross, that I might draw all men unto me, that as I have been lifted up by men even so should men be lifted up by the Father, to stand before me, to be judged of their works, whether they be good or whether they be evil—

"And for this cause have I been lifted up; therefore, according to the power of the Father I will draw all men unto me, that they may be judged according to their works.

"And it shall come to pass, that whoso repenteth and is baptized in my name shall be filled; and if he endureth to the end, behold, him will I hold guiltless before my Father at that day when I shall stand to judge the world.

"And he that endureth not unto the end, the same is he that is also hewn down and cast into the fire, from whence they can no more return, because of the justice of the Father" (3 Nephi 27:13–17).

Jesus clearly defined His objective in being our leader. That objective is to do the will of the Father, to draw all men unto Him, to judge men according to their works, and to forgive the repentant. His objective is to lead us back to dwell eternally with Him and His Father in the mansions He prepared.

Examples of Righteous Leaders

Nephi, like the Savior, defined his objective to lead his people to eternal happiness. In his own concise statement, Nephi said, "For the fulness of mine intent is that I may persuade men to come unto the God of Abraham, and the God of Isaac, and the God of Jacob, and be saved" (1 Nephi 6:4). All that Nephi did and all that he taught was to achieve this objective. He created records that would persuade men to come unto God and he gave instructions that they were for writing "the things which are pleasing unto God" (1 Nephi 6:5). Nephi continued, "Wherefore, I shall give commandment unto my seed, that they shall not occupy these plates with things which are not of worth unto the children of men" (1 Nephi 6:6). Not only did these records serve to persuade his posterity to come unto God, they have been used to persuade millions of people throughout the world to "come unto the God of Abraham, and the God of Isaac, and the God of Jacob, and be saved" (1 Nephi 6:4). Nephi's objective, clearly stated and faithfully followed, continues to produce fruit to this day.

Summary of Examples

- Honorable leaders define their objectives so they align with the objectives of their own leader, as demonstrated by Jesus "to bring to pass the immortality and eternal life of man" (Moses 1:39).

- Honorable leaders define their objectives then inspire people to follow, as Jesus did in drawing all men unto Him.
- Honorable leaders record their objectives so their voice can be carried to the multitudes for generations, as did Nephi.

Questions for Personal Reflection

- Are you aligning your objectives with the Savior's, to bring all men to Him?
- Have you looked over the horizon to see what the ultimate destination is for those you lead?
- What are your objectives for your marriage and your family?
- Do you have a personal and family mission statement?
- How have you conveyed your objectives to those who follow you?

Attribute 37: Lifts Vision

Vision: *The ability to anticipate or plan the future with imagination or wisdom. A mental image of what the future will or could be like.*

Jesus lifts our vision by teaching us new truths and by giving us new experiences. In this way, He is the leaven that causes each of us to rise. Following the feeding of the 5,000, "Jesus constrained [or compelled][1] his disciples to get into a ship, and to go before him unto the other side, while he stayed to send the multitude away. And when he had sent the multitude away, he went up into a mountain apart to pray: and when the evening was come, he was there alone" (Matthew 14:22–23). While the disciples were at sea, a fierce storm arose and during the "fourth watch . . . Jesus went unto them, walking on the sea" (Matthew 14:25).

Could it be that this story was a pre–planned event designed by the Savior to lift the vision and further the development of His disciples? Could it be that His desire to tarry in the mountain and pray apart was to prepare Himself and His disciples for His next teaching experience? Whether it was pre–planned or not, this experience did lift the vision and further the development of His disciples. Think of the growth that occurred as Peter stepped over the side of the ship as he responded to the Savior's simple invitation to "come" (Matthew 14:29). Think of the further learning that occurred as Jesus grabbed the outstretched arms of Peter, and taught us all with these words, "O thou of little faith, *wherefore didst thou doubt?"* (Matthew 14:31, emphasis added).

In another setting, Jesus lifted the vision of His listeners by explaining the benefits of following His teachings. He taught: "Whosoever cometh to me, and heareth my sayings, and doeth them, I will shew you to whom he is like: He is like a man which built an house, and digged deep, and laid the foundation on a rock: and when the flood arose, the stream beat vehemently upon that house, and could not shake it: for it was founded upon a rock" (Luke 6:47–48).

Jesus lifted the vision of His disciples to see their role and impact. He said, "Ye are the salt of the earth . . . Ye are the light of the world"

(Matthew 5:13–14). To the early elders of His restored Church, and indeed to all who have labored since then, He lifted their vision and gave them encouragement when He said, "Wherefore, be not weary in well–doing, for ye are laying the foundation of a great work. And out of small things proceedeth that which is great" (D&C 64:33).

Jesus used another metaphor to help His disciples see new opportunities. He said, "Say not ye, There are yet four months, and *then* cometh harvest? behold, I say unto you, *Lift up your eyes, and look* on the fields; for they are white already to harvest" (John 4:35, emphasis added). All that Jesus taught, all that He did, was to lift our vision to see a better way of living, an expanded way of thinking, a grander view of eternity.

To Abraham, He said:

"My son, my son (and his hand was stretched out), behold I will show you all these. And he put his hand upon mine eyes, and I saw those things which his hands had made, which were many; and they multiplied before mine eyes, and I could not see the end thereof.

"And it was in the night time when the Lord spake these words unto me: I will multiply thee, and thy seed after thee, like unto these; and if thou canst count the number of sands, so shall be the number of thy seeds" (Abraham 3:12–14).

To Moses He said:

"Behold, thou art my son; wherefore look, and I will show thee the workmanship of mine hands; but not all, for my works are without end, and also my words, for they never cease.

"Wherefore, no man can behold all my works . . ..

"And now, behold, this one thing I show unto thee, Moses, my son, for thou art in the world, and now I show it unto thee.

"And it came to pass that Moses looked, and beheld the world upon which he was created; and Moses beheld the world and the ends thereof, and all the children of men which are, and which were created; of the same he greatly marveled and wondered . . ..

"Now, for this cause I know that man is nothing, *which thing I never had supposed*"(Moses 1:4–10, emphasis added).

One of the most quoted of all scriptures is a simple phrase from the Master when He referred to select leaders who had no vision. He said, "Let them alone: they be blind leaders of the blind. And if the blind lead the blind, both shall fall into the ditch" (Matthew 15:14). Yes, leaders need vision, and they need to instill that vision in others and help them see things they have not seen before. Then they need to lead out and say, follow me!

Examples of Righteous Leaders

One of the great Old Testament stories is of the prophet Elisha whose city was surrounded by enemies. When his servant became alarmed, Elisha calmed his fears by saying, "Fear not: for they that *be* with us *are* more than they that *be* with them" (2 Kings 6:16). He then prayed "And the Lord *opened the eyes* of the young man; and he saw: and, behold, the mountain *was* full of horses and chariots of fire round about Elisha" (2 Kings 6:17, emphasis added).

Elisha helped lift the vision of his servant so he could see things he could not see before. This story occurred because of divine intervention, but the principle applies to other leaders as well. Leaders increase their effectiveness as they help people envision things they have not seen before. When people see the vision of their leader, they more readily become supporters who will help achieve that vision. Such was the case with Nephi as he tried to persuade his brothers to assist in securing the plates of brass from Laban.

"And it came to pass that I spake unto my brethren, saying: Let us go up again unto Jerusalem, and let us be faithful in keeping the commandments of the Lord; for behold he is mightier than all the earth, then why not mightier than Laban and his fifty, yea, or even than his tens of thousands?

"Therefore let us go up; let us be strong like unto Moses; for he truly spake unto the waters of the Red Sea and they divided hither and thither, and our fathers came through, out of captivity, on dry ground, and the armies of Pharaoh did follow and were drowned in the waters of the Red Sea.

"Let us go up; the Lord is able to deliver us, even as our fathers, and to destroy Laban, even as the Egyptians" (1 Nephi 4:1–3).

Captain Moroni also lifted the vision of his people as he hoisted the title of liberty throughout the land. These banners stated: "In memory of our God, our religion, and freedom, and our peace, our wives, and our children" (Alma 46:12). These banners, flying freely in the breeze, surely united hearts and fortified determination sufficient enough to win the battle for the privileges he identified.

The Prophet Joseph Smith had the unique ability to help people see that they had greatness inside themselves that they could not see. He understood human nature and their eternal nature and lifted their vision to become better. Consider the insightful analysis from John Henry Evans in his book, *Joseph Smith, an American Prophet.*

"Joseph Smith somehow had the ability to energize people, to imbue them with the thought of a great destiny for them, not only collectively, but individually as well.

"Psychologists have revealed to us an interesting law of human behavior, which may be used to good effect in the handling of men. It is this: If one would win the attachment of others, one must impress them with the idea of their importance. This is called "raising their ego."

"People are always interested in themselves. This interest is deeply fundamental. It can always be counted on. No one likes to be made to feel small. Everyone likes to feel that he is "somebody." Great leaders all know this, and use the fact to their own advantage.

"Benjamin Franklin once got the lasting friendship of an enemy by borrowing a book from him, which no one else in Philadelphia was fortunate enough to own. Theodore Roosevelt always obtained as much information as possible about the man whom he expected to meet, so as to have common ground on which to stand. And it is said that once Lincoln saved a prominent man not a little embarrassment by his quick-wittedness. The two were engaged in conversation just as a cheering crowd called for a speech, and an aide requested the visitor to step aside. 'You see, Mr. Brand,' Lincoln explained, 'they might not know which is president.'"

Mr. Evans continued his analysis of Joseph by comparing him to the other leaders of his day. Joseph differed from them because he lifted people rather than degraded them. Mr. Evans states:

"At the time Joseph Smith lived, religious creeds uniformly made people feel "small" in the sight of God, and preachers helped along this minimizing process not a little.

"The Prophet had different ideas from these. In effect he said this to his disciples: You are eternal, just as God is eternal . . . . You have the will to order your own life . . . .

"And then, in addition, your personality is very sacred. The forces of the universe center in you. You are to be developed, perfected, made happy both here and hereafter. It was never intended that all men should be alike, except in opportunity for growth. Mankind is not inherently bad. Rather mankind is inherently good. Only wrong ideas and influences make men bad, and these are to be displaced by right ideas and influences . . . .

"Joseph Smith, far from being puffed up in pride and wishing to monopolize the prophetic function, sought assiduously to bring every man up to his own level spiritually. This is extraordinary . . . *Joseph Smith never did violence to the ego in his disciples through any coercive measures.* . . . he taught religious ideas that are intimately bound up with the hopes and aspirations of mankind everywhere, and that he put these ideas in such a form as can be readily understood by the average man. In a word, he raises our ego through ideas."[2]

This is lifting vision, helping people see the new heights they can achieve, and then get them moving on the path that leads to that end. This is leadership; it is using your influence to help people become better and do better.

Summary of Examples

- Honorable leaders lift vision by teaching new truths and giving new experiences, as Jesus did by walking on the sea and feeding the 5,000.
- Honorable leaders lift vision by explaining the results of following a certain path, as Jesus taught of building a house on a foundation of rock.
- Honorable leaders lift vision by helping people see their potential, as when Jesus told His disciples they were the light of the world.

- Honorable leaders lift vision by showing their past accomplishments to their people, as Jesus did to Abraham and Moses.
- Honorable leaders lift vision by showing their people what they cannot see, as Elisha did to his servant who was able to behold the mountain filled with horses and chariots.
- Honorable leaders lift vision by reminding them of the past, as Nephi did in reminding his brothers that the Lord helped Moses lead Israel through the Red Sea.
- Honorable leaders lift vision by reminding them what is important, as Captain Moroni did with the Title of Liberty.
- Honorable leaders lift vision by building a sense of self–worth in their followers, and by avoiding offending their ego as demonstrated by Joseph Smith.

Questions for Personal Reflection

- Do you lift your own vision, and dream of doing things never before done?
- Are you leading your associates by lifting their vision to see a future they could achieve?
- How can you avoid offending the ego of other people?
- Do you help people see the future by remembering the past?
- How well do you help others see the consequences of the different paths they are considering?

Attribute 38: Initiates Action

Initiate: *To begin, set going, or originate.*

"Come, follow me" (Luke 18:22). They are three simple words that make a very short sentence, but they are the words that have moved millions of people to change their lives and follow the Savior. In the case of Peter who wanted to go to Jesus as He walked upon the sea, it only took one inviting word, "Come" (Matthew 14:29). This is the first way that Jesus initiates action—He invites people to follow Him.

A second way Jesus initiates action is when He says in essence, "Come, and I will go with you." This suggests a more side–by–side involvement rather than a single–file leader–follower relationship. After the death of Joshua, Ancient Israel was governed loosely for many years by judges rather than by kings. These judges had various degrees of success but one of the most successful was Deborah. She was a prophetess and as Elder Mark E. Peterson explained, she was "Their great female deliverer."[3] At a time when Israel was surrounded by an enemy army of overwhelming strength, Deborah called upon Barak, a man from the tribe of Naphtali, to form an army of ten thousand men to go to battle against this great army. They faced an opposing force that had nine hundred iron chariots and vastly more men that Barak could gather.

With faith and courage, Barak committed to gather that army and go to battle. However, he did not want to go without his spiritual leader. Therefore, he told Deborah, "If thou wilt go with me, then I will go: but if thou wilt not go with me, then I will not go" (Judges 4:8). With strength and conviction, she replied, *"I will surely go with thee"* (Judges 4:9, emphasis added). And with divine help, Barak and his army were victorious and Israel was delivered because this one single woman took the lead and initiated action. She lifted vision, fostered optimism, instilled courage, and restored peace such that "the land had rest forty years" (Judges 5:31). When we think that we cannot make much of a difference, we only need to remember Deborah and like her, lead out, initiate action, and solve problems.

Consider the impact on a young Enoch when God Himself said,

"Walk with me" (Moses 6:34, emphasis added). Consider the comfort Lehi felt when he was called to go into the wilderness and the Savior assured him, "I will also be your light in the wilderness; and I will prepare the way before you . . . and ye shall know that it is by me that ye are led" (1 Nephi 17:13). Years later, when Alma and his people were in bondage, they received this same assurance. "And it came to pass that so great was their faith and their patience that the voice of the Lord came unto them again, saying: Be of good comfort, for on the morrow I will deliver you out of bondage. And he said unto Alma: Thou shalt go before this people, and *I will go with thee* and deliver this people out of bondage" (Mosiah 24:16–17, emphasis added).

Jesus again gave this assurance to the early elders of the restored Church, "I will go before your face. I will be on your right hand and on your left, and my Spirit shall be in your hearts, and mine angels round about you, to bear you up" (D&C 84:88).

The third way Jesus initiates action is when He says "go" instead of "come." For example, He said to the brother of Jared, "Go to work and build" (Ether 2:16). This was direction to build barges so that he and his people could cross the great deep to their Promised Land. Another example came after the Resurrection when Jesus appeared to His eleven Apostles "And he said unto them, Go ye into all the world, and preach the gospel to every creature" (Mark 16:15). He gave the same charge to the elders of His restored Church when He said, "Go ye into all the world, and preach my gospel unto every creature who has not received it" (D&C 112:28).

Whether Jesus said "come, follow me," or "come with me," or "go," He initiated action. He got people moving.

Examples of Righteous Leaders

During the turbulent years of war among the Nephites, a few strong leaders emerged who led their warriors to defeat their enemies and restore peace in the land. Captain Moroni led this effort, but other men like Teancum stood equal with him in their abilities. Teancum was a loyal friend to Captain Moroni and a fearless leader in his own right. He was given command of his own army and fought many successful battles. In him, his men found a leader who led out and demonstrated courage and determination.

On one occasion, Teancum decided he could shorten the war by going directly after the opposing leader. The record states that "Teancum stole privily into the tent of the king, and put a javelin to his heart; and he did cause the death of the king immediately that he did not awake his servants" (Alma 51:34). This brave action likely saved the lives of many of his warriors and made them more determined to fight for him in the future. It was an action Teancum could have assigned to one of his men but he chose to lead out and set the example. It was an action he repeated sometime later, but the circumstances turned out differently and he lost his life. However, he did not lose the respect of his men or his leaders who must have fought with more determination because of his example (Alma 62:36).

The prophet Moroni gives another example of initiating action. Not physical action but spiritual action. He invites those who are considering the truthfulness of the Book of Mormon to learn for themselves by exhorting them to read, remember, ponder, and pray.

"Behold, I would exhort you that when ye shall read these things, if it be wisdom in God that ye should read them, that ye would remember how merciful the Lord hath been unto the children of men, from the creation of Adam even down until the time that ye shall receive these things, and ponder it in your hearts.

"And when ye shall receive these things, I would exhort you that ye would ask God, the Eternal Father, in the name of Christ, if these things are not true; and if ye shall ask with a sincere heart, with real intent, having faith in Christ, he will manifest the truth of it unto you, by the power of the Holy Ghost.

"And by the power of the Holy Ghost ye may know the truth of all things" (Moroni 10:3–5).

Prophets in modern days continue to initiate action in their own way according to current needs. The Prophet Joseph Smith said, "Brethren, shall we not go on in so great a cause? Go forward and not backward. Courage, brethren; and on, on to the victory!" (D&C 128:22).

President Spencer W. Kimball said, "We must lengthen our stride and must do it now."[4] Of President Kimball, Elder Robert D. Hales said, "He is a man of action, demonstrated by the simple sign on his desk that says, 'Do It.'"[5] President Kimball's call to action continued when four years later, he told the Church in a worldwide general conference, "We have paused on some plateaus long enough. Let us resume our journey forward and upward . . . . Let us not shrink from the next steps in our spiritual growth, brothers and sisters, by holding back, or side-stepping our fresh opportunities for service to our families and our fellowmen."[6] These few words led countless members to reach out and do more than they were doing. These words got them moving.

More recently, Elder Dieter F. Uchtdorf also initiated action during one of his sermons. In speaking on how to refrain from judging others, he offered a two-word phrase that was reminiscent of President Kimball's "do it." Elder Uchtdorf said:

"This topic of judging others could actually be taught in a two-word sermon. When it comes to hating, gossiping, ignoring, ridiculing, holding grudges, or wanting to cause harm, please apply the following:

"Stop it!

"It's that simple. We simply have to stop judging others and replace judgmental thoughts and feelings with a heart full of love for God and His children."[7]

When a leader issues a clarion call to "stop it," "do it," "lengthen our stride," or "read, ponder and pray," we are inclined to answer favorably to the question, "Shall we not go on in so great a cause?" There is something unique in a call to action. Especially when it is issued with a few well-chosen words. It seems we have an innate desire to rally around a strong, determined leader who is pressing forward in a noble cause. Perhaps it is because we have seen the example of the Savior demonstrating such leadership.

Summary of Examples

- An honorable leader initiates action by calling his followers to come to him so he can personally influence them, as Jesus did when He invited Peter to walk upon the sea.
- An honorable leader initiates action by rallying the complacent and defeated of heart to band together and fight, as Deborah did with Ancient Israel.
- An honorable leader initiates action by calling his followers to come and go with him as he labors by their side, as Jesus did in leading Lehi to the Promised Land and Alma to freedom.
- An honorable leader initiates action by sending his followers forth to accomplish his work, as Jesus did with the brother of Jared and when He delegates His work to Apostles, prophets, missionaries, and fellow laborers.
- An honorable leader initiates action by taking the first action himself, as did Teancum when he killed the opposing king in his tent.

Questions for Personal Reflection

- Do you interject yourself into daily situations with the plan to guide them to a better outcome?
- How often do you initiate action by saying, "Come with me and let's do it together?"
- Do you initiate action by serving others without being asked to do so?
- Do you initiate action by taking the first step rather than assigning it to others?
- Do you initiate action in yourself by staying fit and healthy, by gaining worthwhile knowledge, and developing beneficial habits?
- Do you find yourself always planning and never starting?

Attribute 39: Visible

Visible: *Recognizable, accessible. Being constantly or frequently in the public view; conspicuous.*

The Prophet Isaiah foretold the birth of the Savior and revealed what name He would be given. He prophesied, "Behold, a virgin shall conceive, and bear a son, and shall call his name Immanuel" (Isaiah 7:14) or "God with us" (Bible Dictionary, "Immanuel"). The thought that a God would dwell on earth to be "with us" and visible for all to see must have been astonishing doctrine in Isaiah's day. In our day, we have the privilege of looking back on the life of Jesus, when a God came as a mortal man to visibly show us how a perfect life is lived.

Throughout His life, Jesus was frequently in public view for all to witness. This way He could influence others by exemplifying the doctrines He taught. In the Sermon on the Mount, He taught His disciples to be visible so they could be examples to all men.

"Ye are the light of the world. A city that is set on an hill cannot be hid.

"Neither do men light a candle, and put it under a bushel, but on a candlestick; and it giveth light unto all that are in the house.

"Let your light so shine before men, *that they may see* your good works, and glorify your Father which is in heaven" (Matthew 5:14–16, emphasis added).

Jesus followed His own counsel. After calling and training the Twelve Apostles, "he departed thence to teach and to preach in their cities" (Matthew 11:1). Now that He had the Twelve Apostles who could carry out His work, He could have resorted to a life of isolation and leisure as so many rulers have done. However, as Mark records, "he went round about the villages, teaching" (Mark 6:6). He wanted to be visible, to be out with the people so they could see for themselves the "light of the world" (John 9:5).

Jesus knew the power of visual imagery and may have designed events that would forever etch their significance in the minds of His disciples. Picture the young Jesus in the temple conversing with a group of mature men of great learning, or sitting on the shore of the beautiful Sea of Galilee as He taught the beatitudes, or calming the mighty waves caused by the tempest, or walking on the water, or reaching down to lift the sinking Peter, or cleansing the temple, or riding into Jerusalem in His triumphal entry, or kneeling in Gethsemane, or hanging on the cross, or ascending to heaven in Jerusalem, or descending from heaven at Bountiful. Yes, He was visible, and He seemed to craft His teaching moments so that an associated visual image would aid in our understanding and retention of His message.

Examples of Righteous Leaders

The book of Exodus records the attack of Amalek against Israel in Rephidim. Moses prepared for this attack by instructing Joshua to create an army and fight with Amalek. Moses then explained, "to morrow *I will stand on the top of the hill* with the rod of God in mine hand" (Exodus 17:9, emphasis added). During this battle, as long as Moses' arms remained raised, Israel prevailed. To aid Moses, Aaron and Hur propped up his arms until the battle was won. This story is usually used to teach of supporting the leader, but it also shows how the leader supports his people by being visible to them. Moses stood on the "top of the hill" (Exodus 17:10) where all his armies could see him and draw strength and determination from him.

During another war in another place, Captain Moroni understood the need for visibility as he led the fight against external enemies and internal corruption. To rally people to his cause, "he rent his coat; and he took a piece thereof, and wrote upon it—In memory of our God, our religion, and freedom, and our peace, our wives, and our children—and he fastened it upon the end of a pole" (Alma 46:12). Who could doubt the impact on the citizens and warriors as they saw their leader "waving the rent part of his garment in the air, *that all might see* the writing which he had written upon the rent part" (Alma 46:19, emphasis added). This garment was known as the title of liberty and became a visual reminder of their leader and the cause for which he was fighting. As this banner was hoisted throughout the land, the citizens recognized what it stood for and many united themselves behind Moroni. In the end, they achieved peace for themselves and their families.

Peace was something that the Prophet Joseph Smith longed for but rarely enjoyed. When possible, he remained visible to the Saints, even when doing so put him in great danger. In the early spring of 1832, Joseph and Emma were living at the John Johnson home 36 miles south of Kirtland. On the evening of March 24, Joseph and Emma nursed their two children who were sick with measles. An angry mob broke into the house and took Joseph outside where they tarred and feathered him in the cold night air. The hot tar blistered his skin, and it took several people all night to remove the caustic substance. The next morning, with great effort amid great pain, Joseph dressed and preached to a congregation about brotherly love and forgiveness. It would have been much easier for him to remain home to heal, but by being visible, he sent a message of resiliency and strength that would fortify his followers through their own trials. It also revealed his character and determination to his assailants, many of whom were in that congregation.

It is important to note that the motivation for being visible makes a tremendous difference, both to the leader and to those he or she wishes to lead. One type of motivation, which is influenced by natural man tendencies, is simply to be seen of man. Some people just like being in the spotlight where they can be viewed as important. The motivation behind the Savior's visibility is to set the example of being the right type of person and doing the right type of behavior.

Summary of Examples

- A visible leader is out among his people, as demonstrated by Jesus.
- A visible leader helps his or her people be as visible as a city set on a hill, as taught by Jesus.
- A visible leader is an encouragement to all his or her people, as Moses was to his armies.
- A visible leader often uses visible imagery to teach his people,

as Jesus did with parables and Captain Moroni with the Title of Liberty.

Questions for Personal Reflection

- How visible are you each day to your family?
- Are you visible to your associates and followers so they can learn from your example?
- Do you teach with visual imagery?
- Are you visible in your neighborhood so you can be available to influence others if the situation arises?
- Are you visibly involved in community affairs?

Attribute 40: Motivates with Persuasion

Persuasive: *To move by explanation, entreaty, or expostulation to a belief, position, or course of action. To plead with, urge.*

The plan of salvation is built on the principle of persuasion rather than compulsion. Persuasion is the action of a teacher. Compulsion is the action of a dictator. As Jesus teaches, He motivates others by explaining why a certain action is beneficial. He persuades by explaining the consequences of various types of actions so that the student can make an informed decision. To Peter, Andrew, James, John, and the other Apostles, He said, "Follow me, and *I will make you fishers of men*" (Matthew 4:18–19, emphasis added). He did not say, "Follow me, because I am the best" or "Follow me, or else!" His method was to "draw all men" unto Him (3 Nephi 27:14). Not by force, but by persuasion. His invitation was to "Come unto me all ye ends of the earth, buy milk and honey, without money and without price" (2 Nephi 26:25).

Throughout His ministry, Jesus taught through parables and the beatitudes that blessings would come from obedience to the commandments. In the Sermon on the Mount, He taught:

- Those who are poor in spirit will receive the kingdom of heaven
- Those who mourn will receive comfort
- Those who are meek will inherit the earth
- Those who hunger for righteousness will be filled
- Those who are merciful will obtain mercy
- Those who are pure in heart will see God
- Those who are peacemakers will be called the children of God
- Those who are persecuted will inherit the kingdom of heaven (Matthew 5:3–10).

Jesus also used persuasion by contrasting the blessings that would come from following Him to the struggles that would come if they did not. For example: "Whosoever cometh to me, and heareth my sayings, and doeth them, I will shew you to whom he is like: He is like a man which built an house, and digged deep, and laid the foundation on a rock: and when the flood arose, the stream beat vehemently upon that house, and could not shake it: for it was founded upon a rock. But he that heareth, and doeth not, is like a man that without a foundation built an house upon the earth; against which the stream did beat vehemently, and immediately it fell; and the ruin of that house was great" (Luke 6:47–49).

Jesus taught His disciples that if they followed His teachings and embraced His doctrine, then rich blessings would come in mortality as well as for eternity. He explained, "In my Father's house are many mansions . . . I go to prepare a place for you" (John 14:2). The thought that they would be rewarded with mansions in heaven must have had a persuasive effect on those trying to endure the challenges that came from following Him.

Not only did Jesus employ the art of persuasion Himself, but He taught His people to use persuasion as they carried out His work. As Nephi taught, "he hath commanded his people that they should persuade all men to repentance" (2 Nephi 26:27). Jesus taught that persuasion was the proper method of influencing others to change their ways and improve their lives. It was the proper method for bringing His Father's children back home to dwell in everlasting happiness.

Examples of Righteous Leaders

Surely, the Prophet Joseph Smith needed a little persuasion to help him endure as he languished in the Liberty Jail. That persuasion came when Jesus reminded him of the blessings that would be his if he could hold on just a little longer. "My son, peace be unto thy soul; thine adversity and thine afflictions shall be but a small moment; And then, *if thou endure it well,* God shall exalt thee on high; thou shalt triumph over all thy foes" (D&C 121:7–8, emphasis added).

Prophets throughout the scriptures continually use persuasion and long–suffering in teaching the wicked of the blessings of right-eousness. For example, when Nephi explains the purpose of his writings he states, "For the fulness of mine intent is that I may persuade men to come unto the God of Abraham, and the God of Isaac, and the God of Jacob, and be saved" (1 Nephi 6:4). Later he said, "For we labor diligently to write, to persuade our children, and also our brethren, to believe in Christ, and to be reconciled to God" (2 Nephi 25:23). A thousand years later, when Mormon combined Nephi's record with those of many other prophets, he echoed Nephi's desires by expressing his own, "And I would that I could persuade all ye ends of the earth to repent and prepare to stand before the judgment-seat of Christ" (Mormon 3:22). These prophets knew that persuasion, instead of compulsion, is the best way to improve lives.

Summary of Examples

- A persuasive leader explains the benefits he can provide to his followers, as Jesus did in the Sermon on the Mount.
- A persuasive leader encourages his followers to be strong in adversity, as Jesus did with Joseph in the Liberty Jail.
- A persuasive leader teaches his followers to also be persuasive in influencing others, as Jesus taught Nephi to persuade people to repent.
- A persuasive leader understands that persuasion is the only proper way to influence others to action, as demonstrated by Jesus, Nephi, and Mormon.

Questions for Personal Reflection

- Do you tend to be a teacher or a dictator?
- Do you lead by persuasion rather than through compulsion, manipulation, intimidation, and so forth?
- Do you use passion, facts, and historical examples to make compelling arguments?
- Do you plead with and urge your associates to make good choices and reach their fullest potential?
- Do you lead people to Christ by helping them understand the blessings He offers?

Attribute 41: Inspires with Oratory

Oratory: *The art of speaking in public eloquently or effectively.*

For a leader to influence people to follow him, he or she must inspire them to act. Often great leaders are great orators and they use that ability to inspire others to action. Some leaders who are not eloquent speakers can still have great influence by the authority they hold and the strength of their character. Moses and Enoch are two such examples. Still, they found a way to inspire large groups of people and were able to effectively persuade them to make significant changes in their lives.

One of the first examples of a leader inspiring others to action occurred in the Council in Heaven. Here, Jesus inspired most of Heavenly Father's children to place their eternal future in His hands. It seems reasonable to assume that He addressed the billions of spirits there with righteous power and earnest persuasion. It seems unlikely He would have played on our emotions with rousing oratory as so many speakers do, but it does seem likely He spoke with authority, power, passion, conviction, persuasion, and clarity.

Referring to Jesus, John records, "Never man spake like this man" (John 7:46) "for he taught them as *one* having authority" (Matthew 7:29). "And they were astonished at his doctrine: for his *word was with power*"(Luke 4:32, emphasis added). People flocked to Jesus wherever He went. His ability as an orator, when coupled with His authority and character, brought people to Him both in masses and individually. There was the Sermon on the Mount, the 5,000 (Matthew 14:21) and the 4,000 (Matthew 15:38), the rich young man, and countless other situations.

We know that Jesus "taught daily in the temple" (Luke 19:47). In fact, "all the people came early in the morning to him in the temple, for to hear him" (Luke 21:38). He spoke with such skill and inspiring doctrine that "all the people were *very attentive* to hear him" (Luke 19:48, emphasis added). Because of this attentiveness, "the chief priests and the scribes and the chief of the people sought to destroy him"

(Luke 19:47) for the wicked do not go without a fight. However, the people liked what Jesus said and how He said it. They saw in Him a leader whom they could follow, for they were persuaded that His vision for their future was better than what was being offered as an alternative.

Examples of Righteous Leaders

Almost every chapter in the scriptures contains an example of oratory. Perhaps it is Nephi who corrects and admonishes his brothers. Perhaps it is a ruler like King Benjamin who gives an accounting of his service to his people. Perhaps it is Alma who gives counsel to each of his children. Perhaps it is Captain Moroni and the title of liberty or his impassioned reprimand of Pahoran. There was Abinadi before King Noah, Paul before King Agrippa, Moses before Pharaoh. Oratory fills the pages of scripture as righteous men and women exercise their faith and use all their influence to persuade others to "come unto Christ" (Jacob 1:7) by using "the words of Christ" for they "will tell you all things what ye should do" (2 Nephi 32:3).

Elder Jeffrey R. Holland used the teachings of Joseph Smith to give additional insight on the power of the spoken word. It is a power far greater than many people realize. "The Prophet Joseph Smith deepened our understanding of the power of speech when he taught, *'It is by words . . . (that) every being works when he works by faith.* God said, "Let there be light: and there was light." Joshua spake, and the great lights which God had created stood still. Elijah commanded, and the heavens were stayed for the space of three years and six months, so that it did not rain . . . . All this was done by faith. . . . *Faith, then, works by words; and with [words) its mightiest works have been, and will be, performed.'*"[8]

Joseph Smith exemplified this doctrine. He moved the Saints forward when so much effort was spent to stop them. His skill as a powerful orator persuaded the Saints to dig deep within his or her character to do great things against tremendous opposition. His power came from his natural personality which was enlarged by the Spirit of God that stirred the hearts of men and women who heard him. They would listen to Joseph in any condition, whether in the heat of the sun or in the damp of the rain.

Joseph F. Smith once noted: "I remember quite well attending one meeting in this grove, that a wagon had been drawn up in front of the audience and the Prophet Joseph stood in the box speaking, when it began to rain. Some one or two persons got up and held umbrellas over him, to shield him from the wet. Many of the people had no umbrellas, and it was very annoying and disagreeable to sit there, but I remember very well, though but a little boy, that there was no one went away from the ground while he spoke."[9]

Joseph F. Smith was a great orator in his own right. Years after he spoke these words of the Prophet Joseph, others said of him, "Spiritually, he was the most high–minded of any man I ever met. I visited the Tabernacle where President Smith blessed the Latter–day Saints. For 20 minutes he blessed them. For 20 minutes there was not a dry eye in the Tabernacle."[10] Bishop Charles W. Nibley said of him, "As a preacher of righteousness, who could compare with him? He was the greatest that I ever heard—strong, powerful, clear, appealing. It was marvelous how the words of living light and fire flowed from him. . . . [When] the heart of President Smith was attuned to the Celestial melodies—he could hear, and [he] did hear."[11] That is the influence a leader with the power of oratory can have—he or she can lift vision, inspire hearts, and change the lives of those who will but listen.

Summary of Examples

- An honorable leader can be persuasive even if not eloquent, as was Moses and Enoch.
- An honorable leader uses persuasive words spoken with power, conviction, and clarity to influence his people to action, as did Jesus, "for his *word was with power*" (Luke 4:32, emphasis added).
- An honorable leader communicates his message to large groups as well as single individuals, as Jesus did with the 5,000 and the rich young man.
- An honorable leader initiates action through powerful words

232

that clearly define the objective, as taught by Joseph Smith, King Benjamin, Alma, Captain Moroni, Abinadi, Paul, and Moses.

- An honorable leader holds the attention of his people even in difficult settings, as Jesus did when the "chief priests and the scribes . . . sought to destroy him" (Luke 19:47), as well as Joseph Smith who often spoke to large congregations in inclement weather.
- An honorable leader uses words to soften hearts, as demonstrated by Joseph F. Smith in the Salt Lake Tabernacle.

Questions for Personal Reflection

- When you find yourself in a meeting or informal conversation, do you guide the group by speaking up and contributing?
- Do you speak with passion, experience, examples, and clarity?
- Do you speak from a position of love for others rather than being condescending?
- Do you intend for your speeches to inspire and lift others rather than to lift you up in their eyes?
- What have you done in your communications with others that have best led them to make better choices or to keep persevering?

Attribute 42: Has Order

Order: *Put persons or things into their proper places in relation to each other. Order suggests a straightening out so as to eliminate confusion or disarray.*

To assist in accomplishing His mission, Jesus set up an organization to teach His gospel and minister unto all who are in need. This organization was ordered so there would be respect for proper authority, freedom from confusion, and so that people would understand their respective roles. Of this organization, Jesus said, "Behold, mine house is *a house of order,* saith the Lord God, and not a house of confusion" (D&C 132:8, emphasis added). The Apostle Paul explained how the Savior provided this order.

"And he gave some, apostles; and some, prophets; and some, evangelists; and some, pastors and teachers;

"For the perfecting of the saints, for the work of the ministry, for the edifying of the body of Christ:

"That we *henceforth* be no more children, tossed to and fro, and carried about with every wind of doctrine, by the sleight of men, and cunning craftiness, whereby they lie in wait to deceive" (Ephesians 4:11–12, 14).

The Savior's organization is built on this foundation of the original Twelve Apostles who "shall sit upon twelve thrones, judging the twelve tribes of Israel" (Matthew 19:28). And they shall judge the Twelve Apostles who were called to judge the Nephites. "Thou rememberest the twelve apostles of the Lamb? Behold they are they who shall judge the twelve tribes of Israel; wherefore, the twelve ministers of thy seed shall be judged of them; for ye are of the house of Israel" (1 Nephi 12:9).

In addition to establishing a body of leaders to guide and judge His people, Christ defined the relationship between these leaders and those whom they lead. He said, "The disciple is not above *his* master, nor the servant above his lord" (Matthew 10:24). Luke records this same phrase with additional insight. "The disciple is not above his master: but every one that is perfect shall be as his master" (Luke 6:40).

Luke suggests that those who learn fully from their leaders can develop into complete representations of the character of their leaders.

To His modern–day Apostles, Jesus continues this theme of how people function within His organization. He taught that each person has a purpose. "Therefore, let every man stand in his own office, and labor in his own calling; and let not the head say unto the feet it hath no need of the feet; for without the feet how shall the body be able to stand? Also the body hath need of every member, that all may be edified together, that the system may be kept perfect" (D&C 84:109–110) (See also 1 Corinthians 12:12–30).

Not only did Jesus establish His organization with order, He operated with order and taught His Apostles how to do so as well. When faced with the need to feed the 5,000 disciples, Jesus told His Apostles to "give ye them to eat" (Mark 6:37). He then taught them how to establish order in such a large group, "And he commanded them to make all sit down by companies upon the green grass. And they sat down in ranks, by hundreds, and by fifties" (Mark 6:39–40).

In the land of Bountiful, Jesus also taught His Twelve Apostles about having order. First, He taught that there are boundaries within which they would operate. He said, "But whoso among you shall do *more or less* than these are not built upon my rock" (3 Nephi 18:13, emphasis added). The Savior then taught the importance of completing assignments when He reminded Nephi of scriptures that were given but not recorded. He said, "Behold, other scriptures I would that ye should write, that ye have not" (3 Nephi 23:6). He then reminded Nephi that the prophecies of Samuel the Lamanite had not been recorded. "And it came to pass that Jesus commanded that it should be written; therefore it was written according as he commanded" (3 Nephi 23:13).

Once all the records were in order, Jesus repeated His charge given in chapter 18 (3 Nephi 18:13) to limit their teaching to the doctrine He gave them, for "he commanded them that they should teach the things which he had expounded unto them" (3 Nephi 23:14). Jesus had set forth the proper order not only for administering His gospel, but also ministering within it. He did so by calling and training the Twelve Apostles and by ensuring His doctrine was recorded properly. Now

His work could spread in purity and with proper oversight because all was in order.

Examples of Righteous Leaders

The Relief Society of the Church of Jesus Christ of Latter–day Saints began as a small group of women who wanted to make a difference. The Prophet Joseph Smith formalized the creation of this organization during one historic meeting, but it was his counsel over many subsequent meetings that added the order necessary for it to grow. Sister Eliza R. Snow served as the first Relief Society secretary and it was her detailed minutes that formed the foundation the organization needed. Her diligence is explained in the book, *Daughters in My Kingdom, The History and Work of Relief Society.*

"On the trek from Nauvoo to the Salt Lake Valley, she had carefully safeguarded her minute book. She understood the importance of what had been taught to the sisters in those meetings. She knew how the society should be structured, and she remembered the principles upon which it was established. She understood that the organization was a fundamental part of The Church of Jesus Christ of Latter–day Saints. "It is no ordinary thing," she explained, "to meet in an organization of this nature. This organization belongs to the organization of the Church of Christ, in all dispensations when it is in perfection." Now, as she traveled from ward to ward, she taught from the minutes again and again."[12]

This small organization of women that started in Nauvoo now numbers in the millions with devoted women around the world. The order that was established in its infancy continues to provide the necessary structure so this great organization can bless the lives of both the giver and the receiver of loving service.

A heaven–designed order can be found all around us, even in the elements of nature. William Shakespeare used his gift of language to explain one such example. Through his character of the Archbishop of Canterbury in *Henry V,* Shakespeare tells of the orderly nature of a beehive to demonstrate a well–ordered organization.

Therefore doth heaven divide
The state of man in divers functions,
Setting endeavour in continual motion;
To which is fixed, as an aim or butt,
Obedience: for so work the honey–bees,
Creatures that by a rule in nature teach
The act of order to a peopled kingdom.
They have a king and officers of sorts;
Where some, like magistrates, correct at home,
Others, like merchants, venture trade abroad,
Others, like soldiers, armed in their stings,
Make boot upon the summer's velvet buds,
Which pillage they with merry march bring home
To the tent–royal of their emperor;
Who, busied in his majesty, surveys
The singing masons building roofs of gold,
The civil citizens kneading up the honey,
The poor mechanic porters crowding in
Their heavy burdens at his narrow gate,
The sad–eyed justice, with his surly hum,
Delivering o'er to executors pale
The lazy yawning drone.[13]

Beehives work because there is order. Each bee has a clearly defined job, works hard, and stays focused on that job. There are also provisions for those bees who do not cooperate with that established order who must face consequences as did the "lazy yawning drone." However, following the Savior's example, every effort should be made to reform rather than remove the uncooperative members.

Summary of Examples

- An honorable leader has order in the organization by establishing roles and responsibilities of those who help lead his effort, as Jesus did in calling the Twelve Apostles.
- An honorable leader has order in the organization by

determining how relationships operate between hierarchal levels, as taught by Jesus when He said, "The disciple is not above his master" (Luke 6:40) and "let not the head say unto the feet it hath no need of the feet" (D&C 84:109).

- An honorable leader has order in the organization by ensuring each person has a responsibility and they do their own work, as Jesus did when He taught "let every man stand in his own office, and labor in his own calling" (D&C 84:109).
- An honorable leader has order in the activities of his organization, such as when Jesus had the 5,000 sit in ranks.
- An honorable leader has order in the organization by establishing operating procedures, such as not altering the message of the organization, as Jesus taught when He said to not do *"more or less"* (3 Nephi 18:13, emphasis added) than assigned.
- An honorable leader has order in the organization by ensuring people fulfill their responsibilities, as Jesus did when He asked Nephi to complete the scriptural record.
- Honorable leaders establish sound principles and constantly adhere to them as demonstrated by the orderly formation and continuing growth of the Relief Society.

Questions for Personal Reflection

- Are you practicing discipline in living an orderly and structured life?
- Can you establish an environment where order and flexibility can coexist?
- Can you function well as a team member and help other team members and leaders function appropriately in their roles?
- Are you content to follow laws and guidelines that have been developed for your safety and success?
- Have you established house rules, such as a curfew with predetermined consequences to eliminate debate if a rule is broken?
- Have you helped in the legislative process to craft or promote the establishment of laws for a more orderly society?

Attribute 43: Gives Clear Direction

Direction: *A guiding, governing, or motivating purpose. A course that must be taken in order to reach a destination.*

Uncertainty leads to instability and contention. The Apostle Paul cautioned against uncertainty when he said, "For if the trumpet give an *uncertain* sound, who shall prepare himself to the battle?" (1 Corinthians 14:8, emphasis added). People will join with a leader if they believe in him and his cause, but they will not follow very long without clarity. In His leadership, Jesus provided a clear and certain message and continually warned His followers not to alter it. He knew if they did, contention would surely follow, and it would divide and weaken His people.

Jesus said to the Nephites, "And according as I have commanded you thus shall ye baptize. And there shall be *no disputations among you,* as there have hitherto been; neither shall there be disputations among you concerning the points of my doctrine, as there have hitherto been. For verily, verily I say unto you, he that hath *the spirit of contention is not of me,* but is of the devil, who is the father of contention, and he stirreth up the hearts of men to contend with anger, one with another" (3 Nephi 11:28–29, emphasis added).

From the peaks of Mount Sinai comes one of the best examples of giving clear direction. As Moses descended those rocky slopes, he carried ten easy-to-understand commandments given by Jehovah. If followed, they would eliminate much of the suffering mortal man experiences.

1. Thou shalt have no other gods before me.
2. Thou shalt not make unto thee any graven image.
3. Thou shalt not take the name of the LORD thy God in vain.
4. Remember the sabbath day, to keep it holy.
5. Honour thy father and thy mother.
6. Thou shalt not kill.
7. Thou shalt not commit adultery.
8. Thou shalt not steal.

9. Thou shalt not bear false witness.

10. Thou shalt not covet (Exodus 20:3–17).

To these Ten Commandments, Jesus adds another commandment that is more powerful, and even more clear and concise. "Love one another; as I have loved you" (John 13:34).

Shortly after receiving the Ten Commandments, Moses received additional direction from the Lord to build several items of sacred importance. He gave clear and precise instructions for each of these because He wanted them constructed exactly as He designed. These instructions are so clear we could build them today almost exactly as Israel built them thousands of years ago. For example, consider some of the instructions to build the ark.

"And they shall make an ark of shittim wood: two cubits and a half shall be the length thereof, and a cubit and a half the breadth thereof, and a cubit and a half the height thereof.

"And thou shalt overlay it with pure gold, within and without shalt thou overlay it, and shalt make upon it a crown of gold round about.

"And thou shalt cast four rings of gold for it, and put them in the four corners thereof; and two rings shall be in the one side of it, and two rings in the other side of it" (Exodus 25:10–12).

Consider some of the instructions to make the tabernacle.

"Moreover thou shalt make the tabernacle with ten curtains of fine twined linen, and blue, and purple, and scarlet: with cherubims of cunning work shalt thou make them.

"The length of one curtain shall be eight and twenty cubits, and the breadth of one curtain four cubits: and every one of the curtains shall have one measure.

"The five curtains shall be coupled together one to another; and other five curtains shall be coupled one to another.

"And thou shalt make loops of blue upon the edge of the one curtain from the selvedge in the coupling; and likewise shalt thou make in the uttermost edge of another curtain, in the coupling of the second.

"Fifty loops shalt thou make in the one curtain, and fifty loops shalt thou make in the edge of the curtain that is in the coupling of the second; that the loops may take hold one of another" (Exodus 26:1–5).

Consider some of the instructions for making the altar:

"And thou shalt make an altar of shittim wood, five cubits long, and five cubits broad; the altar shall be foursquare: and the height thereof shall be three cubits.

"And thou shalt make the horns of it upon the four corners thereof: his horns shall be of the same: and thou shalt overlay it with brass.

"And thou shalt make his pans to receive his ashes, and his shovels, and his basons, and his fleshhooks, and his firepans: all the vessels thereof thou shalt make of brass.

"And thou shalt make for it a grate of network of brass; and upon the net shalt thou make four brasen rings in the four corners thereof.

"And thou shalt put it under the compass of the altar beneath, that the net may be even to the midst of the altar" (Exodus 27:1–5).

Consider some of the instructions to make Aaron's priestly attire.

"And these are the garments which they shall make; a breastplate, and an ephod, and a robe, and a broidered coat, a mitre, and a girdle: and they shall make holy garments for Aaron thy brother, and his sons, that he may minister unto me in the priest's office.

"And they shall take gold, and blue, and purple, and scarlet, and fine linen.

"And they shall make the ephod of gold, of blue, and of purple, of scarlet, and fine twined linen, with cunning work.

"It shall have the two shoulderpieces thereof joined at the two edges thereof; and so it shall be joined together.

"And the curious girdle of the ephod, which is upon it, shall be of the same, according to the work thereof; even of gold, of blue, and purple, and scarlet, and fine twined linen" (Exodus 28:4–7).

These four examples show how a leader gives clear directions on matters where he wants an exact outcome. It is noteworthy that the Lord did not explain how to make the items in these examples, only what they should be like when completed. Thus, He gives directions when needed and refrains from giving directions when not needed. When Jesus does choose to give directions, they are so clear they can produce the desired results without the contention that often comes from uncertainty.

Part of giving clear direction is maintaining consistency. Christ declared, "I *am* the LORD, I change not" (Malachi 3:6). Jesus taught His same doctrine to the Jews, the Jaredites, the Nephites, the Lamanites, and the Gentiles. He also had His disciples teach the same doctrine He gave to them. "And when they had ministered those same words which Jesus had spoken—*nothing varying* from the words which Jesus had spoken—behold, they knelt again and prayed to the Father in the name of Jesus" (3 Nephi 19:8, emphasis added).

Jesus knew the natural tendencies of man and continually taught of the dangers of misunderstanding His doctrine. That is why "he doeth nothing save it be plain unto the children of men" (2 Nephi 26:33). However, there are some who do not want plainness. Jacob taught how the Jews struggled because they did not want simplicity and clear understanding. "But behold, the Jews were a stiffnecked people; and *they despised the words of plainness,* and killed the prophets, and sought for things that they could not understand. Wherefore, because of their blindness, which blindness came by looking beyond the mark, they must needs fall; for God hath taken away his plainness from them, and delivered unto them many things which they cannot understand, because they desired it. And because they desired it God hath done it, that they may stumble" (Jacob 4:14, emphasis added).

Therefore, Jesus taught them with parables so the righteous would learn, and the unrighteous would not. To aid His servants in clearly understanding His doctrine, He taught them using their language. "Behold, I am God and have spoken it; these commandments are of me, and were given unto my servants in their weakness, *after the manner of their language,* that they might come to understanding" (D&C 1:24, emphasis added).

Teaching in this manner goes beyond helping people to understand, it is endeavoring to communicate so well that it avoids misunderstandings. Then, people can put their full efforts toward progression rather than being weakened by contention.

Examples of Righteous Leaders

In addition to having clear doctrine, it is critical to have clear direction in the duties of those who administer the work. This will help fellow laborers from drifting into each other's areas of responsibilities, and limit disputations that surely would arise. Such clarifications were undertaken by President Brigham Young in the early days of the restored Church.

"In his 77th year, President Brigham Young organized the priesthood to give more clear direction to its labors, to unite the Saints, and to gather and care for the sheep of Israel. The effect of President Young's last major project was praised by his assistant counselor, Elder George Q. Cannon. He said that President Young "*set the priesthood in order* as it has never been since the organization of the Church upon the earth. He defined the duties of the apostles, . . . seventies, . . . high priests, . . . elders, . . . lesser priesthood, *with plainness and distinction* and power—the power of God—in a way that is left on record in such unmistakable language that no one need err who has the Spirit of God resting down upon him."[14]

By setting the priesthood in order, the Church was now ready to expand at an accelerated rate while still maintaining the order and harmony one would expect in the Lord's work.

Summary of Examples

- Directions given by a leader should be so clear that they do not lead to disputations, as taught by Jesus to the Nephites when He said, "the spirit of contention is not of me" (3 Nephi 11:29).
- Directions given by a leader should be simple, plain, and concise, as are the Ten Commandments.
- Directions given by a leader can be built upon one single theme, such as "love one another" (John 13:34).

- Directions given by a leader should be consistent, as taught by Jesus when He had the Nephites teach His words with nothing varying.
- Directions given by a leader should be in the language of the listeners, as Jesus demonstrated with the elders of the restored Church.
- Directions given by a leader should be understandable to everyone, and be in "unmistakable" language, as demonstrated by Brigham Young.

Questions for Personal Reflection

- Do you assume too often that others comprehend what you are saying?
- Are you clear in your own mind as to what your objectives are?
- How much do you polish your message before it is delivered to avoid misunderstanding?
- When someone seems unclear with your directions, do you blame them or you?
- How are you testing to see if your directions are actually received as you intended?
- Have you perfected the processes in your organization, and can everyone execute those processes perfectly each time?

Attribute 44: Counsels Together

Counsel: *Consultation, especially to seek or give advice. Interchange of opinions as to future procedure; consultation; deliberation i.e. careful consideration before decision.*

In the premortal realms, the plans for our mortal experiences were "ordained in the midst of the Council of the Eternal God of all other gods before this world was" (D&C 121:32). Abraham teaches that "the Gods took counsel among themselves. . . . And the Gods said among themselves: On the seventh time we will end our work, which we have counseled" (Abraham 4:26; 5:2). How important is counseling together that even the Gods participate in this process of planning and deciding?

In Proverbs we read, "Where no counsel is, the people fall: but in the multitude of counsellors there is safety" (Proverbs 11:14). The act of counseling together allows a group of people to draw upon the experience and wisdom of each member. This allows the leader to make better decisions, but it also benefits the members in the council. Jesus taught, "let us reason together, *that ye may understand"* (D&C 50:10). When members of the council gain greater understanding, they have greater capacity to implement the decisions made in the council.

Jesus trained the Twelve Apostles through continually counseling with them. He asked them questions and discussed their answers. For example, "And Jesus went out, and his disciples, into the towns of Cæsarea Philippi: and by the way he asked his disciples, saying unto them, Whom do men say that I am?" (Mark 8:27). He then counseled, or reasoned, with them that they may more fully understand His divinity.

At the Last Supper, Jesus sat in counsel with his Apostles, for there was much they still needed to understand before the turbulent hours leading to His Crucifixion. After the Crucifixion and Resurrection, Jesus again met with His Apostles to help them better understand His mission and Resurrection. Here, He ate broiled fish and honeycomb and discussed the scriptures with them. He reminded them of the *doctrine He taught before His death and reasoned with them to* deepen their understanding. Then with that understanding, they were better prepared to go forth unto all the world while He ascended to dwell with His Father.

Examples of Righteous Leaders

The prophet Jacob taught the Nephites that there was danger in relying upon their own personal knowledge. He taught that this arrogant over–confidence is a great barrier to counseling together. In particular, he cautioned them against turning a deaf ear to the counsel of God. The message, however, also applies to leaders who turn a deaf ear to the wise counsel of their fellowmen. Jacob said, "O that cunning plan of the evil one! O the vainness, and the frailties, and the foolishness of men! When they are learned they think they are wise, and they hearken not unto the counsel of God, *for they set it aside, supposing they know of themselves,* wherefore, their wisdom is foolishness and it profiteth them not. And they shall perish" (2 Nephi 9:28, emphasis added).

King Mosiah practiced what Jacob preached. His record contains an account of Nephite King Limhi and his people who were in bondage to the Lamanites. They were descendants of Zeniff and his group who left Zarahemla some 80 years earlier to inherit the land of their fathers now under Lamanite control. After those 80 years, Zeniff's descendants wondered about them and repeatedly petitioned King Mosiah to send men to find them. Mosiah demonstrated sound leadership as he counseled with his people, listened to their requests, and then conceded because of their diligence and the worthiness of their desires. Therefore, he sent Ammon and fifteen other strong men to search after them (Mosiah 7:1–2).

After many days in the wilderness, Ammon and his group found them and offered to help lead them back to Zarahemla. However, helping such a great number of people escape would be difficult. To find the best answer, these noble leaders—Ammon and King Limhi— engaged all the people in studying solutions and then discussing together their proposals. "And now *all the study* of Ammon and his people, and king Limhi and his people, was to deliver themselves out of the hands of the Lamanites and from bondage" (Mosiah 21:36, emphasis added). "And now it came to pass that Ammon and king Limhi began to *consult with the people* how they should deliver themselves out of bondage; and even they did cause that all the people should gather themselves together; and this they did that they might have the voice of the people concerning the matter" (Mosiah 22:1, emphasis added).

Ammon and Limhi demonstrated that leaders do not have to be the source of all solutions. If they create the right environment, others can provide solutions based on their varied experiences and expertise. In this open environment, Gideon came forward with a proposal for he was a trusted man of tremendous ability and experience. King Limhi listened to him and "the king hearkened unto the words of Gideon" (Mosiah 22:9). Then Limhi and Ammon did what only they as leaders could do, they organized everyone behind Gideon's proposal. The people united together in a powerful way and gained their cherished freedom.

In more recent times, while many of the early Apostles of the restored Church served in England, they wrote to the Prophet Joseph for guidance. On one such occasion, Joseph responded by deferring the issues back to them by explaining: "There are many things of much importance, on which you ask counsel, but which I think you will be perfectly able to decide upon, as you are more conversant with the peculiar circumstances than I am; and I feel great confidence in your *united wisdom*."[15]

In this one statement, Joseph taught that the leader does not have all the knowledge and that he trusted in their ability to work together to make good decisions. Joseph said, "The way to get along in any important matter is to gather unto yourselves wise men, experienced and aged men, to assist in council in all times of trouble."[16] With the Twelve Apostles, he had such wise and experienced men.

Summary of Examples

- Honorable leaders counsel together with their people to aid their understanding and growth, as taught by Jesus when He said, "let us reason together, *that ye may understand*" (D&C 50:10, emphasis added).

- Honorable leaders counsel together with their people to find the best solution to complex problems, as demonstrated by Ammon and Limhi as they found a way to escape the Lamanites.
- Honorable leaders foster counseling among their people because of the united wisdom they possess, as with the Apostles in England.
- Honorable leaders foster counseling among their people who are more "conversant with [their] peculiar circumstances," as with the Apostles in England.

Questions for Personal Reflection

- Do you use councils to build unity, increase understanding, foster individual growth, and create sound decisions?
- Do you create an environment where the views or recommendations of each person in the council have equal weight without regard to gender, position, experience, or forcefulness?
- How do you ensure each person feels valued?
- Do you guide discussions toward your preferred option, or is the group allowed freedom of discovery?
- How often do you gather together your friends to discuss ways to better influence other friends?
- How are you building consensus and support through counseling with your neighbors?

Attribute 45: Serves Others

Serve: *To furnish or supply with something needed or desired.*

Jesus taught that leaders are servants. After calling His twelve Nephite disciples, He explained that He chose them "from among you to minister unto you, and to be your servants" (3 Nephi 12:1). He taught this same principle to His Apostles in Jerusalem. He taught that "if any man desire to be first, the same shall be last of all, and servant of all" (Mark 9:35). The Savior taught this doctrine to the Apostles in Capernaum after they had "disputed among themselves, who *should be* the greatest" (Mark 9:34). He again had to teach them during the Last Supper when the disciples who sat around the table created an atmosphere of "strife" as they again discussed "which of them should be accounted the greatest" (Luke 22:24). Jesus taught, "he that is greatest among you, let him be as the younger; and he that is chief, as he that doth serve. For whether *is* greater, he that sitteth at meat, or he that serveth? *is* not he that sitteth at meat? but I am among you as he that serveth" (Luke 22:26–27).

Matthew's record states that Jesus said, "but whosoever will be great among you, let him be your minister; And whosoever will be chief among you, let him be your servant: Even as the Son of man came not to be ministered unto, but to minister" (Matthew 20:26–28). The Apostle Paul wrote to the Philippians that Jesus "took upon him the form of a servant" (Philippians 2:7). The Savior did this to serve those in need, but also to set the example for others to serve. He taught how and when to serve when He said, "Therefore, strengthen your brethren in all your conversation, in all your prayers, in all your exhortations, and in all your doings" (D&C 108:7).

Jesus declared, "I am the good shepherd: the good shepherd giveth his life for the sheep" (John 10:11). He also taught, "he that loseth his life for my sake shall find it" (Matthew 10:39). This is more than just dying for them; this is spending His entire life for their benefit. Jesus is teaching that His way of leadership is clearly different from man's ways. Instead of the leader being served by the people, the leader serves the people.

Examples of Righteous Leaders

King Mosiah had four sons who had been rebellious until the Spirit of the Lord touched them and changed their lives. As part of their repentance, they went throughout the land of Zarahemla repairing the damage they had done to their fellowmen. Then they went one step further and desired to go to the Lamanites with the hope of bringing them to the happiness they now enjoyed. These four young men—Ammon, Aaron, Omner, and Himni—wanted this opportunity to serve their brethren, for "they were desirous that salvation should be declared to every creature, for they could not bear that any human soul should perish; yea, even the very thoughts that any soul should endure endless torment did cause them to quake and tremble" (Mosiah 28:3). Because of their love for the Lord, they now desired to be servants to all who would listen. These four young men took the lead and went with a small number of others to the Lamanites and led thousands of them to find the same everlasting joy they had found.

The sons of Mosiah demonstrated that many can be blessed by the efforts of just a few. Their example guides modern leaders who also use their personal influence to bless the lives of many people. Elder Harold G. Hillam gives one such example: "I would like to tell you of a stake conference I was assigned to attend. It was a reorganization. . . . The stake president was young and had served wonderfully for almost 10 years. He was a spiritual giant, but he was also an administrative giant. In my personal interview with him, he told me how he had delegated much of the responsibility for the stake functions to his counselors and to the high council and had thus freed himself to interview those who needed encouragement. Individuals and couples were invited to come to his office. There he got to know them, counseled with them, and invited them to do better, to put their lives in order, and to receive the blessings available to those who follow the Lord. . . . Then he told me that in these interviews he would often ask if they would like a blessing. 'I have placed my hands on the heads of many members of the stake'" he said.

"The next day in the general session of the stake conference, I doubt I have ever seen so many tears—not because they felt the president should not be released, but for the deep love of a young stake president who had blessed their lives. I felt prompted to ask, 'How many of you have had the hands of the president on your heads?' I was amazed at the number of people who raised their hands."[17]

This is the pattern set by the Savior. He delegated to others those things they could help with and then went out and personally served the people.

One of the blessings of serving others is that the person serving is also blessed. For example, Elder Dieter F. Uchtdorf taught: "President Gordon B. Hinckley believed in the healing power of service. After the death of his wife, he provided a great example to the Church in the way he immersed himself in work and in serving others. It is told that President Hinckley remarked to one woman who had recently lost her husband, 'Work will cure your grief. Serve others.'"[18]

Those who have applied this counsel will testify of its truth, for something almost magical happens when one person serves another. That act of service is endorsed by heaven and is accompanied by a healing and lifting power upon the receiver, the giver, and the observer. If a leader truly wants to improve lives, he or she merely needs to serve.

Summary of Examples

- Honorable leaders serve others, as Jesus did with the Apostles.
- Honorable leaders are often called to devote their entire lives to serving others, as Jesus did when He said, "the good shepherd giveth his life for the sheep" (John 10:11).
- Honorable leaders serve others because they want them to have the blessings and privileges they enjoy, as did the sons of Mosiah.
- Honorable leaders will create bonds with their people as they serve them, as taught by Elder Hillam regarding the young stake president.
- As leaders serve others, they are benefited as well, as taught by President Hinckley regarding the healing power of service.

Questions for Personal Reflection

- Is your desire to lead born out of a love to serve others or to be served?
- Are you preparing to serve others by taking care of your own self so you have the strength to lift others?
- Do you periodically assist your associates and neighbors rather than expecting them to always assist you?
- Do you look around your home to find opportunities to serve without being asked?
- How often do you ask your leaders what you can do to lessen his or her load?
- How much are you helping the disadvantaged to have a path toward success?

Attribute 46: Ministers to the One

Minister: *To give aid or service. Attend to the needs of someone.*

The life of a leader is influencing others to become better and do better. It is serving groups of people as well as ministering to individuals. Jesus said, "And whosoever will be chief among you, let him be your servant: Even as the Son of man came not to be ministered unto, *but to minister*" (Matthew 20:27–28, emphasis added). This perspective that Jesus taught is foreign to the natural man who often views leadership as just the opposite. To him, it is often about obtaining and reflecting power and prestige, just as it was with Lucifer. However, Jesus teaches a new way of leading, a way that takes one who is strong and puts him or her in a position to strengthen and guide others.

Such a life of service includes serving large groups of people, like feeding and teaching the 5,000, but it also means attending to one single lost sheep. Jesus taught of serving the one in addition to the group with such clarity that it is one of the most frequently quoted parables.

"And he spake this parable unto them, saying,

"What man of you, having an hundred sheep, if he lose one of them, doth not leave the ninety and nine in the wilderness, and *go after that which is lost, until he find it?*

"And when he hath found *it*, he layeth *it* on his shoulders, rejoicing.

"And when he cometh home, he calleth together *his* friends and neighbours, saying unto them, Rejoice with me; for I have found my sheep which was lost" (Luke 15:3–6, emphasis added).

Not only did Jesus teach this principle of ministering to individuals, He demonstrated it many times. For example, He ministered to Nicodemus who visited one night. As a Pharisee, this private nighttime meeting would have been more comfortable for Nicodemus where he could meet with Jesus out of public view. The fact that he came shows that he felt Jesus was approachable. The fact that he came at night shows that Jesus was also accessible. The scriptures show that

Jesus taught him in a private and personal way, tailoring his message to his needs.

Jesus also ministered to a rich young man who came because he admired what Jesus did. Like Nicodemus, he too came because the Savior was approachable and accessible. He came asking what he needed to do for eternal life, and Jesus gave him an answer tailored to his personal circumstances. He was told to "go *and* sell" (Matthew 19:21) his many possessions, give them to the poor, and follow Him.

Another example is the woman who touched the hem of Jesus's garment with the hope of being healed. Jesus was traveling in a crowded street on His way to other pressing issues but stopped to minister and improve her life. And He ministered with no hint of being inconvenienced (Luke 8:43–48). Neither did He seem annoyed when teaching Martha of the value in setting aside her chores to focus on the words from the Bread of Life (Luke 10:42).

As Jesus traveled through Samaria, He stopped at Jacob's well in Sychar for refreshment. There He ministered to one single Samaritan woman and taught the powerful doctrine that He was the source of living water, even the Christ. He taught, "But whosoever drinketh of the water that I shall give him shall never thirst; but the water that I shall give him shall be in him a well of water springing up into everlasting life" (John 4:14). She then said, "I know that Messias cometh, which is called Christ: when he is come, he will tell us all things" (John 4:25). He then simply said, "I that speak unto thee am *he*" (John 4:26). One of the greatest declarations in history was given to one single Samaritan woman in a private setting by a well.

In the Americas, as the Savior ministered unto those assembled at the temple, He invited them to come forward that He might heal them as He did with some at Jerusalem. And "all the multitude with one accord, did go forth with their sick and their afflicted, and their lame, and with their blind, and with their dumb, and will all them that were afflicted in any manner; and he did heal them *every one*" (3 Nephi 17:9, emphasis added).

After healing every one of the afflicted, Jesus gathered together His newly called Twelve Apostles to bid them farewell. His final act of ministering was to speak with them "one by one, saying unto them:

What is it that ye desire of me, after that I am gone to the Father?" (3 Nephi 28:1). He did not preach to them or remind them of all they needed to do. Instead, He asked each one privately what He could do for them. He sought for some way to minister unto them individually, based on their own personal desires. Then He did for them exactly as they requested. What greater teaching moment could He have given than to show them how to minister one by one?

In each of these examples, great truths were taught to small audiences. The size of the audience does not dictate the leader's level of effort. Sometimes the greatest change comes when the full power of our personal influence is focused on one single individual.

Examples of Righteous Leaders

President Thomas S. Monson made individual ministering a hallmark of his service that spanned several decades. Occasionally, he shared examples of this service and each one was a blessing to the recipient and the observer. One such example is as follows: "One occasion many years ago, I was swimming laps . . . when I felt the inspiration to go to the University Hospital to visit a good friend of mine who had lost the use of his lower limbs. . . . I immediately left the pool, dressed, and was soon on my way to see this good man.

"When I arrived at his room, I found that it was empty. Upon inquiry I learned I would probably find him in the swimming pool area of the hospital, an area which was used for physical therapy. Such turned out to be the case. He had guided himself there in his wheelchair and was the only occupant of the room. He was on the far side of the pool, near the deep end. I called to him, and he maneuvered his wheelchair over to greet me. We had an enjoyable visit, and I accompanied him back to his hospital room, where I gave him a blessing.

"I learned later from my friend that he had been utterly despondent that day and had been contemplating taking his own life. He had prayed for relief but began to feel that his prayers had gone unanswered. He went to the pool with the thought that this would be a way to end his misery—by guiding his wheelchair into the deep end of the pool. I had arrived at a critical moment, in response to what I know was inspiration from on high."[19]

Because of his busy schedule and heavy workload, President Monson could have assigned a million different people to go look after his friend. But he did not. He went himself, just as the Savior did so many times, to minister to someone in need.

At times we may be tempted to think in terms of efficiency when deciding how to help others. We may ask ourselves, "Am I helping the greatest number of people, or am I helping those with the greatest need?" Or do we say, "Lord, just let me help someone in need" without thoughts of a cost/benefit ratio? Consider the following story of a great educator as told by President Harold B. Lee:

"Horace Mann . . . told how he was the speaker at the dedication of a great boys' school, and in his talk he said, "This school has cost hundreds of thousands of dollars; but if this school is able to save one boy, it is worth all that it cost." One of his friends came up to him at the close of the meeting and said, "You let your enthusiasm get away with you, didn't you? You don't mean what you said that if this school, costing hundreds of thousands of dollars, were to save just one boy, it was worth all that it cost? You surely don't mean that."

"Horace Mann looked at him and said, 'Yes, my friend. It would be worth it if that one boy were my son; it would be worth it.'"[20]

Gratefully, the Lord does not consider the costs to Him when He chooses to minister unto us. He ministers because He loves us and desires to improve our lives. That is how Jesus leads, and we can learn to lead like Him also by applying the seven–step process as discussed in chapter 4. Then we can have greater influence to bless lives.

Summary of Examples

- Honorable leaders minister to the one by tailoring their help to the needs and desires of specific individuals, as demonstrated by Jesus to Nicodemus, the rich young man, and the woman who touched His garment.
- Honorable leaders minister to the one when that one person

is in need, even when it is not convenient, as demonstrated by President Thomas S. Monson.

- Honorable leaders minister to the one even if perceived as costly, as taught by Horace Mann.

Questions for Personal Reflection

- As you go throughout your day, do you continually scan your associates and acquaintances for someone you can serve?
- Who do you know that is suffering from misfortune, even if self–inflicted, that could use your hand to lift them up?
- How often do you take time out of your busy schedule to have a warm personal exchange with one in need?
- Is there a lonely young person in your neighborhood whom you can involve in an activity such as little league baseball or dance?
- When you make decisions that affect large numbers of people, do you also consider how they affect each individual?

Attribute 47: Succors the Weak

Succor: *To run to the rescue, bring aid. Assistance and support in times of hardship and distress.*

One manifestation of leadership is when strong people help those who are not strong. It is about running to the rescue and bringing aid to those in distress. As Paul taught the Romans, "We then that are strong ought to bear the infirmities of the weak, and not to please ourselves" (Romans 15:1). The Savior taught this same truth to His restored Church. He said, "And if any man among you be strong in the Spirit, let him take with him him that is weak, that he may be edified in all meekness, that he may become strong also" (D&C 84:106). This is how leaders help others be better and do better. It is putting your arm around them and guiding them to a better place.

The Psalmist has captured so tenderly the feelings of many who have been succored personally by the hands of the Master Healer. In one of the most beloved verses in all scripture, he records these comforting words:

"The Lord is my shepherd; I shall not want.

"He maketh me to lie down in green pastures: he leadeth me beside the still waters.

"He restoreth my soul: he leadeth me in the paths of righteousness for his name's sake.

"Yea, though I walk through the valley of the shadow of death, I will fear no evil: for thou art with me; thy rod and thy staff they comfort me.

"Thou preparest a table before me in the presence of mine enemies: thou anointest my head with oil; my cup runneth over.

"Surely goodness and mercy shall follow me all the days of my life: and I will dwell in the house of the Lord for ever" (Psalms 23:1–6).

The Prophet Joseph Smith must have felt the succoring arms of Jesus as he languished in the cold cellar of Liberty Jail. Those arms must have felt like green pastures and still waters. Following months of opposition and deprivation, Joseph pleaded for relief and Jesus answered:

"My son, peace be unto thy soul; thine adversity and thine afflictions shall be but a small moment;

"And then, if thou endure it well, God shall exalt thee on high; thou shalt triumph over all thy foes (D&C 121:7–8).

"If thou art accused with all manner of false accusations; if thine enemies fall upon thee; if they tear thee from the society of thy father and mother and brethren and sisters; and if with a drawn sword thine enemies tear thee from the bosom of thy wife, and of thine offspring, and thine elder son, although but six years of age, shall cling to thy garments, and shall say, "My father, my father, why can't you stay with us? O, my father, what are the men going to do with you? and if then he shall be thrust from thee by the sword, and thou be dragged to prison, and thine enemies prowl around thee like wolves for the blood of the lamb;

"And if thou shouldst be cast into the pit, or into the hands of murderers, and the sentence of death passed upon thee; if thou be cast into the deep; if the billowing surge conspire against thee; if fierce winds become thine enemy; if the heavens gather blackness, and all the elements combine to hedge up the way; and above all, if the very jaws of hell shall gape open the mouth wide after thee, know thou, my son, that all these things shall give thee experience, and shall be for thy good . . . for *God shall be with you forever and ever"* (D&C 122:6–9, emphasis added).

Mortality brings many experiences that teach and try us, but Jesus has promised to be with us throughout our journey. He knows growth can be painful and difficult. He said to each of us, "These things I have spoken unto you, that in me ye might have peace. In the world ye shall have tribulation: but *be of good cheer;* I have overcome the world" (John 16:33, emphasis added). He continued, "Wherefore, be of good cheer, and do not fear, for I the Lord am with you, and *will stand by you"* (D&C 68:6, emphasis added). How comforting are His words, "I say unto you that mine eyes are upon you. *I am in your midst* and ye cannot see me?" (D&C 38:7, emphasis added).

Jesus promised the Nephites, "the life of my servant shall be in my hand; therefore they shall not hurt him, although he shall be marred because of them. Yet *I will heal him"* (3 Nephi 21:10, emphasis added).

Isaiah taught, "the Lord God will *wipe away tears* from off all faces" (Isaiah 25:8, emphasis added). To His disciples at Jerusalem, He said, "I will *not leave you comfortless:* I will come to you" (John 14:18, emphasis added). He further comforted them when He declared the oft–quoted phrase, "Peace I leave with you, my peace I give unto you: not as the world giveth, give I unto you. Let not your heart be troubled, neither let it be afraid" (John 14:27). Surely, this is succoring the weak—it is giving assistance and support in times of hardship and distress. It is giving hope to the downtrodden with promises such as this: "In my Father's house are many mansions . . . *I go to prepare a place for you"* (John 14:2, emphasis added). When the trials of mortality are past and the weak have become strong, they will find eternal rest in those mansions, having become what Jesus helped them become.

Examples of Righteous Leaders

There is much each of us can do to aid and support those in distress. The Relief Society has a long history with many examples of such service. In April 1921, Sister Clarissa S. Williams was called as Relief Society general president after serving 11 years in the presidency under the leadership of Emmeline B. Wells. During those years, she had seen so much of the sick and destitute who were severely in need. Through her personal ministry and her encouragement to Relief Society sisters worldwide, many sisters stepped forward and succored the weak. For example, the Cottonwood Stake Relief Society followed her leadership and that of their priesthood leaders and formed a maternity hospital. This little hospital grew into a significant resource in the greater Salt Lake City area where countless patients received much needed care. The hospital also provided professional opportunities for many women who were medical providers. This employment helped them become economically self–sufficient. Such is the nature of service where those who give and those who receive are blessed.

News outlets rarely report on the vast numbers of people who follow the example of Jesus in succoring the downtrodden. However, Bishop H. David Burton, Presiding Bishop of the Church of Jesus

Christ of Latter–day Saints, gave such a report. In April 2008 general conference, he said: "In addition to responding to natural disasters, we undertook thousands of public health initiatives during the year. Over 1 million people benefited from Church–sponsored clean water projects in 25 countries. More than 60,500 people received wheelchairs in 60 nations . . . In 11 countries, over 54,000 individuals now enjoy improved vision. Over 16,500 health–care professionals in 23 countries were trained in infant neonatal resuscitation; they, in turn, will train many others. In a quest to eliminate measles, 2.8 million children and youth in 10 countries received immunizations. The combined effects of these outreach endeavors directly touched nearly 4 million people in 85 countries."

Through their guidance, Church leaders have influenced millions of people to donate the resources needed to ease suffering and instill hope in the downtrodden around the globe. They are the strong helping the weak. In doing so, they set the example for other organizations to join in this effort to lift and nourish all of God's children.

Summary of Examples

- Honorable leaders take those who are weak and link them with those who are strong until they become strong, as taught by Jesus.
- Honorable leaders strengthen and encourage those who are downtrodden, discouraged, abused, or seemingly have failed, as Jesus does when He restoreth our souls.
- Honorable leaders relieve the suffering of the disadvantaged, as described by Bishop Burton.

Questions for Personal Reflection

- Do you continually look for opportunities to succor the weak as you go through your daily activities?
- When you succor the weak, do you do so because it makes you seem strong or because you have a genuine desire to relieve human suffering?

- Do you have any condescending feelings toward the disadvan-taged or blame them for their own plight?
- Are you aware that sometimes those who appear the strongest also need help?
- Do you extend kindness and compassion to one who has been disciplined?
- Which of your associates could use your help today?

---

1. Riverside Webster's II Dictionary.
2. John Henry Evans, *Joseph Smith, an American Prophet,* New York: MacMillan Co., 416-20; emphasis added.
3. Mark E. Petersen, *Three Kings of Israel, "The Reign of the Judges,"* 11.
4. Spencer W. Kimball, "Always a Convert Church: Some Lessons to Learn and Apply This Year," *Ensign,* September 1975.
5. Robert D. Hales, "Examples from the Life of a Prophet," *Ensign,* November 1981.
6. Spencer W. Kimball, "Let Us Move Forward and Upward," *Ensign,* May 1979.
7. Dieter F. Uchtdorf, "The Merciful Obtain Mercy," *Ensign,* May 2012.
8. Jeffrey R. Holland, "The Tongue of Angels," *Ensign,* May 2007. See *Lectures on Faith* (1985), 72–73; emphasis added.
9. Joseph F. Smith, "The Spirit of Worship," *Improvement Era,* June 1910, 749–50.
10. LeGrand Richards, cited in Douglas L. Callister, "Seeking the Spirit of God," *Ensign,* November 2000.
11. Joseph F. Smith, *Gospel Doctrine,* 5th ed. (1939).
12. *Daughters in My Kingdom,* 42-43.
13. William Shakespeare, *Henry V,* Act 1, Scene 2.
14. *Teachings of Presidents of The Church: Brigham Young,* 137. See CHC, 5:507, emphasis added.
15. Joseph Smith, B. H. Roberts, *History of The Church of Jesus Christ of Latter-day Saints, vol. 4,* 228; emphasis added.
16. Alma P. Burton, *Discourses of the Prophet Joseph Smith,* 211.
17. Harold G. Hillam, "The Worth of Souls," *Ensign,* May 2005.

18. Dieter F. Uchtdorf, "Happiness, Your Heritage," *Ensign*, November 2008.
19. Thomas S. Monson, "Consider the Blessings," *Ensign*, November 2012.
20. Harold B. Lee, "Today's Young People," *Ensign*, June 1971.

CHAPTER 10

HE PREPARED HIS FOLLOWERS

Attribute 48: Knows Followers and They Know Him

Know: *To be aware of and understand through observation and experience. Discern. To recognize the nature of.*

Jesus knows that people, like sheep, need to know their leader and the leader needs to know them. He explained, "The Lord knoweth them that are his" (2 Timothy 2:19) for "mine eyes are upon you" (D&C 67:2). Therefore, "We see that God is mindful of every people" (Alma 26:37). Jacob gave additional insight when he counseled, "Think of your brethren like unto yourselves, and be familiar with all" (Jacob 2:17). Jesus is unique as a leader because He is intimately aware of each of us. He knows each sheep individually and they know Him. He taught:

"I am the good shepherd: the good shepherd giveth his life for the sheep.

"But he that is an hireling, and not the shepherd, whose own the sheep are not, seeth the wolf coming, and leaveth the sheep, and fleeth: and the wolf catcheth them, and scattereth the sheep.

"The hireling fleeth, because he is an hireling, and careth not for the sheep.

"I am the good shepherd, and know my sheep, and am known of mine" (John 10:11–14, emphasis added).

Knowing people individually is important, but there is a deeper level of understanding that is needed if a leader wants to influence his or her people. The prophet Alma records how Jesus develops this deeper level of understanding. He taught: "And he shall go forth, suffering pains and afflictions and temptations of every kind; and this that the word might be fulfilled which saith he will take upon him the pains and the sicknesses of his people. And he will take upon him death, that he may loose the bands of death which bind his people; and he will take upon him their infirmities, that his bowels may be filled with mercy, according to the flesh, *that he may know according to the flesh how to succor his people according to their infirmities"* (Alma 7:11–12).

As a result, Jesus "knoweth the weakness of man and how to succor them who are tempted" (D&C 62:1). This allows Jesus to personalize His ministering to our individual needs. If leaders paid the price for this understanding, they would know the dreams and frustrations of their people. They would know their strengths and limitations, their temperament and tendencies. They would know where they have potential to improve and where improvement is unlikely. With this knowledge, they would know how to lead them toward higher attainment and greater personal joy.

In the Gospel of Matthew, the Savior teaches a parable about sowers, seeds, and soils. The parable describes four kinds of soils, each one representing the "different states of the hearts of men."[1] "*First* is the 'wayside heart,' which is too hard to receive the word . . . *Second* is the 'thin–soil heart,' which receives the word joyfully, but only briefly . . . *Third* is the 'thorn–infested heart,' which doesn't allow room for the word . . . *Fourth* is the 'good–soil heart,' which is the open and prepared heart."[2] This parable is important for a leader to understand. If a leader understands his followers well enough to know which heart type each possesses, then he or she can work with them, even as a gardener works to improve soil so that it is more receptive.

Knowing those you lead and how to succor them is half of the goal. The other half is for the followers to also know their leaders. The Apostle Paul taught of the need "to know them which labour among you, and are *over you in the Lord, and admonish you"* (1 Thessalonians 5:12, emphasis added). Jesus taught that His disciples followed Him because they knew Him.

"To him the porter openeth; and the sheep hear his voice: and he calleth his own sheep by name, and leadeth them out.

"And when he putteth forth his own sheep, he goeth before them, and the sheep follow him: *for they know his voice.*

"And a stranger will they not follow, but will flee from him: for they know not the voice of strangers" (John 10:3–5, emphasis added).

The Lord gave a choice invitation to the Nephites to come and get to know Him personally when He said: "Arise and come forth unto me, that ye may thrust your hands into my side, and also that ye may feel the prints of the nails in my hands and in my feet, *that ye may know* that I am the God of Israel, and the God of the whole earth, and have been slain for the sins of the world" (3 Nephi 11:14, emphasis added).

After learning of Jesus, the Nephites were better able to follow Him. They understood Him better, trusted Him more, and loved Him deeper. Jesus built a personal relationship with each of them where He could better influence their growth.

Examples of Righteous Leaders

In 1903, President Joseph F. Smith explained that the Relief Society is effective to the degree its leaders know their followers. He told of an experience he had on a recent trip that demonstrated this effectiveness. President Smith had traveled many days to reach an outlying stake of Zion deeply afflicted by widespread sickness. He arrived late one evening and immediately began visiting the sick with the stake president. President Smith tells of visiting one young mother who was extremely ill while her husband and several little children gathered around her. Soon, a matronly woman came to the home with a basket of nourishing food and delicacies for the family.

President Joseph F. Smith recorded, "On inquiry we learned that she had been detailed by the Relief Society of the ward to watch over and administer to the sick woman through the night. She was there prepared to look after the little children, to see that they were properly washed and fed and put to bed; to tidy up the house and make everything as comfortable as possible for the afflicted woman and her family. We also learned that another good sister would be detailed to relieve her the following day; and so on, from day to day."[3]

President Smith learned that the Relief Society was organized to provide this same care to all the sick throughout the settlement. He commented, "Never before had I seen so clearly exemplified the utility and beauty of this grand organization as in the example we here witnessed, and I thought what a gracious thing it was that the Lord inspired the Prophet Joseph Smith to establish such an organization in the Church."[4] The local Relief Society leaders knew each of their followers and understood how to engage their resources to provide needed relief in the midst of great suffering.

Summary of Examples

- Honorable leaders need enough experiences in common with their people so he or she can know how best to help them, as Jesus did with suffering pains and afflictions.
- Honorable leaders need to understand their followers so well that they know how to cultivate each person's heart, as exampled by Jesus as He visited the Nephites.
- Honorable leaders need to be known by their followers so their example can be emulated, as demonstrated by Jesus among the Jews and the Nephites.
- Honorable leaders are capable of pulling together significant resources necessary to meet the needs of their followers, as demonstrated by President Smith's experience with the Relief Society.

Questions for Personal Reflection

- How often do you mingle with those you lead so you can better understand them?
- Have you associated enough with each person in your care to see beneath their outward persona to understand their true self? How well do they know you?
- Are your opinions of others mainly based on your own interactions with them, or are they tainted by the inaccurate views of others?
- Can you tailor learning experiences to the specific needs of an individual rather than using a "one size fits all" approach?

- How much do you know about the dreams and aspirations of your neighbors?
- How well are you enlarging the circle of your influence by getting to know more people on your daily commute, at the office, the gym, or the club?

Attribute 49: Defends Followers

Defend: *Support in the face of argument or hostile criticism. To take action against attack or challenge. To speak or write in favor of an action or person.*

Jesus said to all of us, "Henceforth I call you not servants . . . but I have called you friends" (John 15:15). As such, He will defend us, fight our battles, and be our advocate with the Father. He has promised, "I will fight your battles" (D&C 105:14) and "I will let the sword fall in their behalf" (D&C 35:14). This defense will come in His own time and His own way depending on our need, our obedience, and His wisdom. There may be times when we feel the Lord has forgotten us and not defended us from attacks. Surely, the Jews must have felt that, but the Lord acts in perfect wisdom and He does so for our benefit.

Nephi records the words of the Lord regarding those who have attacked His covenant people. "O ye Gentiles, have ye remembered the Jews, mine ancient covenant people? Nay; but ye have cursed them, and have hated them, and have not sought to recover them. But behold, I will return all these things upon your own heads; for I the Lord have not forgotten my people" (2 Nephi 29:5). The Jews, like many of us, have felt forgotten for a time because the Lord allows our experiences to refine us. Jesus does not forget His followers and will defend them from their abusers in His own time and way.

The scriptures are full of examples where the Lord defends His followers. Nephi taught His people the words of Isaiah who said, "for I will contend with him that contendeth with thee, and I will save thy children" (Isaiah 49:25). The Lord fulfilled this promise as He warned Nephi to flee from his brethren (2 Nephi 5:5). Later, He helped Alma and his people escape King Noah and his armies (Mosiah 23:1). He then warned Mosiah and his people to flee into the wilderness for protection (Omni 1:12). He helped the people of Ammon escape the Lamanite armies and flee to the protection of the Nephites (Alma 27:12). In the record of Ether, He warned Omer to depart out of the land (Ether 9:3). Each of these examples shows the physical protection that Jesus gives to His people from time to time.

Not all enemies come from outside the organization. There are times when the enemy comes from within. In the Sermon on the Mount, Jesus warned against "false prophets, which come to you in sheep's clothing, but inwardly they are ravening wolves" (Matthew 7:15). This concept of ravening wolves in sheep's clothing can be expanded beyond false prophets to include leaders who seek to harm their people. Jesus warned of this as He taught a great leadership principle in the parable of the wicked husbandmen. In this parable, the householder hires husbandmen to manage his vineyard while he is away. Tragically, these husbandmen beat, stoned, and killed the workers in the vineyard (Matthew 21:33–41). When the householder learns of his husbandmen's wickedness, he fires them and installs new husbandmen who will bring forth good fruit. The leadership principle is simple but important. The top leader needs to defend his people from his own people, if needed. He needs to know them so well that he knows if middle management, like the husbandmen, is causing or covering up problems. He needs to know if other individuals are "killing" coworkers by destroying their reputations or misrepresenting their positions or character.

It is obvious in this parable, but not so obvious to some senior leaders, that the wicked husbandmen, or middle managers, hide their wickedness from them. However, in this parable, "the lord . . . cometh" (Matthew 21:40) and discovers their wickedness himself. It is unclear why the lord of the vineyard came. Did he receive a plea for help from the workers or had he heard rumors of trouble? Had he been monitoring the situation from afar, or did he respond to inspiration? Regardless, he came and took action. He was accountable, diligent, and perceptive. As a result, he restored order to his vineyard and made it a place where his people could be productive in doing his work.

In addition to defending us from our enemies, Jesus will also defend us before our loving Heavenly Father. He will do this despite our weaknesses if we have done all He has asked. Jesus said, "Whosoever therefore shall confess me before men, him will I confess also before my Father which is in heaven" (Matthew 10:32). To a small group of elders in Fayette, New York, Jesus said, "I . . . am your advocate with the Father" (D&C 29:5). Regarding the city of Enoch,

He said, "by virtue of the blood which I have spilt, have I pleaded before the Father for them" (D&C 38:4). In each of these scripture references, Jesus sets the example of a leader who defends His followers to His own leader, despite the weaknesses of the people.

Examples of Righteous Leaders

Nephi provides a well-rounded example of the many ways a leader can defend his people. He records that soon after his father Lehi died, he took his people away from the wicked influence of his brothers to a land where they could live after the manner of happiness. Nephi then took the sword of Laban as a guide and fashioned many swords for the defense of his people. As a defense against wickedness, Nephi taught his people the word of God through personal revelation and from the plates of brass. At the end of this great leader's life, Nephi's brother, Jacob, gave this fitting tribute on behalf of his people. "The people . . . loved Nephi exceedingly, he having been a great protector for them, having wielded the sword of Laban in their defence, and having labored in all his days for their welfare" (Jacob 1:10).

Truly, Nephi was a leader who led as Jesus led. He served his people, loved them, defended them, and taught them. He spent his whole life in their service.

Summary of Examples

- Honorable leaders defend their people from external enemies, as Jesus promised to defend the Jews from the Gentiles.
- Top leaders defend their people from internal enemies, as taught by Jesus in the parable of the wicked husbandmen.
- An honorable leader stands with his people before his own leader, as Jesus does in being our "advocate with the Father" (D&C 29:5).
- Honorable leaders defend their people by using a multifaceted approach, as Nephi did in relocating his people, by preparing them for war, and by fortifying them against personal wickedness.

Questions for Personal Reflection

- Do you stick up for the reputations of your associates and your family?
- How do you ensure the "kiss up and spit down" syndrome does not exist in your organization? Do you protect yourself from "kiss up" flattery and protect subordinates from "spit down" abuse?
- If you make a mistake, do you accept responsibility rather than blaming subordinates?
- Do those you lead feel you have their back?
- Are you a leading voice in defending the rights and beliefs of those in your community?

Attribute 50: Delegates

Delegate: *To appoint as one's representative. To assign responsibility or authority.*

When God the Father and His Son appeared in the Sacred Grove, the Father said to Joseph, "This is my Beloved Son. Hear Him!" (JSH 1:17). In those seven words, the Father introduced His son, acknowledged Him, and delegated to Him the opportunity to instruct the boy prophet. Jesus gives another example of delegation when He taught, "For the Father judgeth no man, *but hath committed all judgment unto the Son:* And hath *given him authority to execute judgement* also, because he is the Son of man" (John 5:22, 27). It is interesting to note that not only did the Father delegate the authority to execute judgement, but He then refrained from judging man Himself because it was now Jesus' responsibility. Jesus would now be accountable to Him for how well He exercises that authority.

The Savior does not keep authority and power to Himself. John records, "as many as received him, to them gave he power to become the sons of God" (John 1:12). Jesus uses delegation to enlarge His work and to involve His disciples in their own progression. At the beginning of His Judean ministry, Jesus called, organized, and trained twelve men to administer in the affairs of His church and minister to the people. After their call, He "began to send them forth by two and two; and gave them power over unclean spirits" (Mark 6:7). "And he said unto them, Go ye into all the world, and preach the gospel to every creature" (Mark 16:15). "Heal the sick, cleanse the lepers, raise the dead, cast out devils: freely ye have received, freely give" (Matthew 10:8). He also had the Twelve Apostles baptize those who accepted His gospel rather than doing it Himself. John records, "Though Jesus himself baptized not, but his disciples" (John 4:2).

After preparing the Twelve, Jesus continued with His work. "And it came to pass, when Jesus had made an end of commanding his twelve disciples, *he departed thence to teach and to preach in their cities"* (Matthew 11:1, emphasis added). He did not get bogged down in administrative work or in managing or tracking the Apostles; He got out among the people to serve them. As He did, He continued to delegate by calling others to serve with Him and His Twelve Apostles. Luke records, "the Lord appointed other seventy also, and sent them two and two before his face into every city" (Luke 10:1) and charged them to "heal the sick that are therein" (Luke 10:9).

Before His Crucifixion, Jesus delegated to His Twelve Apostles the high and unique authority to assist Him in "judging the twelve tribes of Israel" (Matthew 19:28). Through the Prophet Joseph Smith, He explained: "Mine apostles, the Twelve which were with me in my ministry at Jerusalem, shall stand at my right hand at the day of my coming in a pillar of fire, being clothed with robes of righteousness, with crowns upon their heads, in glory even as I am, *to judge the whole house of Israel,* even as many as have loved me and kept my commandments, and none else" (D&C 29:12, emphasis added).

After His Crucifixion, Jesus went to the world of spirits and continued to delegate His authority to others. From the Prophet Joseph Smith, we learn "from among the righteous, he organized his forces and appointed messengers, clothed with power and authority, and commissioned them to go forth and carry the light of the gospel to them that were in darkness, even to all the spirits of men; and thus was the gospel preached to the dead" (D&C 138:30).

When Jesus visited the Americas, He called another group of Twelve Apostles (3 Nephi 12:1; 3 Nephi 19:4) and delegated to them the power to preach and administer His gospel. "And the Lord said unto him: *I give unto you power* that ye shall baptize this people when I am again ascended into heaven. And again the Lord called others, and said unto them likewise; and he gave unto them power to baptize. And he said unto them: On this wise shall ye baptize; and there shall be no disputations among you" (3 Nephi 11:21–22, emphasis added).

Now, with these Apostles having the Lord's authority delegated to them, they were able to carry out His work among His people in their portion of the vineyard. As that vineyard expanded or was reestablished, new leaders were called and authority delegated to also serve in His name.

Examples of Righteous Leaders

Many people are familiar with the story of Joseph interpreting Pharaoh's dream regarding the seven years of plenty followed by seven years of famine. It is a story of how the Lord prepared Joseph to be in Egypt at the right time and with the right reputation to be used by Pharaoh to help save his country. Pharaoh was the absolute and unquestioned leader of Egypt; he was considered by his people to be a god. As such, it must have been hard for him to heed to a higher power and a lower power. The higher power was the God of Abraham, Isaac, and Jacob who gave him the prophetic dreams. The lower power was Joseph, a slave, a foreigner, and the one to interpret those dreams. However, this powerful Pharaoh did just that. He trusted in Joseph and his interpretation of his dreams and delegated to him the power to follow the warning they contained.

Pharaoh delegated so much power that Joseph became second only to him. He proclaimed "Thou shalt be over my own house, and according unto thy word shall all my people be ruled: only in the throne will I be greater than thou" (Genesis 41:40). To prepare for the coming famine, Pharaoh helped prepare Egypt by publicly announcing this delegation of authority. "Pharaoh said unto all the Egyptians, *Go unto Joseph; what he saith to you, do*" (Genesis 41:55, emphasis added). He wisely delegated the important task of gathering, storing, and distributing food to Joseph because he could do it better than anyone else. This freed up Pharaoh to make other preparations and together these two men saved Egypt.

One of the most familiar examples of delegation comes from the account of Moses and exiled Israel. Jethro, Moses's father–in–law, gave Moses counsel on how to relieve his heavy burden by delegating to others. There are two important principles Jethro taught. First is to establish laws to follow, and then appoint able men to judge against those laws.

"And thou shalt teach them ordinances and laws, and shalt shew them the way wherein they must walk, and the work that they must do.

"Moreover thou shalt provide out of all the people able men, such as fear God, men of truth, hating covetousness; and place such over them, to be rulers of thousands, and rulers of hundreds, rulers of fifties, and rulers of tens:

"And let them judge the people at all seasons: and it shall be, that every great matter they shall bring unto thee, but every small matter they shall judge: so shall it be easier for thyself, and they shall bear the burden with thee" (Exodus 18:20–22).

By following this counsel, Moses blessed the lives of these able men by allowing them to grow and contribute. He also blessed his own life by easing his burdens. He followed the counsel of the Lord to other leaders when he cautioned them to "not run faster or labor more" than they had strength (D&C 10:4).

At the beginning of the dispensation of the fullness of times, Jesus allowed many of His past prophets to assist Him in the restoration of the gospel. He delegated specific tasks to Peter, James, John, Moses, Moroni, Elias, and many others. In addition to these past prophets, Jesus delegated specific tasks to a new group of leaders. For example, Jesus assigned Oliver Cowdery and David Whitmer the responsibility to identify those men who would serve as new Apostles when He told them to "search out the Twelve" (D&C 18:37). He then instructed them how to find those He had prepared by saying "by their desires and their works you shall know them" (D&C 18:38). It is difficult to imagine the feelings Oliver and David had as they felt the weight of trust that had been bestowed upon them, but that is how a leader develops other leaders.

A unique example of how the Lord involves us in His work is recorded in Doctrine and Covenants 36:2. In blessing Edward Partridge in December 1830, the Lord said, *"I will lay my hand upon you by the hand of my servant* Sidney Rigdon, and you shall receive my Spirit, the Holy Ghost" (D&C 36:2, emphasis added). Jesus made a similar statement while speaking of those who are "unlearned and despised" who will carry on His work. He said, *"their arm shall be my arm"* (D&C 35:14, emphasis added). Jesus added, "whomsoever you bless I will bless, and whomsoever you curse I will curse" (D&C 132:47). The Savior had delegated His authority to His leaders and promised to support them in the use of that authority. Jesus said,

"Whether by mine own voice or by the voice of my servants, it is the same" (D&C 1:38).

Summary of Examples

- Honorable leaders who delegate expand their influence exponentially, as Jesus does when He calls Apostles, prophets, ministers, and missionaries.
- Honorable leaders develop others when they delegate, as Jesus did when He called the Apostles and empowered them to heal the sick, or His disciples to perform baptisms.
- Honorable leaders delegate so that those with specific talents can do what they do best, as Pharaoh did by putting Joseph in charge of gathering and distributing food before and during the famine.
- Honorable leaders delegate so they can be unencumbered to do their own labors, as Jesus did when He returned to ministering after He called the Apostles. Moses also did this so he could focus on the "great matters" of his people.
- Honorable leaders delegate to share their burden and to keep them from running faster or laboring more than they have strength, as Jesus taught and as Moses learned.

Questions for Personal Reflection

- Do you delegate tasks with a pure motive of doing what is best for the growth of people and the best achievement of objectives?
- Do you know each of those you lead well enough to give meaningful responsibility that will lead to his or her growth?
- Do you lead by keeping unencumbered enough to focus on the tasks that only you can do, such as giving overall direction and vision?
- Do you enjoy letting a subordinate shine for doing something you could have done instead?
- Do those you lead feel you are fair in how you delegate assignments, rather than feeling you show favoritism?

- Have you tried giving a responsibility or opportunity to a troubled youth in your neighborhood?

Attribute 51: Allows Freedom

Freedom: *The power or right to act, speak, or think as one wants without hindrance or restraint. The state of not being imprisoned or enslaved.*

Central to the plan of salvation is the principle of individual agency, for "the Lord God gave unto man that he should act for himself" (2 Nephi 2:16). Because of this plan, "they have become free forever to act for themselves and not to be acted upon, save it be by the punishment of the law" (2 Nephi 2:26). Nowhere in this plan is the notion that one person can control another. Leaders and laws can guide a person, but there is no provision for controlling others—not with a spouse, children, friends, subordinates, or coworkers.

At the coasts of Tyre and Sidon, Jesus was approached by a woman of Canaan asking Him to heal her daughter. "But he answered her not a word. And his disciples came and besought him, saying, Send her away; for she crieth after us. But he answered and said, I am not sent but unto the lost sheep of the house of Israel" (Matthew 15:23–24). It was not His mission to minister unto her; however, when Jesus saw her great faith, He used His agency and chose to heal her daughter. Jesus had been given the freedom to act for Himself and utilized that freedom when He felt justified.

Leaders often give direction on *what* should be done, but there is wisdom in allowing individuals some flexibility and creativity in determining *how* to do it. Jesus taught: "Verily I say, men should be anxiously engaged in a good cause, and *do many things of their own free will*, and bring to pass much righteousness; For the power is in them, wherein they are agents unto themselves" (D&C 58:27–28, emphasis added).

Jesus also taught, "For behold, it is not meet that I should command in all things; for he that is compelled in all things, the same is a slothful and not a wise servant" (D&C 58:26). People learn best by taking action themselves and Jesus gives us both the encouragement and the freedom to do so. As we excise our agency, we further our development and find more enjoyment in our lives.

280

Examples of Righteous Leaders

Mosiah was a wise leader who learned how to righteously govern people from his father King Benjamin. Mosiah knew the dangers of an unrighteous king so prior to his death he changed the form of government from kings to judges. He said: "Therefore I will be your king the remainder of my days; nevertheless, let us appoint judges, to judge this people according to our law; and we will newly arrange the affairs of this people, for we will appoint wise men to be judges, that will judge this people according to the commandments of God" (Mosiah 29:11). "Therefore, it came to pass that they assembled themselves together in bodies throughout the land, to cast in their voices concerning who should be their judges, to judge them according to the law which had been given them; and *they were exceedingly rejoiced because of the liberty which had been granted unto them"* (Mosiah 29:39, emphasis added).

People want to be free to act for themselves, and Mosiah had prepared the way for them to do so. Joseph Smith taught something similar when he said, "I teach them correct principles, and they govern themselves."[5] This statement is one of the most quoted from the Prophet Joseph because it resonates in the hearts of men and women who want to be free: Free to dream, free to choose, free to act, free to live their own life as they wish.

There are times when a leader needs to give directions to his or her people, but even then, he can allow for individual freedom where possible. The following three examples show how the Lord gave direction on what He wanted done but did not specify how to accomplish it. On the surface, these examples may not seem to be significant issues, but they reflect a leader who allows freedom.

In the first example of Jesus allowing freedom, the Lord directed Joseph Smith, Sidney Rigdon, and Oliver Cowdery to travel to St. Louis and then to Cincinnati. The Lord declared: "For I, the Lord, rule in the heavens above. . . . But, verily, I will speak unto you concerning your journey unto the land from whence you came. Let there be a craft made, or bought, *as seemeth you good, it mattereth not unto me,* and take your journey speedily for the place which is called St. Louis"

(D&C 60:4–5, emphasis added). Here the Lord gave directions on what to do rather than on how to do it. He avoided micromanaging, which helps keep self-esteem intact and allows people to grow by applying their own solutions.

The second example of Jesus allowing freedom occurred one week later as Joseph met several elders on their way to Zion. The Lord had invited them to come to Zion for an important purpose but gave them no instruction on how to return home. He said, "And then you may return to bear record, yea, even altogether, or two by two, *as seemeth you good, it mattereth not unto me; only be faithful*" (D&C 62:5, emphasis added). Again, the Lord directed what He wanted done but did not dictate how to do it. He granted them their freedom to act using their own judgment.

The third example of Jesus allowing freedom comes a few weeks later when the Lord directed Newel K. Whitney to continue working in the store "yet for a little season" (D&C 63:42). He was instructed to "impart all the money which he can impart, to be sent up unto the land of Zion" (D&C 63:43). However, the Lord gave him the freedom to use his own judgment when he said, "Behold, these things are in his own hands, *let him do according to wisdom*" (D&C 63:44, emphasis added). Here again, Jesus explains *what* He would like to have happen, and then allows people to use their wisdom and best judgment to determine *how* to accomplish the stated objectives. This follows the pattern taught by Helaman who said, "ye are free; ye are permitted to act for yourselves; for behold, God hath given unto you a knowledge and he hath made you free" (Helaman 14:30).

People flourish when a leader, a spouse, a teacher, a coach, or a parent gives them the freedom to act within certain protective parameters. During an interview associated with his 66th wedding anniversary, President Gordon B. Hinckley gave wise counsel on how to have a successful marriage. He said: "You respect one another. Don't try to make over your companion. You respect her qualities, her ambitions, her desires, her talents, her capacities. Don't try to make her in your image. *You let her fly her own kite, and you assist her in doing it.* You'll be happier together."[6]

It is through this freedom that we gain valuable experience and learning. We need to explore different ways of doing something to see what works, what does not work, and what works best. This likely will involve some trial and error, a learning method the Savior uses with each of us.

Summary of Examples

- Honorable leaders are to influence their followers rather than control them, as demonstrated by the contrast between Jesus and Lucifer.
- Honorable leaders establish rules to follow, as Jesus did, then they judge actions against those rules rather than against their ever–changing personal opinions.
- Honorable leaders allow flexibility so their people can adjust to varying circumstances, as demonstrated by Jesus with the Canaanite woman and among the Nephites.
- Honorable leaders teach correct principles and let their people govern themselves, as taught by Joseph Smith.
- Honorable leaders describe *what* they would like their followers to do, then encourage them to figure out *how* to do it, as Jesus did with Joseph, Sidney, Oliver, and Newel K. Whitney.
- Honorable leaders grant freedom to their people to act for themselves, as taught by Helaman and President Hinckley who lets people "fly their own kite."

Questions for Personal Reflection

- Are you making a difference among your associates by being tolerant of those with differing views or personalities?
- Do those you lead have the freedom to determine *how* to do what you have asked them to do?
- How often do you allow people to learn from their own mistakes by focusing on learning rather than punishing?
- Do those you lead feel imprisoned by you? Can you get an honest reading from them?

- Can you use your influence to turn a heated argument back into a civil discourse where each person can speak freely?

Attribute 52: Avoids Favoritism

Favoritism: *The practice of giving unfair preferential treatment to one person or group at the expense of another.*

The Savior's earthly ministry was primarily to the house of Israel but after His Resurrection, He directed Peter to take the gospel to the Gentiles as well. Peter learned from this direction that "God is no respecter of persons" (Acts 10:34). Further insight was given by James when he explained, "if any of you lack wisdom, let him ask of God, that *giveth to all men liberally,* and upbraideth not" (James 1:5, emphasis added). The phrase *upbraideth not* is translated from a Greek word which means *reproaches* or *censures* (see Bible footnotes). Therefore, each of God's children can approach Him and receive His blessings without being scolded and without any hint of favoritism toward a select few.

The principle of avoiding favoritism applies also to disciplining. The Prophet Joseph Smith was called to lead the restoration of the gospel in the dispensation of the fullness of times. He was chosen in the pre-earth life to fulfill this great assignment because of his faithfulness. Yet because of a mistake influenced by Martin Harris, Joseph was disciplined when 116 pages of the Book of Mormon were lost. The Lord said to Joseph, "thou hast lost thy privileges for a season" (D&C 3:14). Furthermore, He told Joseph that if he did not repent he would "have no more gift" (D&C 3:11). Jesus, who at other times referred to Joseph as His friend, chastened him for his mistakes just as He does anyone else. There was no favoritism shown to Joseph because of his high calling.

Examples of Righteous Leaders

Joseph Smith, likewise, refrained from showing favoritism during his ministry. For example, he chose three men, then another eight men to be witnesses of the gold plates from which the Book of Mormon was translated. None of these eleven men were family members. As another example, he did not place family members in prominent leadership positions. Although, the Lord did call Hyrum to be "a prophet, and a seer, and a revelator" three years before his death (D&C 124:94).

Joseph was friendly with the wealthy and wise, the poor and uneducated, and the young and playful. If needed, he was not afraid to rebuke anyone, whether an enemy of the Church, a new convert, or even high-ranking leaders like Brigham Young. Joseph's example of leadership is reflected in John Taylor's statement who said, "We want no favoritism shown to any man, or to any woman, or to any set of men."[7]

Perhaps these modern prophets learned from mistakes made by earlier men. For example, in the Old Testament, Jacob showed so much favoritism toward his son Joseph that it almost cost Joseph his life. Because of that favoritism, the Lord established a law in Israel to protect against it. President Joseph F. Smith summarized Joseph's story and then explained the reason for this law.

"He was a rather remarkable little boy, and his father loved him, and was a little partial toward him, perhaps because he was the firstborn of his beloved Rachel, and Rachel was dead. Jacob erred perhaps a little in the partiality that he showed to Joseph on this account. He may have made a mistake there like some other parents do when they make a favorite of one of their sons. This is a mistake, no matter who the mother of the boy is. Whenever a father begins to discriminate in favor of one son as against another, it begets jealousy in the hearts of the brothers, and possibly hatred toward their fathers. It is a dangerous thing to do. Because Jacob erred somewhat in this matter, the Lord gave to Israel a law on the subject (Deuteronomy 21:15–17). The Lord endeavored to correct the evil that grew out of what Jacob did in his favoritism, by giving a law on this subject to govern the people thereafter."[8]

This law, found in Deuteronomy states:

"If a man have two wives, one beloved, and another hated, and they have born him children, both the beloved and the hated; and if the firstborn son be hers that was hated:

"Then it shall be, when he maketh his sons to inherit that which he hath, that he may not make the son of the beloved firstborn before the son of the hated, which is indeed the firstborn:

"But he shall acknowledge the son of the hated for the firstborn, by giving him a double portion of all that he hath: for he is the beginning of his strength; the right of the firstborn is his" (Deuteronomy 21:15–17).

The practice of showing a little favoritism can seem so innocent at first, but it can become detrimental to all within its influence. Following the pattern set by the Savior, all are deserving of a leader's attention and care.

Summary of Examples

- Honorable leaders refrain from favoritism by giving of themselves liberally to all their people as Jesus does, for they are "no respecter of persons" (Acts 10:34).
- Honorable leaders hold all people accountable for their actions, even the actions of other leaders, as Jesus did with Joseph when the 116 pages were lost.
- Honorable leaders avoid showing favoritism to friends or relatives, as practiced by Joseph Smith with the eleven witnesses.
- Honorable leaders avoid following the example of Jacob who showed favoritism to his son Joseph.

Questions for Personal Reflection

- Do you seek for the well–being and improvement of everyone regardless of gender, race, culture, income, religion, or other defining features?
- Are you as willing to correct a loved one as you are someone who is not as close to you?
- Do you delegate assignments based on who is best for that assignment rather than who you would most like to succeed?
- When making decisions, are you swayed by who can best reciprocate a favor for a favor?
- If you were a coach of your daughter's little league soccer

team, would you give her more play time than better team-mates?

Attribute 53: Overcomes Obstacles

Obstacle: *Something that impedes progress or achievement.*

In the parable of the sower, the seeds grow differently based on the readiness of the soils in which they are planted. "One of the primary differences between the different kinds of soils (hearts) is their preparation. The soils that rejected the word were intrinsically no different from the good soil, except that the good soil had been prepared. It had been plowed, unlike the hard soil on the wayside. It had had the rocks removed, including those hiding under the surface. It had many of the thorns pulled out of it."[9] Then, with obstacles removed, the soil is ready for the seeds to grow just as the sower had planned.

During His ministry, Jesus helped many people overcome their obstacles. For example, physical limitations were removed as "Jesus went about all Galilee . . . healing all manner of sickness and all manner of disease among the people" (Matthew 4:23). These healings were given out of compassion for their suffering but also as a symbol of the more necessary spiritual healings that Jesus offered. It was the spiritually blind, lame, and deaf who truly had barriers removed through the Atonement so that individual progress could occur.

Jesus also helped Lehi and his family overcome obstacles that kept them from accomplishing the things needed to bless their lives. For example, as Lehi and his sons endeavored to obtain the brass plates as they had been commanded to do, they found Laban to be an obstacle to their success. Therefore, the Lord did what Lehi and his family could not do, He provided a way for Laban to be removed so they could obtain the plates. Before embarking on this mission, Nephi expressed his trust in the Lord to remove the obstacles standing in the way: "I will go and do the things which the Lord hath commanded, for I know that the Lord giveth no commandments unto the children of men, *save he shall prepare a way* for them that they may accomplish the thing which he commandeth them" (1 Nephi 3:7, emphasis added).

The Lord prepared the way and the plates were obtained. He

continued to prepare the way as Lehi and his family put their faith in Him and acted on the directions received. Jesus said: "And I will also be your light in the wilderness; and *I will prepare the way before you,* if it so be that ye shall keep my commandments; wherefore, inasmuch as ye shall keep my commandments ye shall be led toward the promised land; and ye shall know that it is by me that ye are led" (1 Nephi 17:13, emphasis added).

Jesus also helped overcome other obstacles by providing the Liahona. This compass pointed the path Lehi's family should follow through the unknown wilderness so they could have sustenance and protection (1 Nephi 16:10). Jesus also removed another obstacle when He said, "I will make thy food become sweet, that ye cook it not" (1 Nephi 17:12). These were temporal obstacles, but temporal needs often hold back spiritual development. As a wise leader, Jesus addressed both the temporal and the physical needs of His people.

Examples of Righteous Leaders

When Brigham Young announced plans to build a temple in the harsh climate of southern Utah, he knew there would be tremendous obstacles that would need to be overcome. Brigham began by allocating all tithing and contributions received south of Beaver, Utah, to be used for constructing the temple. Later, he expanded that area so most of the state was making some sort of contribution. Brigham also called additional families, including skilled craftsman, to relocate to St. George to assist with the construction and with the support of the workers. Brigham even donated a steam sawmill and other machinery to help build the local economy and support the construction of the temple.[10]

Under Brigham's leadership, the boggy soil on the temple site was stabilized by driving thousands of stones into the mud using an iron cannon as a pile driver.[11] Timber was harvested at Mt. Trumball some 80 miles away and was transported over dirt roads back to St. George.[12] Glass was manufactured in the East and shipped to Utah by rail. It was then transported by wagon to St. George.[13] One by one, each obstacle in this great undertaking was faced by determined men and women who followed their visionary leader and raised a magnificent building in the most inhospitable place possible.

Summary of Leadership Examples

- Honorable leaders help overcome obstacles by softening hearts so they are more receptive to guidance, as Jesus taught in the parable of the soils.
- Honorable leaders help overcome obstacles by relocating or removing people who thwart the efforts of their people, as Jesus did in removing Laban.
- Honorable leaders help overcome obstacles that limit their people's physical capacities to do their work, such as providing guidance to find food and building a ship, as Jesus did for Lehi's family.
- Honorable leaders help overcome obstacles that obscure the path by providing clear directions, as Jesus did with the Liahona.

Questions for Personal Reflection

- What are you doing to remove barriers to the intellectual, emotional, physical, and emotional needs of those you influence?
- Are you removing barriers to your own growth by humbly identifying them and diligently working hard to limit their influence on you?
- If one of your associates is socially awkward, have you rallied your friends to help teach him or her necessary social skills?
- Is there someone you encounter during your daily activities for whom you can identify a barrier to their progress and help remove it?

Attribute 54: Teaches

Teach: *To instruct by precept, example, or experience.*

Almost all the words from Jesus recorded in the scriptures are the words of a teacher. Whether teaching the Beatitudes or the parables, or whether at the temple, the synagogues, the Mount of Transfiguration, the Sea of Galilee, the upper room, the garden, on the road to Emmaus, or at the temple in Bountiful, Jesus was a teacher.

Jesus taught to non-believers, to mixed audiences of believers and non-believers, and directly to believers. He taught His followers how to live better lives, to choose the good part, and the consequences of their choices. He lifted their vision, expanded their minds, and encouraged them to improve in all aspects of their lives. He taught the 7,000, the 5,000, and the one. However, as the Savior explains in the parable of the seed growing by itself (Mark 4:27), even though the teacher may teach, it is up to the student to learn.

The prophet Isaiah beckons all to come and learn from Jesus, the Master Teacher. He invites us: "Come ye, and let us go up to the mountain of the Lord, to the house of the God of Jacob; and he will teach us of his ways" (Isaiah 2:3). Jesus will be our teacher if we will be His pupil or His disciple. "The word for disciple and the word for discipline both come from the same Latin root—*discipulus*, which means *pupil.* It emphasizes practice or exercise."[14] Jesus teaches His disciples, or pupils, by example and by explaining the principles of His gospel. He then gives them opportunities to practice those principles through the exercises of mortality.

Jesus tailored His teaching to each individual or group. For example, He taught *lovingly* to Martha who meant well but misunderstood her priorities. "But Martha was cumbered about much serving, and came to him, and said, Lord, dost thou not care that my sister hath left me to serve alone? bid her therefore that she help me. And Jesus answered and said unto her, Martha, Martha, thou art careful and troubled about many things: But one thing is needful: and Mary hath chosen that good part, which shall not be taken away from her" (Luke 10:40–42).

Jesus taught *hopefully* when He tried to persuade people of the benefits in following Him. "Whosoever cometh to me, and heareth my sayings, and doeth them, I will shew you to whom He is like: He is like a man which built an house, and digged deep, and laid the foundation on a rock: and when the flood arose, the stream beat vehemently upon that house, and could not shake it: for it was founded upon a rock. But he that heareth, and doeth not, is like a man that without a foundation built an house upon the earth; against which the stream did beat vehemently, and immediately it fell; and the ruin of that house was great" (Luke 6:47–49).

Jesus taught *clearly and patiently* to His inexperienced elders of His restored Church. He said to them, "Let us reason together, that ye may understand" (D&C 50:10). He taught them "after the manner of their language that they might come to understanding" (D&C 1:24). If they did not understand, He patiently continued to teach. For example, His original Twelve Apostles did not understand all He taught while He dwelt among them, so He continued teaching after His Crucifixion.

"And he said unto them, These *are* the words which I spake unto you, while I was yet with you, that all things must be fulfilled, which were written in the law of Moses, and *in* the prophets, and *in* the psalms, concerning me.

"Then *opened he their understanding, that they might understand* the scriptures,

"And said unto them, Thus it is written, and thus it behoved Christ to suffer, and to rise from the dead the third day:

"And that repentance and remission of sins should be preached in his name among all nations, beginning at Jerusalem.

"And ye are witnesses of these things" (Luke 24:44–48, emphasis added).

Frequently, Jesus responded to questions with a teaching moment rather than simply answering the question. When the lawyer asked Jesus, "And who is my neighbour?" (Luke 10:29), Jesus responded with the parable of the good Samaritan. After giving the parable, Jesus continued the teaching moment by testing the lawyer if the message had been understood. Jesus asked, "Which now of these three, thinkest thou, was neighbour unto him that fell among the thieves?" (Luke 10:36). The lawyer answered, "He that shewed mercy on him. Then said Jesus unto him, Go, and do thou likewise" (Luke 10:37).

Jesus taught all men to repent. The Bible Dictionary explains, "The Greek word of which this [repentance] is the translation denotes a change of mind, i.e., a fresh view about God, about oneself, and about the world" (Bible Dictionary, "Repentance"). This repenting, or changing our minds, happens when we learn from our own experience that His ways are the right way to lasting happiness. Repenting results in a fresh and clear view of what we need to be and to do. It comes from implementing what we have learned from our teacher, the Lord Jesus Christ.

Jesus often taught with parables because they are effective teaching tools. "The word *parable* is Greek in origin, and means a setting side by side, a comparison" (Bible Dictionary, "Parable"). Therefore, the Savior used parables where "divine truth is presented by comparison with material things" (Bible Dictionary, "Parable"). Putting these truths in a parallel comparison with something His students already understood helped them learn the principles He taught.

Teaching with parables is also effective because they teach a truth while limiting personal injury. For example, instead of directly accusing a person of having a hardened heart, Jesus taught the results of having a hardened heart by likening it to hard, rocky, or thorn-infested soil. By avoiding personal attacks and a condescending "let me teach you" attitude, the teacher presents the lesson in a way so that the student can focus more on introspection rather than self-defense.

Examples of Righteous Leaders

Alma was a man of tremendous influence who knew how and when to shift his focus from being an executive to being a teacher. This shift occurred because he was perceptive to the needs of his people. He left his role as chief judge to become a full-time teacher because he had learned "the preaching of the word had a great tendency to lead the people to do that which was just—yea, it had had more powerful effect upon the minds of the people than the sword, or anything else"

(Alma 31:5). He explained: "We have entered into their houses and taught them, and we have taught them in their streets; yea, and we have taught them upon their hills; and we have also entered into their temples and their synagogues and taught them" (Alma 26:29).

Alma taught everywhere he could find listeners. He was an example of the words of the Savior, "whosoever shall . . . teach . . . shall be called great in the kingdom of heaven" (Matthew 5:19). This high acclaim comes because of the importance of the role. And if the teacher is successful in that role, minds are opened, hearts are changed, and lives are improved.

There were many great teachers during the early days of the Restoration of the gospel. These were men and women who opened minds and changed hearts both within and outside the Church. Sister Emmeline B. Wells, fifth Relief Society general president was one whose influence was widely felt both through her personal associations and as editor of the *Woman's Exponent*, a newsletter to sisters in the Church. In her diary, she expressed a desire to teach the sisters in the Church how to become better than they were. She wrote, "I desire to do all in my power to help elevate the condition of my own people, especially women."[15] Continuing this theme, she later wrote, "I have desired with all my heart to do those things that would advance women in moral and spiritual as well as educational work and tend to the rolling on of the work of God upon the earth."[16]

The ministry of Emmeline Wells served a large audience, but it grew to worldwide proportions as World War I raged throughout Europe. With members of the Church on both sides of that terrible conflict, she taught the sisters what the Savior would have taught them in order to bring forgiveness and healing. With all the wisdom that her 90 years of life experiences provided, and being guided by divine inspiration, she issued the following counsel to women throughout the world.

"Administer in the spirit of love and patience to your husbands and to your children; guard the little ones; do not permit them to imbibe the spirit of intolerance or hatred to any nation or to any people; keep firearms out of their hands; do not allow them to play at war nor to find amusement in imitating death in battle; inculcate the spirit of loyalty to country and flag, but help them to feel that they are soldiers of the Cross and that if they must needs take up arms in defense of liberty, or country and homes they shall do so without rancor or bitterness. . . . Teach the peaceable things of the kingdom [and] look after the needy more diligently than ever."[17]

This message that Sister Wells taught was offered to help stabilize families during one of the greatest trials mankind has experienced. It was given with clarity, timeliness, and great sensitivity by a skilled teacher seeking to improve the lives of all within her influence.

Summary of Examples

- Honorable leaders teach their people by providing experiences that allow them to practice a new idea or principle, as Jesus does with us.
- Honorable leaders teach but recognize that ultimately it is up to the student to grow, as Jesus taught about the seed growing by itself.
- Honorable leaders teach in different ways to different people, as demonstrated by Jesus who taught lovingly, hopefully, clearly, and patiently.
- Honorable leaders teach by involving the student in the learning process, as Jesus did with the lawyer who wondered who was his neighbor.
- Honorable leaders teach because they know it is the most effective way to change behavior, as demonstrated by Jesus who taught all men to repent, i.e. change their mind and heart, and Alma who knew that teaching is more powerful than the sword.
- Honorable leaders who teach are highly esteemed, as taught by Jesus when He said, "whosoever shall . . . teach . . . shall be called great in the kingdom of heaven" (Matthew 5:19).
- Honorable leaders turn their people into teachers because they will learn better as they teach others, as Jesus did with His prophets, Apostles, and each of His disciples.

- Honorable leaders teach because they want to lift their people to be better and do better, as did Sister Emmeline B. Wells.

Questions for Personal Reflection

- Do those you teach respect you enough to want you as their teacher?
- How can you improve your teaching skills?
- Do you guide people through carefully planned learning experiences that are individually tailored to their varied needs?
- Do you teach rather than condemn?
- Can you teach without taking on an attitude of superiority?
- What parables using modern imagery can you create?

Attribute 55: Nourishes

Nourish: *To promote growth or development.*

The prophet Alma taught the Zoramites that a seed would grow if it had proper nourishment. Then Alma likened a seed to his gospel message and encouraged the Zoramites to nourish it so it would grow into a tree, which represented a full conviction of the truth. Alma then warned that if that nourishment ended, their conviction would also come to an end. He taught "But if ye neglect the tree, and take no thought for its nourishment, behold it will not get any root; and when the heat of the sun cometh and scorcheth it, because it hath no root it withers away" (Alma 32:38). The Apostle Peter continued this theme when he counseled Church leaders to take responsibility for the nourishment of the Saints. He taught, "Feed the flock of God which is among you, taking the oversight *thereof*"(1 Peter 5:2). For as the Lord said, "Woe be to the shepherds of Israel that . . . feed not the flock" (Ezekiel 34:2–3).

The Savior's parable of the good Samaritan is one of the most familiar examples of providing nourishment. He tells of a man who was traveling from Jerusalem down through the mountain passes into Jericho. During that journey, thieves robbed and beat him and left him near death. A priest and a Levite passed him by, but a Samaritan stopped and nourished him back to health. The Samaritan bound his wounds, poured oil and wine upon him, and took him to an inn. There he continued to nourish him until it came time to resume his journey. The Samaritan paid the host to continue caring for the injured man until he healed. There are multiple lessons to learn from this parable, and one of the most important is our responsibility to help nourish our fellow travelers along our mortal journey.

The prophet Zenos, as quoted by Jacob, gives an example of how the Lord nourishes His people and provides for their growth. In his allegory of the tame and the wild olive trees, we see one of the best explanations of the Savior's leadership. We see how the Lord constantly monitors His vineyard and gives directions on how to improve it such as fertilizing, pruning, grafting, and balancing between the strength of the roots and the strength of the branches. At times, He even went with the servants into the vineyard to labor with them. Below is a brief description of how Jesus showed overall leadership for His vineyard and nourished all that grew therein.

1. Jesus demonstrates how a leader can be so aware that he sees the beginning of trouble and then creates a plan to address the problem. "And it came to pass that the master of the vineyard went forth, and he saw that his olive-tree *began* to decay; and he said: I will prune it, and dig about it, and nourish it, that perhaps it may shoot forth young and tender branches, and it perish not" (Jacob 5:4, emphasis added).

2. Jesus demonstrates how a leader can take a personal interest in nourishing young talent rather than limiting their growth opportunities. "And behold, saith the Lord of the vineyard, I take away many of these young and tender branches and I will graft them whithersoever I will" (Jacob 5:8).

3. Jesus demonstrates how a leader can delegate with clear, concise directions. "And the Lord of the vineyard *caused* that it should be digged about, and pruned, and nourished . . . Wherefore, go thy way; watch the tree, and nourish it, according to my words" (Jacob 5:11–12, emphasis added).

4. Jesus demonstrates how a leader can leave his central location to extend his reach. By getting out among his people, they can nourish even the most remote locations. "Come, let us go to the nethermost part of the vineyard" (Jacob 5:19).

5. Jesus demonstrates how a leader can turn things around through diligence, patience, and developing his people. "This long time have I nourished it, and it hath brought forth much fruit" (Jacob 5:20).

6. Jesus demonstrates how a leader can be so aware of each person that he knows what nourishment each one needs. "And it came to pass that the Lord of the vineyard did taste of the fruit, every sort according to its number" (Jacob 5:31). Therefore, he could personally say, "Behold, I knew that all the fruit of the vineyard, save it were these, had become corrupted" (Jacob 5:42).

7. Jesus demonstrates how a leader can be introspective and learn from his own actions. Jesus also shows some emotion as He grieves over His losses. "And it came to pass that the Lord of the vineyard wept, and said unto the servant: What could I have done more for my vineyard?" (Jacob 5:41). "Have I slackened mine hand, that I have not nourished it? Nay, I have nourished it, and I have digged about it, and I have pruned it, and I have dunged it; and I have stretched forth mine hand almost all the day long, and the end draweth nigh. And it grieveth me that I should hew down all the trees of my vineyard, and cast them into the fire that they should be burned. Who is it that has corrupted my vineyard?" (Jacob 5:47).

8. Jesus demonstrates how a leader can listen to and follow the suggestions of a servant. "But, behold, the servant said unto the Lord of the vineyard: Spare it a little longer. And the Lord said: Yea, I will spare it a little longer, for it grieveth me that I should lose the trees of my vineyard" (Jacob 5:50–51).

9. Jesus demonstrates how a leader should know enough about the work to give detailed directions. For the Lord said, "Graft in the branches; begin at the last that they may be first, and that the first may be last, and dig about the trees, both old and young, the first and the last; and the last and the first, that all may be nourished once again for the last time. Wherefore, dig about them, and prune them, and dung them once more" (Jacob 5:63–64).

10. Jesus demonstrates how a leader can labor alongside his workers rather than being aloof and elitist. "The servants did go and labor with their mights; and the Lord of the vineyard labored also with them" (Jacob 5:72).

11. Jesus demonstrates how a leader can express his gratitude for the work of his servants, and how he can share the rewards with them. "And *blessed art thou,* for because ye have been diligent in laboring with me in my vineyard, and have kept my commandments, and have brought unto me again the natural fruit, that my vineyard is no more corrupted, and the bad is cast away, behold *ye shall have joy with me* because of the fruit of my vineyard" (Jacob 5:75, emphasis added).

All leaders have vineyards, and all vineyards need nourishing. People are like the seed that Jesus referenced in the parable of the seed growing by itself. The farmer plants the seed in the soil, then it grows, "he knoweth not how" (Mark 4:27). Not only does he not know how the seed grows, he doesn't even know if it will grow. All he knows is that if he doesn't provide the necessary nourishment, growth is unlikely. Leaders are like farmers in that they don't know how or if their people will grow, but with the proper nourishment, earnest encouragement, and well-chosen opportunities, growth is likely.

Like the Lord of the vineyard, in order to have each tree produce good fruit, the leader may need to make some changes. In a business setting, this may mean relocating some people to other parts of the organization or reducing their number if the leadership (i.e. roots) cannot give them proper support. It may mean reducing the number of managers to better balance with the number of employees. It may mean pairing up a creative person with a methodical person or a rookie with a veteran. It may mean sending some back to school or terminating the so called "dead wood" who are unproductive. It may mean paying more attention to the younger workers who are the future of the organization.

There is always a need to fertilize or provide nutrients to make the mind and heart grow through seminars, lectures, continuing education, cross-training, apprenticeships, books, and so forth. There is also the need to give enough space to get unfiltered light without being shaded by others. Leaders who lead like the Savior diligently nourish their vineyard with fertilizing, pruning, and grafting so that each person in their care can bring forth good fruit. This way, the laborers and their leaders can rejoice together in their results (i.e. harvest of fruit).

Examples of Righteous Leaders

About 90 years before the birth of Christ, Ammon and his brothers—all sons of King Mosiah—departed into the land of the Lamanites to minister unto them. Over the next 14 years they brought thousands of people unto Christ. Because of increasing hostility from their unbelieving brethren, these converts followed Ammon's lead and migrated to Zarahemla to dwell with the Nephites. There, they were called Ammonites, or the people of Ammon.

As they approached Zarahemla, Ammon went ahead to test the heart of the Nephites to see if they would welcome these Ammonites. From his first inquiry, the Nephites willingly accepted them and offered to nourish them. To aid in nourishing them, they vacated the city of Jershon and gave it to them as an inheritance. Then they assisted the Ammonites with all their needs and protected them as they became established. In short, they created an environment where they could grow safely in the gospel of Christ.

Before long, the Ammonites had the opportunity themselves to nourish another group of refugees as they had been nourished by the Nephites. These refugees were Zoramites who were taught by Alma and Amulek. Many of the Zoramites accepted the gospel of Christ and left their wicked ways. Because of their conversion, they were compelled to leave their homeland and flee to Jershon. Here, things came full circle as the Ammonites "did receive all the poor of the Zoramites that came over unto them; and they did nourish them, and did clothe them, and did give unto them lands for their inheritance; and they did administer unto them according to their wants" (Alma 35:9).

These examples show that many lives can be blessed when people live the gospel of Christ and provide nourishment so that the children of God can grow in righteousness.

Summary of Examples

- An honorable leader nurtures his people by overseeing their growing process, as Jesus does for all of God's children.
- An honorable leader nurtures his or her people by following the principles of the allegory of the tame and the wild olive trees. We learn from this allegory that a leader nurtures people by:
    1. Seeing the beginning of trouble and then creating a plan to address the problem

2. Taking a personal interest in developing young talent rather than limiting their growth opportunities
3. Delegating
4. Leaving his central location to extend his reach, and getting out among his people even in the most remote locations
5. Turning things around through diligence, patience, and developing his people
6. Being so aware of each person that he knows the characteristics of each one
7. Being introspective to learn from his own actions
8. Listening to and following the suggestions of a servant or subordinate
9. Knowing enough about the work to give specific directions
10. Laboring alongside his workers rather than being aloof and elitist
11. Expressing his gratitude for the work of his servants, and sharing the rewards with them

- Honorable leaders create growth environments for their people by assisting where possible to ensure their physical and emotional needs are met both at home and work, as Ammon did for his people and for the Zoramites.

Questions for Personal Reflection

- Are you creating a growth environment for everyone you lead?
- How do you balance the learning experiences of those you lead so that people can stretch themselves without burning out?
- Do you have the love, patience, and desire needed to labor alongside those you are developing?
- Can you find enjoyment in the growth of your children without feeling resentment that your time with them could have been spent on your own development?

- Are you rallying your friends around associates who would fall by the wayside without your collective effort to nourish them?
- Can you create an environment where people choose to come to you for nourishment?

Attribute 56: Sets an Example

Example: *One that serves as a pattern to be imitated.*

Jesus set the perfect example of what a leader should be and what a leader should do. In setting that example, He gave a simple invitation to "Come, follow me" (Luke 18:22). He expanded on that invitation to Nephi when He said, "follow me, and do the things which ye have seen me do" (2 Nephi 31:12). While visiting the Nephites, Jesus taught the proper way to administer the sacrament, and then said, "And this shall ye always observe to do, even as I have done" (3 Nephi 18:6). He taught them to pray, "as I have prayed among you even so shall ye pray in my church. . . . Behold I am the light; I have set an example for you" (3 Nephi 18:16). As Jesus concluded His ministry among the Nephites, He again invited them to follow His example when He said, "Therefore, what manner of men ought ye to be? Verily I say unto you, even as I am" (3 Nephi 27:27).

One of the most quoted of Jesus's examples was when He offered a prayer that we now call the Lord's Prayer. He said: *"After this manner therefore pray ye:* Our Father which art in heaven, Hallowed be thy name. Thy kingdom come. Thy will be done in earth, as it is in heaven. Give us this day our daily bread. And forgive us our debts, as we forgive our debtors. And lead us not into temptation, but deliver us from evil: For thine is the kingdom, and the power, and the glory, for ever. Amen" (Matthew 6:9–13, emphasis added).

In all that He did, in everything He said, Jesus set the example to emulate. He taught us what to do, He showed us how to do it, and now He invites us to try ourselves.

Examples of Righteous Leaders

Almost daily, the Prophet Joseph Smith set an example for his followers to emulate. He set an example of serving a mission by partnering with Sidney Rigdon in Upper New York and Canada. He set an example of enduring physical and emotional strain when, in an effort to relieve the suffering of Saints in Missouri, Joseph organized

Zion's Camp where he led a large group of men hundreds of miles during the heat of summer. During this journey, "Joseph took full share of the fatigues of the journey. In addition to the care of providing for the camp and presiding over it, he walked most of the time and had a full portion of blistered, bloody and sore feet. . . . But during the entire trip he never uttered a murmur or complaint."[18] During this long and difficult journey, many of the future leadership of the Church traveled with him and were taught firsthand by his noble and Christlike example. What they learned would guide them as they guided others in following the example of Jesus.

In another setting, Joseph set an example of service as told by Bishop H. David Burton: "A group of men were talking with the Prophet Joseph Smith one day when news arrived that the house of a poor brother who lived some distance from town was burned down. Everyone expressed sorrow for what had happened. The Prophet listened for a moment, then put his hand in his pocket, took out five dollars and said, 'I feel sorry for this brother to the amount of five dollars; how much do you all feel sorry?'"[19] Joseph, like Jesus, was always the teacher. He taught by example, by precept, and by sermons. Joseph led the way and said in essence, "Come follow me as I follow Christ."

In more recent times, another great prophet set an example in his private life of the doctrines he taught in his public life. President Gordon B. Hinckley's daughters said this of their father: "Family life was full of laughter and adventure, not heavy with expectations or rules. As a parent, President Hinckley taught much the way he leads, through quiet example. He would talk about other people at the dinner table and say 'he's a fine man,' and would talk about the characteristics and attributes of the person, and we would know that these are the things that you value."[20]

These great leaders followed the example of the Savior, and in the process, they set the example for others. They lived what *He* taught, and they lived what *they* taught. We learn by hearing, by watching, and by doing. We learn by following someone we can imitate. A popular child's game is called "Follow the Leader" where each youth follows the actions of their appointed leader. This simple little game teaches how to follow the actions of another person. Perhaps the next lesson they need to be taught is how to choose a leader who is worthy of following.

Summary of Examples

- An honorable leader becomes and does what he wants his people to become and do, as Jesus did when He taught, "Follow me, and do the things which ye have seen me do" (2 Nephi 31:12).
- An honorable leader demonstrates to his people what they should do, then asks them to do it themselves, as Jesus did with "The Lord's Prayer," and Joseph Smith in serving a mission, enduring his own trials, and in serving others.
- An honorable leader shows how to live a happy life, as did Gordon B. Hinckley.

Questions for Personal Reflection

- Is the example you set based on a solid personal character rather than on a skillfully enacted persona?
- How often do you take the time to show someone what you mean rather than just tell them?
- At the end of a long day at work, does your family also have the opportunity to see you at your best rather than seeing a shut–down version of you?
- Are you leading your associates to follow the example of their leaders?
- How well will others learn the gospel by studying your example?
- When you attend a game of a heated rivalry, do you lead others to being civil by your example?

Attribute 57: Mentors

Mentor: *An influential senior sponsor or supporter. A wise and trusted counselor or teacher.*

The record of Moses tells of a young Enoch who "heard a voice from heaven, saying: Enoch, my son, prophesy unto this people and say unto them—Repent. . . . And when Enoch had heard these words, he bowed himself to the earth, before the Lord, and spake before the Lord, saying: Why is it that I have found favor in thy sight, and *am but a lad*, and all the people hate me; for I am slow of speech; wherefore am I thy servant?" (Moses 6:26–31, emphasis added). Enoch, in his formative youth, had just been given an enormous assignment to cry repentance to a wicked world. However, he would not be expected to fill it alone. God reassured Enoch by declaring that He Himself would be his mentor, saying, "My Spirit is upon you . . . thou shalt abide in me, and I in you; therefore *walk with me*" (Moses 6:34, emphasis added). Enoch did walk with God all his days and eventually became one of the greatest prophets, a prophet whose people became the most righteous of any who have ever lived.

Jesus understands that His followers are weak and incomplete. He said, "for all have not every gift given unto them; for there are many gifts . . . . To some is given one, and to some is given another, that all may be profited thereby" (D&C 46:11–12). He also stated, "They cannot bear meat now, but milk they must receive . . . lest they perish" (D&C 19:22). Acknowledging our infancy, He reassured us that He would guide and mentor us one step at a time through our individual developmental process. He continued, "Behold, ye are little children and ye cannot bear all things now; ye must grow in grace and in the knowledge of the truth" (D&C 50:40), "nevertheless, be of good cheer, for *I will lead you along*" (D&C 78:18, emphasis added).

The work Jesus had been given by His Father was to "bring to pass the immortality and eternal life of man" (Moses 1:39). As such, He understands that each of us has varied talents and gifts, and to have eternal life, He needs to help us fully develop. He acts as a personal mentor in arranging experiences that will teach and develop us more completely. There are many examples from the scriptures that demon-strate this mentoring. Each example shows that learning is more intensified and effective as we become involved in the experience. It seems we learn more as participants on the playing field than as spectators in the bleachers.

One of the great teaching moments of Jesus was when He taught the 5,000 on the banks of the sea. He taught them all day long and into the evening. When they were hungry, He engaged His disciples in providing for the multitude's needs. The disciples proposed the easiest solution which was to send them all away. However, Jesus used this situation to teach, to build, and to give experience. He sent His disciples to count the people and determine how much food was collectively among them. He then had them organize the people into "ranks, by hundreds, and by fifties" (Mark 6:40). The well-known miracle then followed where so little food fed so many people. The Lord used this event for multiple purposes, such as demonstrating His divine nature, but it also provided an opportunity to mentor His disciples. It gave them valuable leadership experience in front of thousands of people without feeling the full weight of the situation that was borne by Jesus. After His death, His disciples would feel that full weight.

Later, in a more intimate setting, Jesus mentored Peter by involving him in the miracle of paying the tax collectors with money he received from the mouth of a fish (Matthew 17:24–27). The money could have been provided in many other ways, but Jesus was mentoring Peter for the important role he would yet fill in His work.

Jesus involved the brother of Jared in preparing a way for his family to cross the great deep. He instructed him to "go to work and build, after the manner of barges which ye have hitherto built" (Ether 2:16). He allowed the brother of Jared to do that which he knew how to do and then allowed him to struggle to learn that which he did not know. In one such situation, the brother of Jared asked the Lord what he should do for light in the vessels. Continuing the growing experience, the Lord said, "What will ye that I should do that ye may have light in your vessels? For behold, ye cannot have windows, for they will be dashed in pieces; neither shall ye take fire with you" (Ether

2:23). The brother of Jared then came up with a solution on his own. He prepared sixteen small stones and asked the Lord to touch them to give them light (Ether 3:4). In addition to providing light for his vessels, this line–upon–line mentoring produced faith sufficient for the brother of Jared to see "the finger of the Lord" (Ether 3:6) and from there the Lord was able to fully reveal Himself to him (Ether 3:13).

Several hundred years later, the Lord mentored Nephi to accomplish the same work of building a vessel to take his family across the great waters. "The Lord *did show me from time to time* after what manner I should work the timbers of the ship. Now I, Nephi, did not work the timbers after the manner which was learned by men, neither did I build the ship after the manner of men; but I did build it after the manner which the Lord had shown unto me; wherefore, it was not after the manner of men. And I, Nephi, did go into the mount oft, and I did pray oft unto the Lord; wherefore the Lord showed unto me great things" (1 Nephi 18:1–3, emphasis added).

Nephi saw firsthand how the Lord also mentored his father Lehi. This line–upon–line process started when Jesus sent prophets to preach to Lehi (1 Nephi 1:4). He answered Lehi's prayers with a vision (1 Nephi 1:6). He sent him to preach His gospel to others (1 Nephi 1:18). He directed him to take his family into the wilderness (1 Nephi 2:2). He had Lehi send his sons back to Jerusalem to get the plates of brass (1 Nephi 3:3–4). He had Lehi send his sons back again to "take daughters to wife" (1 Nephi 7:1). He prepared the Liahona to guide him through the wilderness (1 Nephi 16:10). He led him to Bountiful (1 Nephi 17:5). He directed the building of a ship (1 Nephi 17:8) and so forth. Each step built upon the previous steps.

Through this methodical progression, the Lord built Lehi into a great prophet who became a righteous influence for his people. Therefore, Lehi could testify that the Lord had led him along the way as He promised He would (1 Nephi 17:13). Later, his son Nephi taught this doctrine to his brethren: "For behold, thus saith the Lord God: I will give unto the children of *men line upon line, precept upon precept, here a little and there a little;* and blessed are those who hearken unto my precepts, and lend an ear unto my counsel, for they shall learn wisdom; for *unto him that receiveth I will give more;* and from them that shall say, We have enough, from them shall be taken away even that which they have" (2 Nephi 28:30, emphasis added).

Centuries later, Joseph Smith was also mentored, starting with the First Vision, and then followed by visits from Moroni and other prophets and apostles. He was told that the Lord "will give unto the faithful line upon line, precept upon precept" (D&C 98:12) and they would "receive knowledge from time to time" (D&C 1:28).

Part of the mentoring process is knowing the capacity and needs of those being mentored. In the example of the Prophet Joseph Smith, we see how the Lord regulates the pace of growth. While translating the Book of Mormon, the Lord told Joseph, "I will grant unto you no other gift until it is finished" (D&C 5:4). Later, Joseph received the same message regarding the completion of the translation of the Bible where he was told, "I give no more unto you at this time" (D&C 73:6). It seems the Lord wanted Joseph to stay focused on the task at hand to avoid overwhelming him.

Later, the Lord told Joseph, "I will order all things for your good, as fast as ye are able to receive them" (D&C 111:11). One of the major roles of leadership, whether in the home or place of business, is the proper pacing of growth of those we lead. This requires constant monitoring to prevent the extremes of burnout or stagnation. This is true with tasks and assignments as well as with learning knowledge. Knowledge is usually added upon a sound foundation of prerequisite knowledge.

The prophet Alma explained to the people in Gideon that he had learned some things but not all things. "For behold, I say unto you there be many things to come; and behold, there is one thing which is of more importance than they all—for behold, the time is not far distant that the Redeemer liveth and cometh among his people. Behold, I do not say that he will come among us at the time of his dwelling in his mortal tabernacle; for behold, *the Spirit hath not said unto me that this should be the case.* Now as to this thing I do not know; but this much I do know, that the Lord God hath power to do all things which are according to his word" (Alma 7:7–8, emphasis added).

Later, as Alma was teaching his son Helaman about the records of his people and wondering what impact the records would have, he explained, "Now these mysteries are not yet fully made known unto me. And it may suffice if I only say they are preserved for a wise purpose, which purpose is known unto God" (Alma 37:11–12). Again, as the Lord mentored Alma; He showed the mentoring process is line upon line. John states that even Jesus followed this pattern. "And I, John, saw that he received not of the fulness at the first, but received grace for grace . . . until he received a fulness; And thus he was called the Son of God, because *he received not of the fulness at the first*" (D&C 93:12–14, emphasis added).

This is the step–by–step process of building perfect, or complete, lives. One well designed step builds upon a previous step until a person's growth is complete.

Examples of Righteous Leaders

Much of the focus of a mentor is to help the young and inexperienced learn from those who have gone through many of the experiences they will yet face. The need for mentoring was expressed by Alexander Pope who said, "As the twig is bent, so the tree's inclined."[21] Therefore, to grow a straight and strong tree, the twig must be attached to a straight and sturdy guide during its formative years. The Apostle Paul taught that the straight and sturdy guides are the "aged men" who exhort young men and "aged women" who "teach the young women . . . shewing thyself a pattern of good works" (Titus 2:3–7).

These wise and experienced men and women recognize that many youth are very capable and can do great things. Often, they just need an opportunity and a mentor. President Boyd K. Packer said the following: "There are many accounts in the scriptures of young men serving. Samuel served in the tabernacle with Eli. David was a young man when he faced Goliath. Mormon's service began when he was 10. Joseph Smith was 14 when he received the First Vision. And Christ was 12 when He was found in the temple teaching the wise men. Paul told young Timothy, 'Let no man despise thy youth.'"[22]

Not all young or inexperienced people will render great service, but all can grow and contribute if given an opportunity and a mentor. The Lord counseled prospective mentors when He said, "And if any man among you be strong in the Spirit, let him take with him him that is weak, that he may be edified in all meekness, that he may become strong also" (D&C 84:106). One can envision a strong and capable man or woman putting his or her arm around the shoulder of a hesitating and unsure youth and walking off to face new experiences together. It has been said of the learning process, "Tell me and I forget. Teach me and I remember. Involve me and I learn."[23] This is the method of learning the Savior uses as He continues to mentor each of us.

Sister Eliza R. Snow led many people to self–development and new opportunities through her example and encouragement. She told the sisters, "Do not let your president have to say all . . . . Has not God endowed you with the gift of speech? . . . If you are endowed with the Spirit of God, no matter how simple your thoughts may be, they will be edifying to those who hear you."[24] One sister who followed Eliza's lead was Emily S. Richards who learned to speak in public because of prodding and instruction she received from Sister Snow. Emily said of Eliza, "The first time [she] asked me to speak in meeting, I could not, and she said, 'Never mind, but when you are asked to speak again, try and have something to say.' And I did."[25]

Sister Richards acted on her new–found faith in herself and became tremendously influential on a much larger stage. In 1889, she had the opportunity to speak in Washington, D.C., at the National Woman Suffrage Association convention. Because of the influence of an experienced mentor like Eliza R. Snow, Emily Richards was able to use her own influence and help improve individual lives and to shape society in general.

Summary of Examples

- Honorable mentors walk alongside those they mentor to teach, support, train, and influence them, as God did with Enoch.
- Honorable mentors know that each person has some gifts but

not all gifts, as Jesus taught when He said, "To some is given one, and to some is given another" (D&C 46:11–12).

- Honorable mentors give carefully designed assignments that take advantage of their people's talents and also develop their areas of weakness, as Jesus did with the brother of Jared.
- Honorable mentors give needed instruction from time to time, line upon line, as Jesus did with the brother of Jared, Lehi, Nephi, and Joseph Smith.
- Honorable mentors keep their people focused on the task at hand, as Jesus did with Joseph Smith while translating the Book of Mormon and the Bible.
- Honorable mentors keep their people moving forward at a proper speed to prevent burn out or stagnation, as Jesus did with Joseph Smith when He said, "I will order all things for your good, as fast as ye are able to receive them" (D&C 111:11).
- Honorable mentors are mentored themselves, as demonstrated by Alma when he acknowledged that he was still being taught and did not have all the answers. Also, Joseph Smith was mentored as he received various revelations from time to time.
- Honorable mentors acknowledge that young people can do great things if an experienced mentor oversees their growing process, as demonstrated by Samuel, David, Jesus, Timothy, Mormon, and Joseph Smith.
- Honorable mentors set expectations then give encouragement as people grow into those expectations, as Emily Richards did while being mentored by Eliza R. Snow.

Questions for Personal Reflection

- Are you regulating the speed of growth of your people based on their individual capacity to do more?
- Are you balancing your mentoring by helping when needed but holding back when appropriate?
- Are you a better mentor than were your mentors?

- Who are you personally mentoring right now?
- Can you expand the number of people you are mentoring?

---

1.   Jay A. and Donald W. Parry, *Understanding the Parables of Jesus Christ,* 2.

2.   Parry, 7-8.

3.   *Woman's Exponent,* May 1903, 93.

4.   *Woman's Exponent,* May 1903, 93.

5.   John Taylor, "The Organization of the Church," *Millennial Star,* Nov. 15, 1851, 339. Also, cited in *Teachings of Presidents of the Church: Joseph Smith,* (2011), 281-91.

6.   Gordon B. Hinckley, "Time a friend, ally after 66 years together," *Church News,* April 26, 2003; emphasis added.

7.   John Taylor, *Conference Report,* April 1880, "Third Day," Thursday, 10 A.M.

8.   *General Authorities, Collected Discourses* v3, Joseph F. Smith, October 8, 1893.

9.   Jay A. and Donald W. Parry, *Understanding the Parables of Jesus Christ,* 8.

10. Blaine M. Yorgason, *All That was Promised,* 189.

11. Yorgason, 102.

12. Yorgason, 106.

13. Yorgason, 147.

14. James E. Faust, "Discipleship," *Ensign,* November 2006. emphasis added.

15. *Diary of Emmeline B. Wells,* Jan. 4, 1878, Harold B. Lee Library Special Collections, Brigham Young University; punctuation standardized.

16. *Diary of Emmeline B. Wells,* Aug. 1, 1895, Harold B. Lee Library Special Collections, Brigham Young University; punctuation standardized.

17. "Epistle to the Relief Society Concerning These War Times," *Relief Society Magazine,* July 1917, 364.

18. *Teachings of Presidents of the Church: Joseph Smith,* 287.

19. H. David Burton, "Tender Hearts and Helping Hands," *Ensign,* May 2006. See Andrew Workman, in "Recollections of the Prophet Joseph Smith," *Juvenile Instructor,* Oct. 15, 1892, 641.

20.   Virginia Pearce, Kathleen Walker, "LDS Pres. Hinckley gentle, unpretentious," *Deseret* News, December 25, 2005.

21.   Alexander Pope, *Moral Essays*, vol. 2 of *The Works of Alexander Pope,* Esq., "Epistle I: To Sir Richard Temple, Lord Cobham," (1776), 119; line 150.

22.   Boyd K. Packer, "Counsel to Young Men," *Ensign*, May 2009.

23.   This statement has been attributed to Benjamin Franklin and to Confucius but both claims are disputed by some scholars. The concept behind the quote is found in *Xunzi, the collected works of Xun Kuang* (a Chinese Confucian philosopher who lived from 312-230 BC) compiled by Liu Xiang in about 818 AD. Book 8, Chapter 11. (See Quora.com)

24.   Eliza R. Snow, in *Tenth Ward Relief Society Minutes*, Jan. 22, 1874, Church History Library, 24; punctuation and capitalization standardized.

25.   Emily S. Richards, in "General Conference Relief Society," *Woman's Exponent*, Dec. 1901, 54.

CHAPTER 11

HE OVERSEES FOLLOWER'S PERFORMANCE

Attribute 58: Provides Hands-on Leadership

Hands-on: *Involving or offering active participation rather than theory.*
Micromanaging: *Controlling or critiquing every detail of someone else's work.*

Soon after delivering Abraham from Pharaoh's sacrificial altar, Jehovah said to him, "Behold, I will lead thee by my hand" (Abraham 1:18) "into a strange land" (Abraham 1:16). Abraham had been living in Chaldea, which was the land of his fathers, but it had become so wicked that Jehovah intervened. He saved Abraham by loosening the bands that bound him to the altar and led him to a better land where he could grow into the person Jehovah knew he could be. Then Jehovah stepped back and guided from a distance until stronger intervention was again needed.

Each of us can benefit from a mentor who guides us through our learning experiences. However, learning is best done when this mentor can then back away far enough so we can learn without fear of each move being critiqued. This is the pattern the Savoir followed with His Twelve Apostles. After He called and trained them, He resumed His own work and allowed them space to perform the work He had given them. As Matthew records, "when Jesus had made an end of commanding his twelve disciples, *he departed thence to teach and to preach in their cities"* (Matthew 11:1, emphasis added).

Jesus continued to monitor His Apostles as He does each of us, always ready to step in and assist if necessary. Jesus said to ancient Israel, *"Am* I a God at hand . . . and not a God afar off?" (Jeremiah 23:23). To His Saints in the latter-days, He said, "Lift up your hearts and be glad, for *I am in your midst"* (D&C 29:5, emphasis added). Later, He reassured them, *"mine eyes are upon you. I am in your midst* and ye cannot see me" (D&C 38:7, emphasis added). Even Jesus had the benefit of having a mentor who was in His midst to watch over Him. He said, "The Father hath not left me alone" (John 8:29). Although He was not alone, Jesus was not micromanaged. He had been given enough space and freedom to act on His own. He had been allowed to find that balance between being guided by the wishes of His leader and being guided by His own agency.

In the parable of the talents, the Savior gave an example of a hands–on leader who does not micromanage. In the parable, a "man travelling into a far country . . . called his own servants, and delivered unto them his goods. And unto one he gave five talents, to another two, and to another one; to every man according to his several ability; and straightway took his journey" (Matthew 25:14–15). The leader was hands–on enough that he knew the "several ability" of each servant and proportioned his goods accordingly. Then, he got out of their way long enough for them to do their work. Two of them did well while one did not, but each had been given the freedom to act for himself.

A portion of our learning needs to be self–initiated. Jesus said, "I prepared all things, and have given unto the children of men to be agents unto themselves" (D&C 104:17). He explained further: "For behold, it is not meet that I should command in all things; for he that is compelled in all things, the same is a slothful and not a wise servant; wherefore he receiveth no reward. Verily I say, men should be anxiously engaged in a good cause, and *do many things of their own free will, and bring to pass much righteousness;* For the power is in them, wherein they are agents unto themselves. And inasmuch as men do good they shall in nowise lose their reward" (D&C 58:26–28, emphasis added).

People want to "do many things of their own free will." They yearn for the freedom to act and only need to be allowed to do so. This desire is divinely initiated and should not be inhibited, only guided by wise, experienced, and trusted leaders.

Examples of Righteous Leaders

After arriving in the land of Bountiful, the Lord directed Nephi to build a ship. Of this experience, Elder L. Tom Perry said: "This is one of the more interesting stories we have in the scriptures because it tells of an instance in which the Lord provided help *but then stepped aside* to allow one of His sons to exercise his own initiative. I have sometimes wondered what would have happened if Nephi had asked the Lord for tools instead of a place to find the ore to make the tools. I doubt the Lord would have honored Nephi's request. You see, the Lord knew that Nephi could make the tools, and it is seldom the Lord will do something for us that we can do for ourselves."[1]

This is the Lord's pattern of helping only when needed. Allowing someone to use his or her previously developed skills builds a stronger sense of self–worth and allows more skills to be developed.

During the final days of construction on the St. George Temple, workers who were weary from many years of strenuous effort were encouraged by President Young to quicken the pace. Brigham Young was in failing health and needed the temple to be complete so he could finalize the presentation of the endowment as assigned by the Prophet Joseph Smith. To help with this effort, Brigham Young and George Albert Smith "mingled with workers and supervisors, listened to problems, encouraged, and counseled. They did the same with townspeople, at celebrations, evening events, and at church." During this time, President Young "suffered from rheumatism and a throat problem that made speaking difficult"[2] but he knew the power of his influence and he rendered it to the fullest extent possible. He did not take over the management of the project as a micromanager would, he and Brother Smith only offered encouragement to weary hands.

Summary of Examples

- Honorable leaders need to be available to lead by the hand if necessary, as Jehovah did while leading Abraham out of the land of his fathers.
- Honorable leaders need to know when to be out among their people and when to back away and leave them alone, as did the man in the parable of the talents.

- Honorable leaders need to help when needed and avoid helping when not needed, as Jesus demonstrated when Nephi built the ship.
- Honorable leaders need to let their people do many things of their own free will, as Jesus taught.
- Leaders can revitalize weary arms by mingling and encouraging, as demonstrated by Brigham Young and George Albert Smith.

Questions for Personal Reflection

- Do you allow others to accomplish as much as they can before interjecting yourself?
- Do you stay close enough so you can step in at the proper time to give the proper level of assistance?
- If you need to step in and assist, can you do so without offending egos?
- Do you mingle with those you lead long enough to know and understand each of them?
- When you give an assignment to an inexperienced person, do you walk beside them long enough to guide them?
- If you taught piano or violin, would you balance your instruction between showing how to play a phrase and then sitting back and letting the student emulate your example?

Attribute 59: Places Faith in Followers

Faith: *Confidence. Loyalty.*

There is such a disparity between Jesus and all mortal men that it seems difficult to understand how He could have faith and confidence in us. Yet He does. Otherwise, He would not delegate His authority to act in His name. He involves us in His work because He has faith in our potential and His faith allows us to have confidence in ourselves. It is the confidence to act, to do, to become, to try, to experiment, to learn; even if by trial and error.

On the Mount of Olives, Jesus gave His disciples the parable of the talents. This parable provides an example of a leader who has faith in his people and operates based on individual accountability. The man in the parable gave his servants "his goods," then left for a long time. It is likely that the master had the ability to create a larger return on his investment than his three servants could. However, he had faith in them and wanted them to learn diligence and accountability. He wanted them to grow through their own experiences. This is what leaders do—they build others, and that requires taking a risk while having faith in them.

The Savior demonstrated faith in His servants when He said, "What I the Lord have spoken, I have spoken, and . . . shall all be fulfilled, whether by mine own voice *or by the voice of my servants*, it is the same" (D&C 1:38, emphasis added). Here, Jesus demonstrates that He has enough faith in His servants that He will honor what they do or say. By placing this faith in them, He encourages them to rise to the level of His expectations. The ancient prophets must have felt those expectations as well as the Apostles in Jerusalem, in the land Bountiful, and in Fayette, New York.

The calling of the new Apostles in Fayette is a clear demonstration of the faith the Savior places in His followers. Jesus delegated to Oliver Cowdery and David Whitmer the responsibility to "search out the Twelve" (D&C 18:37). They were to find 12 men who would become the Twelve Apostles in the restored Church. To help them identify who they would be, Jesus said, "By their desires and their works you shall know them" (D&C 18:38). What great faith Jesus placed in Oliver and David as He delegated this most important responsibility. Consider the growth that must have occurred as they struggled to live up to the faith their Lord placed in them. They learned firsthand that a leader often can cause more growth by placing faith in others than by directing their every action.

Examples of Righteous Leaders

The year 1840 was a busy season for the Church of Jesus Christ of Latter-day Saints. Congregations were flourishing in many parts of the United States, especially in Nauvoo. The city now had over 3,000 people with more arriving by steamboat and wagons every day. The building of the Nauvoo temple had commenced where the Saints were giving labor one day in ten to its construction. Missionaries were being sent far and near as the Church enjoyed accelerated growth. While the Prophet Joseph provided overall leadership from Nauvoo, many of the Apostles provided leadership in remote locations such as England where they oversaw the printing of the Book of Mormon, the creation of a hymn book, and the writing of several editorials and publications. They oversaw the care of the poor that made up a large portion of English converts and prepared for their immigration to Zion.

The scale of Church operations had grown so extensive that Joseph Smith could not make all the decisions or keep abreast of all the issues facing this expanding effort. After having received several letters from the Apostles and other leaders in England, Joseph penned a reply. In essence, he deferred many issues back to these seasoned leaders in whom he placed great faith. In that letter he said, "There are many things of much importance, on which you ask counsel, but which I think you will be perfectly able to decide upon, as you are more conversant with the peculiar circumstances than I am; and I feel great confidence in your united wisdom; therefore you will excuse me for not entering into detail. If I should see anything that is wrong, I would take the privilege of making known my mind to you."[3]

Surely, Joseph must have wanted to weigh in on every aspect of the Church's operations like Moses did with ancient Israel, but as

Jethro counseled Moses, so the Lord counseled Joseph to "not run faster or labor more than you have strength." (D&C 10:4) As a result, Joseph placed his faith in his follower and allowed them the freedom to study, ponder, pray, and make their own decisions. Joseph taught, "I teach them correct principles and they govern themselves."[4] By leveraging the leadership of these remote Apostles, Joseph led the Church to exponential numerical and spiritual growth.

Summary of Examples

- An honorable leader builds his people by placing faith in them and their efforts, even though the leader may have done better himself, as Jesus taught in the parable of the talents.
- An honorable leader demonstrates faith by giving significant assignments to his people, as Jesus did with Oliver Cowdery and David Whitmer in identifying the Twelve Apostles.
- An honorable leader allows his people to make their own decisions for their own growth, as demonstrated by Joseph with the apostles in England.

Questions for Personal Reflection

- Do those who follow you know you have faith in them?
- Do you give others significant responsibility rather than only delegating unimportant tasks?
- Can you allow a subordinate to take the lead on an important assignment?
- How do you feel when someone completes an assignment in a different manner than you would have done?
- Are you willing to let a person fail in an assignment if it brings about needed learning?

Attribute 60: Expects Results

Results: *Consequences, effects, or outcomes of something.*

Results validate teaching. Jesus is ever the teacher, but who are the learners? Learners are those who produce results based on what is taught. Jesus expects all His followers to grow and develop into more capable people; men and women of faith, obedience, compassion, integrity, endurance, and so forth. His mission centers on our eternal progression, and mortality is designed to allow us the opportunity to progress individually. Jesus likens us unto a tree and measures our progression by the fruit, or results, we produce. In the Sermon on the Mount, Jesus taught, "Wherefore by their fruits ye shall know them" (Matthew 7:20). He taught that productivity is evidence of character.

One of the Savior's great teaching moments came on the road from Bethany to Jerusalem at the beginning of His final week. "And seeing a fig tree afar off having leaves, he came, if haply he might find any thing thereon: and when he came to it, he found nothing but leaves; for the time of figs was not *yet*" (Mark 11:13). "All present knew that fig trees bring forth their fruit before their leaves. All were equally aware that it would be some weeks before fig trees normally gave fruit. Yet the profusion of leaves on this tree constituted an announcement that it was laden with fruit. . . . The symbol was perfect—a tree professing fruits and having none."[5] Jesus uses this tree to teach that the appearance of results is not acceptable; it is in the actual fruit that the worth of the tree is manifest.

The Savior also teaches the need for producing results in the parable of the talents. This parable, as with all parables, teaches multiple lessons. This parable was discussed in previous chapters to show how to be a hands–on leader and to have faith in your people. However, it also teaches that Jesus clearly expects us to produce great results with the talents we are given. Not just for the sake of the results or return on investment, but for the growth of the individual. In this parable, a man gives his goods to his servants, and then travels into a far country. When he returns, he asks for an accounting of the results of their labors. The servants who produced good results were entrusted with more of his goods, while the one who did poorly had his talent withdrawn (Matthew 25:14–28).

Jesus, like the master in the parable, will fully reward all who have labored for Him. He declared, "For the Son of man shall come in the glory of his Father with his angels; and then he shall reward every man according to his works" (Matthew 16:27), "they that have done good, unto the resurrection of life" (John 5:29). These are they who have tried, who have experimented, who have labored to do something of worth and to become someone of worth. These are they who have added upon the talents they have been given and have grown into more complete or perfect individuals.

Not only does Jesus expect results from everyone, He has higher expectations for His followers than for others. He knows our potential, and His mission is to assist us in growing to the fullest extent possible. One way He does this is by expecting much from us. The Apostle Paul taught that Jesus "is the mediator of a better covenant, which was established upon better promises" (Hebrews 8:6). The higher law Jesus taught, (no anger, no lust, no swearing at all, loving your enemies, and praying for persecutors) replaced the Law of Moses (no murder, no adultery, no profanity, and an eye for an eye).

Jesus taught Peter, "For unto whomsoever much is given, of him shall be much required" (Luke 12:48, D&C 82:3). Each of His disciples has indeed been given much. They have access to the Atonement, which brings peace in this life and mansions in the next life. They understand the purpose of life and the glories that await them hereafter. They have His life as an example of how to live properly. However, with these great blessings come higher expectations as Jesus taught in His Sermon on the Mount and in other settings.

Regarding *righteousness* He said:

> For I say unto you, That except your righteousness shall exceed *the righteousness* of the scribes and Pharisees, ye shall in no case enter into the kingdom of heaven (Matthew 5:20).

Regarding *killing* He said:

> Ye have heard that it was said by them of old time, Thou shalt not kill; and whosoever shall kill shall be in danger of the judgment:

But I say unto you, That whosoever is angry with his brother without a cause shall be in danger of the judgment: and whosoever shall say to his brother, Raca, shall be in danger of the council: but whosoever shall say, Thou fool, shall be in danger of hell fire (Matthew 5:21–22).

Regarding *adultery* He said:

Ye have heard that it was said by them of old time, Thou shalt not commit adultery:

But I say unto you, That whosoever looketh on a woman to lust after her hath committed adultery with her already in his heart (Matthew 5:27–28).

Regarding *divorce* He said:

It hath been said, Whosoever shall put away his wife, let him give her a writing of divorcement:

But I say unto you, That whosoever shall put away his wife, saving for the cause of fornication, causeth her to commit adultery: and whosoever shall marry her that is divorced committeth adultery (Matthew 5:31–32).

Regarding *oaths* He said:

Again, ye have heard that it hath been said by them of old time, Thou shalt not forswear thyself, but shalt perform unto the Lord thine oaths:

But I say unto you, Swear not at all (Matthew 5:33–34).

Regarding *retaliation* He said:

Ye have heard that it hath been said, An eye for an eye, and a tooth for a tooth:

But I say unto you, That ye resist not evil: but whosoever shall smite thee on thy right cheek, turn to him the other also.

And if any man will sue thee at the law, and take away thy coat, let him have *thy* cloke also.

And whosoever shall compel thee to go a mile, go with him twain.

Give to him that asketh thee, and from him that would borrow of thee turn not thou away (Matthew 5:38–42).

Regarding *enemies* He said:

Ye have heard that it hath been said, Thou shalt love thy

neighbour, and hate thine enemy.

But I say unto you, Love your enemies, bless them that curse you, do good to them that hate you, and pray for them which despitefully use you, and persecute you (Matthew 5:43–44).

Regarding giving *alms* He said:

Take heed that ye do not your alms before men, to be seen of them: otherwise ye have no reward of your Father which is in heaven.

Therefore when thou doest *thine* alms, do not sound a trumpet before thee, as the hypocrites do in the synagogues and in the streets, that they may have glory of men. Verily I say unto you, They have their reward.

But when thou doest alms, let not thy left hand know what thy right hand doeth:

That thine alms may be in secret: and thy Father which seeth in secret himself shall reward thee openly (Matthew 6:1–4).

Regarding *praying* He said:

And when thou prayest, thou shalt not be as the hypocrites *are*: for they love to pray standing in the synagogues and in the corners of the streets, that they may be seen of men. Verily I say unto you, They have their reward.

But thou, when thou prayest, enter into thy closet, and when thou hast shut thy door, pray to thy Father which is in secret; and thy Father which seeth in secret shall reward thee openly. But when ye pray, use not vain repetitions, as the heathen *do* (Matthew 6:5–7).

Regarding *fasting* He said:

Moreover when ye fast, be not, as the hypocrites, of a sad countenance: for they disfigure their faces, that they may appear unto men to fast. Verily I say unto you, They have their reward.

But thou, when thou fastest, anoint thine head, and wash thy face;

That thou appear not unto men to fast, but unto thy Father which is in secret: and thy Father, which seeth in secret, shall reward thee openly (Matthew 6:16–18).

Regarding *forgiving* He said:

> Then came Peter to him, and said, Lord, how oft shall my brother sin against me, and I forgive him? till seven times?
>
> Jesus saith unto him, I say not unto thee, Until seven times: but, Until seventy times seven (Matthew 18:21–22).

Regarding *choices* He said:

> And Jesus answered and said unto her, Martha, Martha, thou art careful and troubled about many things:
>
> But one thing is needful: and Mary hath chosen that good part, which shall not be taken away from her (Luke 10:41–42).

In each of these examples and many more, Jesus taught that He expects His disciples to continually rise above average performance and stretch their souls to progress eternally. This is how they become like Him and prepare to live with Him in kingdoms of glory.

Examples of Righteous Leaders

In just one oft-quoted sentence, the Prophet Joseph Smith taught a great leadership principle. He said, "I teach them correct principles and they govern themselves."[6] His expectations were clear. He taught his people foundational principles that should govern their life and then expected them to apply these throughout their life. It was not his desire to control people, but rather that they should control themselves, their own thoughts and actions, according to the divinely revealed principles he taught. Those who did so received the promised blessings, and those who did not bore the resulting consequences.

Joseph taught his people that adherence to the commandments of God would bring about results far greater than they could imagine. In a very real sense, it was the expectations of these results that led so many to follow him. It was the hope of divine knowledge and protection that led an impoverished and persecuted people to build the Kirtland Temple with a hammer in one hand and a rifle in the other. It was this hope that led a people stricken with malaria to rise out of their sick beds and begin construction on yet another temple on the banks of the Mississippi River. These Saints dreamed of living in a Zion community where all were righteous and had pure hearts. They dreamed of one day entering into the presence of God, to sit at His feet and to live with Him and their families for eternity.

Indeed, it was the expectation of results that set Joseph Smith apart from other religious leaders who did not link faith and works together. Faith combined with works is a characteristic of the restored gospel of Christ and was adopted by many leaders trained by Joseph. This clearly was evident in his successor, Brigham Young.

There are many examples of how Brother Brigham led the pioneers to accomplish great things by placing one expectation after another in front of them. There was Brigham's determination to finish the Nauvoo Temple before being driven west. There was the establishment of communities across the plains to help resupply the pioneers on their trek. There was the expectation of getting crops into the soil early enough in the year to provide food for their first winter in the Salt Lake Valley. Brigham gave directions that hundreds of communities should be established throughout the intermountain west, from Canada to Mexico. In addition, there was the building of more temples in St. George, Logan, Manti, and Salt Lake City.

The call to build more temples must have been expected by most of the Saints, for they understood their purpose and were grateful for their blessings. To a group of these Saints, Brigham said, "This I do know—there should be a temple built here. I do know it is the duty of this people to commence to build a temple."[7] Some who feared the attending opposition protested and said, "I do not like to do it, for we never began to build a temple without the bells of hell beginning to ring."[8] However, Brigham countered with conviction and determination, "I want to hear them ring again. All the tribes of hell will be on the move. . . . But what do you think it will amount to? You have all the time seen what it has amounted to."[9]

Brigham expected the Saints to build a temple and by following his leadership, they did just that. And millions of people have benefited from that great endeavor.

Summary of Examples

- Honorable leaders influence their people to act by expecting results from them, as Jesus taught when He said, "Wherefore by their fruits ye shall know them" (Matthew 7:20).

- Honorable leaders wisely discern if the labors of their people produce actual results or an illusion, as demonstrated by Jesus with the barren fig tree.
- Honorable leaders reward those who do produce, by giving them more opportunities to produce, as taught by Jesus with the man who traveled into a far country.
- Honorable leaders establish high expectations for their people to rise above mediocrity and then help them reach those expectations, as Jesus does regarding righteousness, killing, adultery, divorce, oaths, retaliation, enemies, alms, praying, fasting, forgiving, and choices.

Questions for Personal Reflection

- What results do you expect from yourself?
- How do you determine the level of expectations for those who follow you?
- How do you determine how much more to stretch a person's growth without breaking them?
- Are the expectations you set fair and realistic?
- How willing are you to adjust your expectations?

Attribute 61: Accepts People's Best

Accept: *To receive willingly, to appreciate*

Jesus teaches the principle that to bring the best out of people, a leader must expect great things from them. However, these expectations need to be within the bounds of the person's ability. Expecting more than a person can give will likely harm him or her. Jesus had high expectations for the Prophet Joseph Smith, yet He cautioned Joseph, "Do not run faster or labor more than you have strength and means provided" (D&C 10:4). A wise leader knows each person's limits and then influences growth within those limits. Expecting too little provides no growth, but so does expecting too much. Jesus teaches His disciples that when someone such as a widow or a poor person gives his or her all, He accepts that and expects no more.

"And Jesus sat over against the treasury, and beheld how the people cast money into the treasury: and many that were rich cast in much.

"And there came a certain poor widow, and she threw in two mites, which make a farthing.

"And he called *unto him* his disciples, and saith unto them, Verily I say unto you, That this poor widow hath cast more in, than all they which have cast into the treasury:

"For all *they* did cast in of their abundance; but she of her want *did cast in all that she had, even* all her living" (Mark 12:41–44, emphasis added).

Each of us can be likened to the poor widow in that our offerings are meager, but if we offer all that we can, the Master asks no more.

In the parable of the seed growing by itself, Jesus teaches that the gardener can make all the necessary preparations for a seed to grow, but ultimately, the seed grows by itself. Also, the gardener must accept what the seed grows into, whether it is some variety of grass, or flower, or bush, or tree. Jesus can help the seed be the best it was designed to be, but that is all He can do. The same is true for leaders. They can provide all the help possible, but in the end, they cannot make people be what they are not.

331

The Lord taught that each person has his own gifts and should be respected for the gifts he has and not be condemned for those he does not have. "For all have not every gift given unto them; for there are many gifts, and to every man is given a gift by the Spirit of God. To some is given one, and to some is given another, that all may be profited thereby" (D&C 46:11–12).

The Lord demonstrated this with regard to Joseph Smith and Sidney Rigdon when He explained the differences between these two men's gifts. He said Joseph would have "power to be mighty in testimony" (D&C 100:10), and Sidney would be "mighty in expounding all scriptures" (D&C 100:11). Jesus explained that Sidney would "be a spokesman unto [Joseph]" and Joseph "shall be a revelator unto [Sidney]" (D&C 100:11). The Lord also states the differences in gifts between Joseph and Oliver Cowdery:

"For thou [Joseph] shalt devote all thy service in Zion; and in this thou shalt have strength.

"And in temporal labors thou shalt not have strength, for this is not thy calling. Attend to thy calling and thou shalt have wherewith to magnify thine office, and to expound all scriptures, and continue in laying on of the hands and confirming the churches.

"And thy brother Oliver shall continue in bearing my name before the world, and also to the church" (D&C 24:7, 9–10).

These individual gifts served the Lord's purposes well and created a specific place for each of these men to serve. This same pattern continues today in each of our lives. We are strong in some things and not as strong in others. The key for leaders is to be perceptive and know each of their followers well. For instance, not every man has it in him to hike twenty miles in the rain, endure the night in a muddy sleeping bag, and then remain pleasant eating burnt scrambled eggs cooked by twelve–year–old Boy Scouts. Not everyone will be able to captivate congregations with their oratory, but they can stir spiritual feelings through a simple heartfelt testimony.

Jesus asks that we give our best because that is the only way growth can occur. However, He lovingly accepts our best offerings and wisely prepares us for our next learning experiences. Each learning experience is designed to help us become more like Him by acquiring

His attributes. Using the seven–step process discussed in chapter 4 will aid in acquiring these attributes so we can have a greater influence for good.

Examples of Righteous Leaders

Sister Eliza R. Snow played a prominent role in the early days of the restored Church. She was widely respected for her skill with the English language and has been called "Zion's poetess."[10] Sister Snow was concerned that many women in the early days of the Church lacked the skills and courage to speak up and contribute. She taught, "Do not let your president have to say all . . . . Has not God endowed you with the gift of speech?... If you are endowed with the Spirit of God, no matter how simple your thoughts may be, they will be edifying to those who hear you."[11] With an admonition like that, consider the emotions that must have flowed when this highly skilled speaker asked the humblest of sisters to express her views. That invitation came to Sister Emily S. Richards.

Sister Richards explained, "The first time [she asked me to speak in meeting], I could not, and she said, 'Never mind, but when you are asked to speak again, try and have something to say.'"[12] Sister Snow asked Sister Richards to contribute but she couldn't, so Sister Snow simply accepted that and gave a little encouragement to be prepared for future opportunities. Had Sister Snow shown any hint of disappointment, Sister Richards likely would not have tried to improve. However, she did improve, and in a few short years, Sister Richards became such an accomplished public speaker that in 1889 she spoke in Washington, D. C., at the National Woman Suffrage Association convention. This is how leaders help people become better and do better—by accepting their best and encouraging continual growth.

Summary of Examples

- Honorable leaders need to help prevent their people from burning out, as Jesus did with counseling Joseph Smith to not run faster than he had strength.

- Honorable leaders may provide a great environment for their people to grow, but it is up to the individual to grow, as taught by Jesus in the parable of the seed growing by itself.
- Honorable leaders need to know when a person has given all she can give, as the widow did with her mite.
- Honorable leaders should respect a person for the gifts she has and not condemn her for those she does not have, as demonstrated by Jesus and Eliza R. Snow.

Questions for Personal Reflection

- How well can you accept yourself when you have given your very best and it still was not good enough to achieve your goal?
- Do those you lead know your high expectations but also know you will accept them if they do not measure up to those expectations?
- How do you differentiate between someone who has insufficient aptitude as opposed to dormant skills? For example, not everyone has the aptitude or desire to be an athlete.
- Do you know when to stop asking more of another person?
- How much can you admire someone who has given their best effort even though they have fallen short of the objective?
- When is good enough, good enough?

Attribute 62: Follows Up

Follow-up: *Maintaining contact with a person in order to progress or reach a desired end.*

When Jesus visited the Nephites soon after His ascension into heaven, He ministered unto the righteous who had survived the destruction associated with His Crucifixion. He prayed with them, healed them, and taught them. He expounded on the words of Isaiah and other prophets. But He also corrected them. At one point, Jesus said, "Behold, other scriptures I would that ye should write, *that ye have not*" (3 Nephi 23:6, emphasis added). Jesus found that something was missing from their records.

"And it came to pass that he said unto Nephi: Bring forth the record which ye have kept.

"And when Nephi had brought forth the records, and laid them before him, he cast his eyes upon them and said:

"Verily I say unto you, I commanded my servant Samuel, the Lamanite, that he should testify unto this people, that at the day that the Father should glorify his name in me that there were many saints who should arise from the dead, and should appear unto many, and should minister unto them. And he said unto them: *Was it not so?*" (3 Nephi 23:7–9, emphasis added).

The Savior's question may have seemed like a rebuke to His faithful disciples who had been diligent but incomplete in their assignment. However, that assignment was important, and Jesus was following up to ensure it was completed properly. The disciples responded:

"And his disciples answered him and said: Yea, Lord, Samuel did prophesy according to thy words, and they were all fulfilled.

"And Jesus said unto them: *How be it that ye have not written this thing,* that many saints did arise and appear unto many and did minister unto them?

"And it came to pass that Nephi remembered that this thing had not been written.

"And it came to pass that Jesus commanded that it should be

written; therefore it was written according as he commanded" (3 Nephi 23: 10–13, emphasis added).

One can only imagine the anxiety Nephi felt when Jesus followed up on a previously given assignment that had not been completed. Jesus had instructed the Nephites to record the words of the prophets so they would know what to teach. But there had been a significant omission that Jesus wanted corrected. The Savior showed no hint of condescension toward Nephi, but He was not reticent either. He matter-of-factly asked for an accounting, and when He identified the omission, He simply asked that it be corrected. Jesus then waited patiently until it was complete. "And now it came to pass that when Jesus had expounded all the scriptures in one, which they had written, he commanded them that they should teach the things which he had expounded unto them" (3 Nephi 23:14).

Jesus demonstrated that following up is an important responsibility of a leader to ensure results are achieved. For without results, there is no need to lead. Those results vary based on the objective, such as building a successful business or building an associate's self-esteem. Results validate effort.

Examples of Righteous Leaders

One of the great sermons in the scriptures is when King Benjamin addressed all his people who were gathered around the temple. He taught them the gospel of Christ and that they serve Him by serving their fellow men. After his sermon, King Benjamin followed up to see if the people believed his words. "And now, it came to pass that when king Benjamin had thus spoken to his people, he sent among them, desiring to know of his people if they believed the words which he had spoken unto them" (Mosiah 5:1).

In response to King Benjamin's inquiry, the people testified they did believe what he had taught. Then they manifested it by entering into a covenant. King Benjamin then again followed up by recording the names of each person who had entered that covenant. "And now, king Benjamin thought it was expedient, after having finished speaking to the people, that he should take the names of all those who had entered into a covenant with God to keep his commandments" (Mosiah 6:1). Now with that list of names, King Benjamin would better know how to minister unto the people so he could continually lead them to Christ.

In today's Church setting, the follow–up process is often used and is based on the principles of consistency, simplicity, personal growth, and accountability. One high counselor, Brother Ralph Christensen, explained a method that was used by his busy stake president and business leader. Speaking to a large audience in the Church Office Building in Salt Lake City, Brother Christensen explained that once a month, he was invited to President Bill Marriott's home for an interview. President Marriott would open a folder that he had for Brother Christensen. A folder was kept for each of his high counselors. He read his notes from their last visit that listed what Brother Christensen said he would do during the month. The president then asked for a report on each item. He took careful notes of the report. Finally, he asked what Brother Christensen planned to do during the next month. Again, notes were taken, and the folder closed. The next month, the pattern was repeated.[13] This pattern of following up is consistent with the example of the Savior who is a hands–on leader without being a micromanager. He is one who has faith in His people and expects greater results from them.

Summary of Examples

- Honorable leaders influence their people to act by following–up on assignments given, as Jesus did with Nephi and the unrecorded scriptures.
- Honorable leaders determine if they have been effective at influencing others by testing the results of those efforts, as King Benjamin did when he first sought out the feelings of those who heard him and then recorded the names of those who accepted.
- Honorable leaders are consistent at following up, as demonstrated by President Bill Marriott who met monthly with his high counselors.

Questions for Personal Reflection

- When following–up on assignments you have given, do you also follow–up on lessons learned?
- How do you follow up without micromanaging?
- How do you follow up without being condescending?
- Are your motives in following up to help people be successful rather than avoiding your own embarrassment for appearing unsuccessful?
- How do you help your associates complete assignments without taking over their responsibility to manage their own affairs?

Attribute 63: Steps In When Needed

Steps in: *To intervene in an affair or dispute. To act as a replacement.*

When Lehi's family began their journey into the wilderness, they acted in faith and obedience. They did not know where, for how long, or how far they would go. This approach developed their faith, but eventually, the Lord deemed it appropriate to step in, remove obstacles, and give greater help and assurance. Therefore, He provided the Liahona to guide them along a safe path through an unknown wilderness. It was a wilderness they could not have navigated without divine help. He emphasized this point when He said: "And I will also be your light in the wilderness; and I will prepare the way before you, if it so be that ye shall keep my commandments; wherefore, inasmuch as ye shall keep my commandments ye shall be led toward the promised land; and ye shall know that it is by me that ye are led" (1 Nephi 17:13).

Jesus did the same thing when He asked Philip to solve the problem of feeding the 5,000 disciples. Jesus knew Philip could not provide a solution, but He let him struggle with it to deepen the learning process. Then at the proper time, He stepped in to solve the problem through miraculous means. Jesus is ever the perfect mentor.

Perhaps an even more dramatic example of Jesus stepping in was when Peter came to Him on the water. "And in the fourth watch of the night Jesus went unto them, walking on the sea. And when the disciples saw him walking on the sea, they were troubled, saying, It is a spirit; and they cried out for fear. But straightway Jesus spake unto them, saying, Be of good cheer; it is I; be not afraid. And Peter answered him and said, Lord, if it be thou, bid me come unto thee on the water. And he said, Come. And when Peter was come down out of the ship, he walked on the water, to go to Jesus. But when he saw the wind boisterous, he was afraid; and beginning to sink, he cried, saying, Lord, save me. And *immediately Jesus stretched forth his hand, and caught him,* and said unto him, O thou of little faith, wherefore didst thou doubt?" (Matthew 14:25–31).

Peter learned more about faith than perhaps any other person through this experience. He was under the constant tutelage of the Master Teacher who provided meaningful learning experiences and who was always nearby to step in and help if necessary. As Giles Fletcher so eloquently expressed regarding the Savior:

> He is a path, if any be misled;
> He is a robe, if any naked be;
> If any chance to hunger, he is bread;
> If any be a bondman, he is free;
> If any be but weak, how strong is he!
> To dead men life he is, to sick men, health;
> To blind men, sight,
> and to the needy, wealth;
> A pleasure without loss, a treasure without stealth.[14]

Those who have felt Jesus step into their lives will surely testify of the truths so eloquently expressed in this poem. And as He steps in, He demonstrates to other leaders how to lead, how to teach, how to nurture, and how to minister.

Examples of Righteous Leaders

The Prophet Joseph Smith echoed the words of this poem as he said, "If any man is hungry, let him come to me, and I will feed him at my table. If any are hungry or naked . . . come and tell me and I will divide with them to the last morsel."[15] These few words reveal the heart of this great leader who willingly stepped in to help anyone in need, sharing his all with them if necessary.

Following the death of Joseph, Brigham Young stepped in to a difficult circumstance and provided solid leadership when Joseph's followers needed to be led. Those followers were unclear on the succession of leadership as various men tried to fill that role. However, there was only one who could, and that was Brigham Young who was serving as the President of the Quorum of the Twelve. Years later, another Apostle said this of Brother Brigham: "As we look at Brigham Young and reflect upon the inspiration and direction that came to that most unusual man, we recall how he was able to fill the tragic void caused by the death of the Prophet Joseph Smith, how he *stepped in* and was able under inspiration and revelation to guide and direct the closing of Nauvoo and the planning of the trip west."[16]

Brigham stepped in with certainty, capability, and confidence that united the Church. He had been prepared for this moment through years of tutoring at Joseph's side. He drew upon prior experience such as when he took charge of evacuating the Saints from Missouri to Nauvoo in the dead of winter. Soon, he would lead a larger group over a longer journey in the dead of winter as he evacuated the Saints from Nauvoo and into the valley of the Great Salt Lake.

Today, great leaders follow the example of past leaders and unify people around noble causes. Often, only the collective resources and efforts of many people can accomplish these causes. Those people, however, need a leader to bring them together, to determine the objective, and to initiate action. They need someone to lead them. Consider this story from Thailand: "Recently in the small village of Ubon, Thailand, a member family by the name of Tan was beset with what seemed to be insurmountable problems. The father had lost his job, they had no money, the children were sick and malnourished. They were being forced to remove their humble home from the government land upon which it was built, and they had no place to go.

"At this point a fine priesthood leader, who had been using welfare services missionaries as a resource, *stepped in* and averted what could otherwise have been a tragic situation. Under his guidance and with the assistance of all the branch members, a piece of land was obtained, and the Tan family home was dismantled, transported, and rebuilt. Brother Tan began farming the land and started a family produce business which is now flourishing. Some hard work, dedication, and love from local leaders and members, aided by the suggestions of welfare services missionaries, caused a miracle for one family and a great learning and growing experience for a whole branch.[17]

This is what can happen when people step forward and lead. People's lives are blessed and obstacles to their success are removed. It often starts with one person who has the desire and a vision who can then persuade others to join the cause.

Summary of Examples

- Honorable leaders do for their people what they cannot do for themselves, as demonstrated by Jesus who was the "light in the wilderness" for Lehi's family (1 Nephi 17:13).
- Honorable leaders step in when their people are sinking, as Jesus did with Peter.
- Honorable leaders prepare themselves to be ready to step in when vacancies arise, as Brigham did when following Joseph.
- Honorable leaders step in whenever a situation needs a leader, as demonstrated with the family in Thailand.

Questions for Personal Reflection

- Do you know when to step in if someone is sinking and when to hold back and allow them to struggle through a learning experience?
- Are you keeping your skill set sharp so you can fill in and do specific tasks as needed?
- When have you stepped in to finish the work of someone who has fallen short of the objective?
- When you step in, do you act with love and compassion as the Savior would?
- When you step in, can you avoid being condescending?

---

1. L. Tom Perry, "Becoming Self-Reliant," *Ensign*, November 1991; emphasis added.
2. Blaine M. Yorgason, *All That Was Promised*, 169.
3. B. H. Roberts, *History of The Church of Jesus Christ of Latter-day Saints, vol. 4*, 228; emphasis added.
4. James R. Clark, *Messages of the First Presidency*, 6 vols., Salt Lake City: Bookcraft (1965-75), 3:54. Also cited in *Teachings of Presidents of the Church: Joseph Smith* (2011), 281-91.
5. Joseph Fielding McConkie, *Gospel Symbolism*, 10-11.
6. Clark, 3:54.
7. John A. Widtsoe, *Discourses of Brigham Young*, 410.

8. Widtsoe, 410.
9. Widtsoe, 410.
10. *Daughters in My Kingdom*, 49.
11. Eliza R. Snow, in *Tenth Ward Relief Society Minutes*, Jan. 22, 1874, Church History Library, 24; punctuation and capitalization standardized.
12. Emily S. Richards, in "General Conference Relief Society," *Woman's Exponent*, Dec. 1901, 54.
13. Story told by Brother Christensen; used by permission.
14. Giles Fletcher, "*Poems of Giles Fletcher, B.D.,*" 126.
15. Joseph Smith, *History of the Church* 5:286.
16. David B. Haight, "Faith of Our Prophets," *Ensign*, November 2001, 22; emphasis added.
17. James E. Faust, "Establishing the Church: Welfare Services Missionaries Are an Important Resource," *Ensign*, November 1979, 91; emphasis added.

CHAPTER 12

HE JUDGES

Attribute 64: Is Just and Merciful

Just: Guided by truth, reason, and fairness. Done or made according to principle; conforming to a standard.
Merciful: Bringing someone relief from something unpleasant. Compassionate treatment of those in distress.

Jesus said, "I the Lord cannot look upon sin with the least degree of allowance" (D&C 1:31). He also said, "With everlasting kindness will I have mercy on thee" (3 Nephi 22:8). As our leader, His role is to help us reach our full potential. To accomplish this, He sets rules and consequences to guide our actions. He continually teaches these rules and consequences and grants us the freedom to make our choices. He then judges our actions against those rules and allows the consequences to take their course. For example, He said to the Nephites, "Whosoever breaketh this commandment suffereth himself to be led into temptation" (3 Nephi 18:25, emphasis added). When we choose to break His rules, we are choosing to bear the consequences.

Following the triumphal entry into Jerusalem, Jesus taught, "He that rejecteth me, and receiveth not my words, hath one that judgeth him: the word that I have spoken, the same shall judge him in the last day" (John 12:48, emphasis added). He judges us against the rules He sets. When we choose the wrong path, the predetermined consequences are then in force. However, if those unpleasant consequences lead us to change our beliefs and actions, then He stands ready to plead for mercy on our behalf. All leaders, including parents, will find this pattern also works in their sphere of influence. It removes conflicts between them and others and keeps the conflicts where they belong— between the individual and the rules and consequences.

When Joseph Smith was given ancient plates to translate, he was given specific instructions concerning their safekeeping. Tragically, mistakes were made and a portion of that record was lost. As a result, Joseph had to bear painful consequences according to a just God. However, in God's mercy, Joseph regained his opportunity after he repented. "But remember, God is merciful; therefore, repent of that which thou hast done which is contrary to the commandment which I gave you, and thou art still chosen, and art again called to the work" (D&C 3:10).

Joseph was chastened for the mistake, but he was not cast off forever. Yes, the mistake was serious and the repentance process painful, but the price was paid, the lesson learned, and the Prophet Joseph grew. As a result, he became a more just and merciful leader himself.

Being just and merciful goes beyond rules, consequences, and forgiveness. It also includes an element of compassion towards others. Part of the definition of mercy is "compassionate treatment of those in distress." In the parable of the great supper, Jesus taught that if we show mercy to those in need, then He will repay. "But when thou makest a feast, call the poor, the maimed, the lame, the blind: And thou shalt be blessed; for they cannot recompense thee: for thou shalt be recompensed at the resurrection of the just" (Luke 14:13–14).

Leaders who apply this parable will find opportunities to bless those who bless others. As they do, they create a culture for their people to replace pride and envy with mercy and love.

William Shakespeare used his writings masterfully to convey the virtue of mercy. Using the character of Portia in The Merchant of Venice, Shakespeare explains the divine relationship between justice and mercy.

> The quality of mercy is not strain'd,
> It droppeth as the gentle rain from heaven
> Upon the place beneath: it is twice blest;
> It blesseth him that gives and him that takes:
> 'Tis mightiest in the mightiest: it becomes
> The throned monarch better than his crown;

His sceptre shows the force of temporal power,
The attribute to awe and majesty,
Wherein doth sit the dread and fear of kings;
But mercy is above this sceptred sway;
It is enthroned in the hearts of kings,
It is an attribute to God himself;
And earthly power doth then show likest God's
When mercy seasons justice.[1]

Wise leaders who lead as Jesus leads allow mercy to "season justice." Although mercy cannot rob justice, it can soften its influence in appropriate circumstances.

Examples of Righteous Leaders

During the summer of 1834, the Prophet Joseph gathered a group of men to march to Jackson County Missouri to help restore the Saints' land from which they were driven by mobs. Parley P. Pratt was assigned to gather men, money, and supplies for this effort known as Zion's Camp. As they marched on their thousand–mile journey to Missouri, Parley traveled to many communities along the way, gathering whatever support he could. During those months away from home, his wife was very ill and incurred significant debt for her care. When Zion's Camp disbanded, Parley returned home and began working to pay the debt and take care of his family.

Parley began preaching in the vicinity surrounding his home until he received letters from W. W. Phelps censuring him for having that debt. Phelps was acting as President of the Church in Missouri and suspended Parley's authority to preach. He told Parley his conduct of incurring debt "was not the way of the pure in heart." Parley responded by making a written defense of his actions and in February 1935, he traveled 50 miles to Kirtland to meet with Joseph. Parley explained to Joseph, "I had once offered the money on the same, but the person to whom it was due, in view of my public services, refused to take it."

After Parley pleaded "the injustice of the accusation," Joseph stood and said, "Brother Parley, God bless you, go your way rejoicing, preach the gospel, fill the measure of your mission, and walk such things under your feet; it was a trick of Satan to hinder your usefulness; God Almighty shall be with you, and nothing shall stay your hand." In response to Joseph's balance between justice and mercy, Parley recorded, "I was comforted, encouraged, filled with new life, thanking God that there was one noble spirit on the earth who could discern justice and equity, appreciate the labors of others, and had boldness of soul to judge and act accordingly." Not only did Joseph release the oppressive bands that confined Parley, but within two weeks, Joseph called and ordained Parley as an Apostle. With such a calling, Parley's voice was raised in preaching the gospel of Christ wherever he traveled for the remainder of his days—all because his leader wisely balanced justice and mercy.

Summary of Examples

- Honorable leaders set rules and consequences, then judge actions against those rules, as Jesus does.
- Honorable leaders set consequences to reform rather than destroy a person, as demonstrated by Jesus when Joseph Smith lost a portion of the translated records.
- Honorable leaders show mercy, as Jesus does to those who have a change of heart.
- Honorable leaders reward those who are merciful and compassionate toward others, as taught by Jesus of those who invite to the feast "the poor, the maimed, the lame, the blind" (Luke 14:13–14).
- Honorable leaders weigh facts accurately and with a desire to bless lives, as demonstrated by Joseph Smith regarding Parley P. Pratt.

Questions for Personal Reflection

- Do you apply justice and mercy to yourself?
- How well do you keep justice and mercy in balance?

- When you encounter a situation which leads you to make a judgment, is your first inclination to seek justice or to render mercy?
- When a person makes a mistake, is your objective to punish them or reform them?
- Are you compassionate towards those in distress even if the distress is self–inflicted?
- If an associate has broken established rules, do you help them find a way to escape punishment? Or, do you help them own up to their actions and pay the required price?

Attribute 65: Judges Righteously

Judge: *To form an opinion through the careful weighing of evidence and testing of premises.*

Jesus has established a straightforward pattern for judging righteously. He first sets clear rules and then judges actions against those rules. This pattern requires the rules to be recorded accurately and completely. Jesus then judges with wisdom, justice, and mercy based on those rules. He taught this pattern to Nephi when He said: "For I command all men, both in the east and in the west, and in the north, and in the south, and in the islands of the sea, that they shall write the words which I speak unto them; *for out of the books which shall be written I will judge the world,* every man according to their works, according to that which is written" (2 Nephi 29:11, emphasis added).

Jesus taught this pattern later to the newly called Nephite Apostles. He explained: "And behold, all things are written by the Father; therefore *out of the books* which shall be written shall the world be judged. And know ye that ye shall be judges of this people, according to the judgment which I shall give unto you, which shall be just. Therefore, what manner of men ought ye to be? Verily I say unto you, even as I am" (3 Nephi 27:26–27, emphasis added).

At the conclusion of the Sermon on the Mount, Jesus told His disciples, "Judge not, that ye be not judged" (Matthew 7:1). The Prophet Joseph Smith added this clarification, "Judge not *unrighteously,* that ye be not judged; *but judge righteous judgment"* (Joseph Smith Translation, Matthew 7:1–2).

To judge righteously, we must endeavor to discern the truth rather than rely solely on what has been reported or what is first apparent. Discernment is an ability that can be developed through effort and experience and should be aided by the whisperings of the Holy Ghost. The clearer we understand the truth of a situation or a person, the better we are able to make a righteous judgment. In addition to discernment, the Savior has given the following principles to guide our judgment:

1. **Things are not always as they appear.** Jesus taught, "Judge not according to the appearance" (John 7:24).

2. **Judge against established rules.** Jesus taught, *"the word that I have spoken, the same shall judge him* in the last day" (John 12:48, emphasis added).

3. **Do not rely on your personal desires but rely on what is right.** Jesus explained, "I can of mine own self do nothing: as I hear, I judge: and *my judgment is just; because I seek not mine own will,* but the will of the Father which hath sent me" (John 5:30, emphasis added).

4. **Plead to prevent wrong choices.** The prophet Isaiah indicates that pleading to prevent wrong choices is as important as judging with righteousness. He taught, "The Lord standeth up to *plead,* and standeth to judge the people" (2 Nephi 13:13).

5. **Judge with wisdom, understanding, knowledge, righteousness, and reprove with equity.** Again, Isaiah teaches us about the judgments of Jesus when he said:

> "And there shall come forth a rod out of the stem of Jesse, and a branch shall grow out of his roots.
>
> "And the Spirit of the Lord shall rest upon him, the spirit of *wisdom* and *understanding,* the spirit of counsel and might, the spirit of *knowledge* and of the fear of the Lord;
>
> "And shall make him of quick understanding in the fear of the Lord; and he shall not judge after the sight of his eyes, neither reprove after the hearing of his ears.
>
> "But with *righteousness shall he judge* the poor, and *reprove with equity* for the meek of the earth; and he shall smite the earth with the rod of his mouth, and with the breath of his lips shall he slay the wicked.
>
> "And righteousness shall be the girdle of his loins, and faithfulness the girdle of his reins" (2 Nephi 21:1–5, emphasis added).

These five principles are the foundation upon which leaders can judge as Jesus does. If they judge wisely and righteously they can be a blessing in many lives. However, judging the Savior's way takes effort. Making a quick decision is easy, making the right decision is harder. It requires study, observation, and deliberation. It requires setting aside your own wishes and drawing upon all the wisdom and knowledge available.

When leaders judge in righteousness, they can protect their people from bad influences that weaken their ability to progress. In Proverbs we learn that "A king that sitteth in the throne of judgment scattereth away all evil with his eyes" (Proverbs 20:8). If a leader can judge righteously and keep constant watch, he or she can do much to keep pride, resentment, mischief, retaliation, posturing, intrigue, or any other evil from derailing the efforts their people.

Examples of Righteous Leaders

Alma had a great desire to judge righteously but felt he lacked the wisdom when faced with a significant need early in his ministry. Soon after he established the church in Zarahemla, many members of the Church were led into sin by unbelievers. These unbelievers were brought before Alma to be judged, but Alma referred them to King Mosiah who referred them back to Alma. "Now the spirit of Alma was again troubled; and he went and inquired of the Lord what he should do concerning this matter, for he feared that he should do wrong in the sight of God. And it came to pass that after he had poured out his whole soul to God, the voice of the Lord came to him" (Mosiah 26:13–14).

The Lord then gave Alma great insight and instructions for judging his people. Alma valued this divine direction so much that he wrote it down to guide all his future decisions. "And it came to pass when Alma had heard these words he wrote them down that he might have them, and that he might judge the people of that church according to the commandments of God" (Mosiah 26:33). Alma now had the guidelines needed to judge righteously, but he received them only after much effort. His earnest seeking for wisdom enabled his judgments to bless many lives.

Summary of Examples

- Honorable leaders base their judgment on the following principles established by Jesus:
    1. Things are not always as they appear.
    2. Judge against established rules.
    3. Do not rely on your personal desires but rely on what is right.
    4. Plead to prevent wrong choices.
    5. Judge with wisdom, understanding, knowledge, and righteousness, and reprove with equity.
- Honorable leaders judge based on specific standards established in advance, as taught by Jesus who judges based on the words He has given. Alma also demonstrated this when he obtained the standards by which he should judge.

Questions for Personal Reflection

- Do you judge with consistency, fairness, compassion, justice, and mercy?
- Do you keep alert to the possibility that you are being misled, either intentionally or not?
- When forming an opinion, how much effort do you spend in gathering information by personal association and from trusted sources?
- When tempted to judge another person, can you remember that things are not always as they appear?
- When judging, do you seek to bless lives rather than destroy them?

Attribute 66: Disciplines with Kindness

Discipline: *Training that corrects, molds, or perfects the mental faculties or moral character.*

In order for Jesus to "draw all men unto [him]" (John 12:32), He needs to correct those who have separated themselves from Him through disobedience. The scriptures give many examples of how He corrects all people regardless of their standing among other men. They record that He corrected and disciplined prophets and kings, as well as ordinary people. For example, He forbade Moses from entering the promised land because of a mistake. Moses had struck a rock to provide water miraculously for the people, but Moses did not acknowledge the source by which the miracle occurred. It would be easy to think that Moses should earn a pass on this mistake because of all He had done to serve the Lord. Entering the promised land would have been the culminating experience after more than four decades of service. However, Jesus was more interested in developing Moses for more glorious rewards through eternity, "For whom the Lord loveth he correcteth; even as a father the son *in whom* he delighteth" (Proverbs 3:12).

King Saul once ruled with God's favor over Israel and did much good for the people, but when he turned from the Lord, he was disciplined by the Him. The prophet Samuel said to Saul, "Thou hast rejected the word of the Lord, and the Lord hath rejected thee from being king over Israel" (1 Samuel 15:26). Samuel continued, "The Lord hath rent the kingdom of Israel from thee this day, and hath given it to a neighbour of thine, *that is* better than thou" (1 Samuel 15:28).

David replaced Saul as king and reigned over all Israel during the height of its glory. He, like Saul, did much good for the kingdom but was disciplined for committing adultery with Bathsheba and the connected sin of causing the death of her husband Uriah (2 Samuel 11:3–27). The Lord declared, "Therefore he hath fallen from his exaltation, and received his portion; and he shall not inherit them out of the world, for I gave them unto another, saith the Lord" (D&C 132:39).

Later, as all Israel came under condemnation for their sins and were scattered among nations, the Lord told them "I am with thee . . . to save thee . . . but I will correct thee in measure" (Jeremiah 30:11). In this very specific language, the Lord taught that measured correction is to save the sinner and is done under the attentive direction of the leader. Then after the needed correction occured, the Lord assured Israel "I will restore" (Jeremiah 30:17) and "Again I will build thee" (Jeremiah 31:4). Part of the restoring and building process is instructing those who have repented. The Lord said:

"I have surely heard Ephraim bemoaning himself *thus*; Thou hast chastised me, and I was chastised, as a bullock unaccustomed to the *yoke*: turn thou me, and I shall be turned; for thou art the Lord my God.

"Surely after that I was turned, I repented; and after that I was instructed.

"Is Ephraim my dear son? *Is he* a pleasant child? For since I spake against him, I do earnestly remember him still (Jeremiah" 31:18–20).

This is the Lord's way of disciplining: to correct, restore, build again, and instruct. In addition, He taught that disciplining or chastening should be done with love for proper growth to occur. He said: "Verily, thus saith the Lord unto you whom I *love*, and whom I *love* I also chasten that their sins may be forgiven, for with the chastisement I prepare a way for their deliverance in all things out of temptation, and I have *loved* you" (D&C 95:1, emphasis added). In this one single sentence where Jesus talked about chastening, He used the word "love" three times. Clearly, He was teaching as much about *how to chasten* as He was the *need for chastening.*

The Savior continued this theme when He instructed His elders on the proper use of priesthood power. He said: "No power or influence can or ought to be maintained by virtue of the priesthood, only by persuasion, by long–suffering, by gentleness and meekness, and by love unfeigned; By kindness . . . and without guile, Reproving betimes with sharpness, when moved upon by the Holy Ghost; and then showing forth afterwards an increase of love toward him whom thou hast reproved, lest he esteem thee to be his enemy" (D&C 121:41–43).

If a leader provides correction in a hostile way and creates an enemy, he or she has weakened the ability to provide influence in the future. Then, the only thing accomplished was the venting of anger rather than improving behavior. A sincere expression of love can make all the difference.

In the story of Peter walking on water, Jesus showed how to correct with kindness at a time when Peter came up short. Despite his shortcoming, how could Jesus feel anything but love and compassion for Peter? When Peter saw Jesus walking on the water toward his ship, Peter asked if he could come to Him. Following the Savior's invitation, Peter slipped over the side of the ship and walked on the water towards his Master. To begin with, his faith was strong enough, "But when he saw the wind boisterous, he was afraid; and beginning to sink, he cried, saying, Lord, save me. And immediately Jesus stretched forth *his* hand, and caught him, and said unto him, O thou of little faith, wherefore didst thou doubt?" (Matthew 14:30–31). Peter had fallen short because he doubted, but the Savior's gentle rebuke must have been offered with all the kindness and love possible.

Later in the Garden of Gethsemane, Peter again received kind chastening. It came after the Savior repeatedly asked the Apostles to watch while He prayed. He said to Peter and his fellow Apostles, James and John, "Could ye not watch with me one hour?" (Matthew 26:40). Jesus said, in a spirit of understanding, "The spirit indeed *is* willing, but the flesh *is* weak" (Matthew 26:41). After the third time the Apostles fell asleep, Jesus simply said, "Sleep on now, and take *your* rest" (Matthew 26:45). Even though Peter, James, and John didn't do as He asked, and even though He chastened them, Jesus still showed kindness and understanding towards them.

Following the Savior's suffering in Gethsemane, Peter was again chastened as he attempted to defend his Master with his sword. Jesus must have viewed Peter's actions as an expression of his love, but again there was a lesson to be taught, and it was taught in kindness. "And, behold, one of them which were with Jesus stretched out *his* hand, and drew his sword, and struck a servant of the high priest's, and smote off his ear. Then said Jesus unto him, Put up again thy sword into his place: for all they that take the sword shall perish with the sword.

Thinkest thou that I cannot now pray to my Father, and he shall presently give me more than twelve legions of angels? But how then shall the scriptures be fulfilled, that thus it must be?" (Matthew 26:51–54).

Any leader would be pleased with such a noble heart as Peter demonstrated, but Jesus needed to correct Him. He needed to help Peter understand that He had come to atone for the sins of man, and as such, His mission must be allowed to proceed.

Examples of Righteous Leaders

The brother of Jared was one of the most righteous men in the scriptures. His family continually asked him to pray on their behalf because of his ability to commune with God. Yet at one point, he went four years without praying and was chastened for this sin. "And it came to pass at the end of four years that the Lord came again unto the brother of Jared, and stood in a cloud and talked with him. And for the space of three hours did the Lord talk with the brother of Jared, and chastened him because he remembered not to call upon the name of the Lord" (Ether 2:14).

After this chastening, "the brother of Jared repented of the evil which he had done, and did call upon the name of the Lord for his brethren who were with him. And the Lord said unto him: I will forgive thee" (Ether 2:15). It is interesting to note what happened next. After having gone through this correcting process, the brother of Jared was now more wise and experienced. This allowed the Lord to reveal things greater than had been revealed to any other prophet (see Ether 3:15–25). The Lord did not cast him out, as some leaders do following a mistake, but lifted him up instead.

One of the great accounts of Jesus disciplining with kindness occurs on the American continent after His death. He caused many cities to be destroyed along with their wicked inhabitants, yet with compassion, He ministered unto those who remained. When Jesus appeared to those gathered at the temple in the land Bountiful, He was "troubled" by the wickedness, yet He pleaded to the Father in their behalf.

"And it came to pass that when they had knelt upon the ground, Jesus groaned within himself, and said: Father, I am troubled because of the wickedness of the people of the house of Israel.

"And when he had said these words, he himself also knelt upon the earth; and behold he prayed unto the Father, and the things which he prayed cannot be written, and the multitude did bear record who heard him.

"And after this manner do they bear record: The eye hath never seen, neither hath the ear heard, before, so great and marvelous things as we saw and heard Jesus speak unto the Father;

"And no tongue can speak, neither can there be written by any man, neither can the hearts of men conceive so great and marvelous things as we both saw and heard Jesus speak; and no one can conceive of the joy which filled our souls at the time we heard him pray for us unto the Father" (3 Nephi 17:14–17).

Those who heard Him said His voice "was not a harsh voice, neither was it a loud voice; nevertheless, and notwithstanding it being a small voice it did pierce them that did hear to the center" (3 Nephi 11:3). Later, the voice was described as "not a voice of thunder, neither was it a voice of a great tumultuous noise, but behold, it was a still voice of perfect mildness, as if it had been a whisper, and it did pierce even to the very soul" (Helaman 5:30). It was the voice of a leader chastening His people, but the tone of perfect love changed their hearts and their descendant's hearts for the next two hundred years.

In the fall of 1830, the Prophet Joseph Smith had occasion to correct a Church member who was having a negative influence on the Church. This member, Hiram Page, had found a stone that he felt brought him revelations "concerning the upbuilding of Zion and the order of the Church" (D&C 28 section heading). Joseph prayed for guidance and was told by the Lord how to correct Hiram in the proper manner. He was told, "thou shalt take thy brother, Hiram Page, *between him and thee alone,* and tell him that those things which he hath written from that stone are not of me and that Satan deceiveth him" (D&C 28:11, emphasis added). Out of kindness toward Hiram, the Savior told Joseph to correct him in private but to be specific about his mistake so that he could learn what he had done was wrong. This is what the Apostle Paul meant when he said, "speaking the truth in love" (Ephesians 4:15) or as the Savior said, "speak the truth in soberness" (D&C 18:21).

Jesus showed this same kindness toward Oliver Cowdery as He withdrew his ability to translate. The Savor said, "And, behold, it is because that you did not continue as you commenced, when you began to translate, that I have taken away this privilege from you. *Do not murmur, my son,* for it is wisdom in me that I have dealt with you after this manner. Behold, you have not understood" (D&C 9:5-7, emphasis added). The Master Teacher is always teaching.

The Savior also corrected David Whitmer with very specific detail. He said: "Behold, I say unto you, David, that you have feared man and have not relied on me for strength as you ought. But your mind has been on the things of the earth more than on the things of me, your Maker, and the ministry whereunto you have been called; and you have not given heed unto my Spirit, and to those who were set over you, but have been persuaded by those whom I have not commanded" (D&C 30:1-2). There is no hint of unkindness in either the tone or content of the Savior's instruction. He simply and succinctly taught David what he had done wrong so he could correct it and move forward.

The scriptures show that Jesus corrected in a variety of circumstances, not just the severe ones mentioned above, but for lesser ones as well.

- Regarding doubting Thomas, "Jesus saith unto him, Thomas, because thou hast seen me, thou hast believed: blessed *are* they that have not seen, and *yet* have believed" (John 20:29).
- Regarding Heman Basset, He said, "In consequence of transgression, let that which was bestowed upon Heman Basset be taken from him, and placed upon the head of Simonds Ryder" (D&C 52:37).
- Regarding Ziba Peterson, He said, "Let that which has been bestowed upon Ziba Peterson be taken from him; and let him stand as a member in the church, and labor with his own hands, with the brethren, until he is sufficiently chastened for all his sins;

for he confesseth them not, and he thinketh to hide them" (D&C 58:60).

- Regarding Martin Harris, He said, "Let him repent of his sins, for he seeketh the praise of the world" D&C (58:39).
- Regarding W. W. Phelps, "I, the Lord, am not well pleased with him, for he seeketh to excel, and he is not sufficiently meek before me" (D&C 58:41).
- Regarding Edward Partridge, "But if he repent not of his sins, which are unbelief and blindness of heart, let him take heed lest he fall" (D&C 58:15).
- Even regarding Joseph Smith, the Lord said, "Thou art not excusable in thy transgressions; nevertheless, go thy way and sin no more" (D&C 24:2).

In each of these cases, Jesus acts to correct, to redirect, to refocus, and retrain those who have strayed. He did this to draw all men unto Him that they may have a place in the mansions He prepared for them.

Summary of Examples

- Honorable leaders make corrections out of love for their people and in a spirit of love, as demonstrated by Jesus. "For whom the LORD loveth he correcteth" (Proverbs 3:12).
- Each person, regardless of his standing, needs someone to correct him, as Jesus did with Moses, Joseph Smith, and many others.
- Honorable leaders ensure that consequences from mistakes are appropriate for the level of the mistake, as demonstrated by Jesus in dealing with Moses and Joseph Smith differently than Saul and David.
- Chastening should be done in love and because of love, as Jesus taught the leaders of the restored Church.
- Honorable leaders continue to show kindness after the chastening, as demonstrated by Jesus with His Apostles in Gethsemane.
- Chastening should be done to teach and reform, as Jesus did

with Oliver Cowdery who had not continued as he commenced, and the brother of Jared who had not prayed for four years.

- Chastening should be done in a voice of perfect mildness, as demonstrated by Jesus with the Nephites in Bountiful.
- Correcting should be done in private, as Joseph did with Hiram Page.
- Some leaders may need to be removed from their positions because of their mistakes, as was Saul, David, Heman Bassett, Ziba Peterson, and others.

Questions for Personal Reflection

- Is there an element of your discipline that is simply a release of your anger or resulting from your embarrassment?
- When you correct someone, is your voice and demeanor one of perfect mildness yet accurate in explaining the shortcoming?
- Do you discipline others to demonstrate your authority, or are you motivated by love and a sincere desire to improve behavior?
- How well have you set rules and consequences and communicated them to those you lead?
- Can you allow those whom you have corrected to rise again, even to a more esteemed standing than before the correction?
- If you are disciplined by another person, can you view it as a means to correct your character rather than a punishment?
- If you are disciplined by someone who is misguided in his or her approach, can you overlook their weakness and focus only on what you need to do to improve?

Attribute 67: Forgives

Forgive: *Stop feeling angry or resentful toward someone for an offense, flaw, or mistake.*

Some people may feel it is odd for forgiveness to be a leadership attribute, but it may be one of the most important. Forgiveness gives people a chance to move forward and incorporate in their future the lessons learned from their past. Forgiveness by a leader can engender feelings of trust and respect for that leader and can foster a love that will lead to more earnest performance and compliance.

Before the Savior's Crucifixion, Peter thrice denied his Lord. Yet, Jesus forgave him. More than that, He still made Peter the leader of His Church and used him in the restoration of the gospel in the latter days (Luke 22:34–62). Jesus forgave the soldiers who were assigned to crucify Him. "Then said Jesus, Father, forgive them; for they know not what they do" (Luke 23:34). He forgave Moses for striking a rock and making water flow without acknowledging the source from whence the miracle came. Moses was kept from leading Israel into the promised land, but he was restored to good standing and allowed to serve at the Mount of Transfiguration and play a role in the restoration of the gospel. Jesus forgave Alma. Despite Alma's many sins early in his life, Jesus changed the course of his life and used him to establish His Church (Alma 36:14–21).

The Savior forgave the Prophet Joseph Smith for losing the first 116 pages of the Book of Mormon. Although Joseph *"reluctantly* allowed these pages to pass from his custody to that of Martin Harris,"[2] but their loss was attributed to Joseph. He was the one who had been "entrusted" (D&C 3:5) with the record and was, therefore, disciplined. He lost his ability to translate for a season, but the Savior, ever the mentor, fashioned the punishment to the mistake. Soon, He restored Joseph's ability to translate and continued to use him in the work of the Restoration (D&C 3:10).

Examples of Righteous Leaders

Sibling rivalries can be vicious and often tear families apart for generations. Had Joseph of old not forgiven his brothers who put him

362

in a pit and then sold him into Egypt, his family would have perished in the famine. Joseph did forgive them, however, and he was the means for restoring peace and prosperity to his family and to Egypt.

In another land and another time, one man who forgave another also saved a nation. This example comes from a time of terrible conflict between the Nephites and Lamanites. Adversity can sometimes bring out the worst in people, but in this example, it revealed the greatness of character of the Nephites' two top leaders, Pahoran and Moroni. In this account, Moroni, who was the commander of all the Nephite armies, wrote a stinging rebuke to Pahoran, the chief judge and governor. In that rebuke, Moroni accused him of failing to do his part to support the Nephite armies with the men and supplies necessary to defeat the Lamanites.

Regarding this rebuke, Elder David A. Bednar said, "Pahoran might easily have resented Moroni and his message, but he chose not to take offense. Pahoran responded compassionately and described a rebellion against the government about which Moroni was not aware. And then he responded, 'Behold, I say unto you, Moroni, that I do not joy in your great afflictions, yea, it grieves my soul. . . . And now, in your epistle you have censured me, but it mattereth not; I am not angry, but do rejoice in the greatness of your heart'" (Alma 61:2, 9).[3]

A leader who can respond as Pahoran responded manifests his greatness while promoting greatness, nobility, and confidence in the hearts of the people. Pahoran quickly forgave Moroni, who acted boldly but with incomplete information. When Moroni learned he had misjudged Pahoran, he repented by taking his armies to Pahoran's defense. Had these two leaders not forgiven each other and instead taken offense, they likely would have led the entire Nephite nation to its destruction.

Both of these examples were well known to the Prophet Joseph Smith. He was named after the Joseph in the first example, and he translated the account from an ancient text in the second example. Undoubtedly, these examples guided him in his great need to forgive others. One such example occurred in the life of W. W. Phelps, who had been a close friend and associate. During a period of great tribulation, he turned against the Prophet and contributed to his imprisonment in the Liberty Jail. When W. W. Phelps regained his bearings and sought forgiveness, he sent a letter to Joseph on June 29, 1840:

"I have seen the folly of my way, and I tremble at the gulf I have passed. . . . I will repent and live, and ask my old brethren to forgive me, and though they chasten me to death, yet I will die with them, for their God is my God. The least place with them is enough for me, yea, it is bigger and better than all Babylon. . . .

"I have done wrong and I am sorry. . . . I have not walked along with my friends according to my holy anointing. I ask forgiveness in the name of Jesus Christ of all the Saints, for I will do right, God helping me. I want your fellowship; if you cannot grant that, grant me your peace and friendship, for we are brethren, and our communion used to be sweet."

The Prophet Joseph replied:

"It is true, that we have suffered much in consequence of your behavior—the cup of gall, already full enough . . . was indeed filled to overflowing when you turned against us. One with whom we had oft taken sweet counsel together, and enjoyed many refreshing seasons from the Lord— 'Had it been an enemy, we could have borne it.'

"However, the cup has been drunk, the will of our Father has been done, and we are yet alive. . . . And having been delivered from the hands of wicked men by the mercy of our God, we say it is your privilege to be delivered from the powers of the adversary . . . and again take your stand among the Saints of the Most High, and by diligence, humility, and love unfeigned, commend yourself to our God, and your God, and to the Church of Jesus Christ.

"Believing your confession to be real, and your repentance genuine, I shall be happy once again to give you the right hand of fellowship, and rejoice over the returning prodigal. . . .

"Come on, dear brother, since the war is past,
For friends at first, are friends again at last.
Yours as ever, Joseph Smith, Jun."[4]

By demonstrating forgiveness, Joseph Smith helped restore peace in a Church fractured by persecution by demonstrating forgiveness. A reminder of his forgiveness lives on today as Saints often sing the tribute W. W. Phelps wrote of the man who had forgiven him. That tribute begins with these words:

> Praise to the man who communed with Jehovah!
> Jesus anointed that Prophet and Seer.
> Blessed to open the last dispensation,
> Kings shall extol him, and nations revere.
>
> Great is his glory and endless his priesthood.
> Ever and ever the keys he will hold.
> Faithful and true, he will enter his kingdom,
> Crowned in the midst of the prophets of old.[5]

Forgiveness is the power of leadership in action. It is a power to change lives, to unify a people, and to lead them through difficulties to arrive safely on peaceful shores. Forgiveness is a power to remove obstacles that hold people and organizations back from achieving their full potential. Forgiveness is a power to heal, to nurture, and to grow tender young trees into something that produces wonderful fruit.

Summary of Examples

- Honorable leaders forgive their own leaders, as Joseph of old did with his elder brothers.
- Honorable leaders fashion consequences to fit the mistake, as Jesus did with Joseph Smith following the loss of the 116 pages of manuscript.
- Honorable leaders restore opportunities when forgiveness is given, as Jesus did with Joseph Smith by returning the gift to translate.
- Honorable leaders can defuse tension by forgiving, by staying calm, and by not taking offense, as Pahoran did in response to Moroni's scorching letter.
- Honorable leaders forgive, even when they have been severely

harmed, as Joseph did with W. W. Phelps who had contributed to his persecution and imprisonment.

Questions for Personal Reflection

- Who do you need to forgive today?
- Have you felt the damaging effects of lingering resentfulness towards someone you have not forgiven?
- Can you truly let go of resentful feelings toward someone who has offended or abused you regardless of their level of repentance?
- Can you resist the urge to remind a person of his or her former mistakes?
- Have you noticed that love and loyalty toward you can grow from one whom you have forgiven?

Attribute 68: Looks on the Heart

Heart: One's innermost character, feelings, or inclinations.

During the feast of the tabernacles, Jesus taught, "Judge not according to the appearance, but judge righteous judgment" (John 7:24). It is so difficult for man to judge other people accurately because the outward persona often masks true personality and character. We can learn a little through observation, but a deeper understanding comes over time through close association during many varied circumstances. In the Old Testament, the Lord taught this same truth to Samuel: "But the Lord said unto Samuel, Look not on his countenance, or on the height of his stature; because I have refused him: for the Lord seeth not as man seeth; for man looketh on the outward appearance, but the Lord looketh on the heart" (1 Samuel 16:7, emphasis added).

A leader who understands the heart of a person such as an employee, client, family member, patient, or competitor will better understand how to influence him or her. This understanding takes time to develop because personas are effective camouflages. However, a perceptive leader who diligently seeks for understanding will soon find it.

In the parable of the Pharisee and the Publican, one of the truths the Savior teaches is that the heart of a man is not readily apparent. In this parable, two men go to the temple to pray. The Pharisee appears to be the righteous one, but his private prayer reveals his prideful heart. By contrast, the publican normally would be viewed as a prideful tax collector, but his private prayer reveals humility when he pleads, "God be merciful to me a sinner" (Luke 18:13). Jesus can see past the persona. Wise leaders can learn to do so as well.

In the parable of the mustard seed, Jesus compares "the least of all seeds" (Matthew 13:32) to the kingdom of heaven. He taught that His kingdom may appear small at present but will eventually grow as the mustard seed to become "the greatest among herbs" (Matthew 13:32). Here again, multiple truths can be taught by one simple parable. One truth is that great things can come from unlikely sources. As it is with mustard seeds, so it is with each child of God. A wise leader will see great potential in each person even if that potential is obscured. For as Isaiah said, "He shall not judge after the sight of his eyes, neither reprove after the hearing of his ears" (Isaiah 11:3). Jesus will look on a person's heart, see his or her innermost feelings, character, and inclinations, and lead them accordingly.

Examples of Righteous Leaders

It is not unusual for multiple attributes to be demonstrated from one example. As such, there is value in continuing the examination of Parley P. Pratt who was censured by W. W. Phelps. This example demonstrates how Joseph Smith was "Just and Merciful" (see attribute #65) as he considered Parley's defense. In addition, we see Joseph's ability to look at Parley's heart to better understand his intentions that influenced his actions.

During the summer of 1834, the Prophet Joseph gathered a group of men to march to Jackson County Missouri to help restore the Saints' land from which they were driven by mobs. Parley P. Pratt was assigned to gather men, money, and supplies for this effort known as Zion's Camp. As they marched on their thousand-mile journey to Missouri, Parley traveled to many communities along the way, gathering whatever support he could. During those months away from home, his wife was very ill and incurred significant debt for her care. When Zion's Camp disbanded, Parley returned home and began working to pay the debt and take care of his family.

Parley began preaching in the vicinity surrounding his home until he received letters from W. W. Phelps censuring him for having that debt. Phelps was acting as President of the Church in Missouri and suspended Parley's authority to preach. He told Parley his conduct of incurring debt "was not the way of the pure in heart." Parley responded by making a written defense of his actions and in February 1935, he traveled 50 miles to Kirtland to meet with Joseph. Parley explained to Joseph, "I had once offered the money on the same, but the person to whom it was due, in view of my public services, refused to take it."

368

After Parley pleaded "the injustice of the accusation," Joseph stood and said, "Brother Parley, God bless you, go your way rejoicing, preach the gospel, fill the measure of your mission, and walk such things under your feet; it was a trick of Satan to hinder your usefulness; God Almighty shall be with you, and nothing shall stay your hand." In response to Joseph's balance between justice and mercy, Parley recorded, "I was comforted, encouraged, filled with new life, thanking God that there was one noble spirit on the earth who could discern justice and equity, appreciate the labors of others, and had boldness of soul to judge and act accordingly." This discernment came from looking at Parley's heart to understand his motives, and in doing so, this leader helped his follower become better and do better by judging him righteously.

Summary of Examples

- Honorable leaders judge by looking at a person's heart, desires, opinions, and feelings—all of which are often disguised behind well–crafted personas, as taught by the parable of the Pharisee and the Publican.
- Honorable leaders know that great things come from unlikely sources, as taught by the parable of the mustard seed.
- Honorable leaders consider a person's intent and desires when judging his or her actions, as demonstrated by Joseph Smith regarding Parley P. Pratt.

Questions for Personal Reflection

- Are you creating an environment where people are free to let their guard down and express their personal feelings?
- Do you try to understand the heart of other people as well as you understand the heart of your children?
- How often do you consider the desires of a person when making decisions that affect them?
- If someone acts unusual, do you get offended or do you try to understand the root cause of his or her actions?

- Do you keep in mind that it takes time and effort to break through a person's persona to begin to understand his or her heart, hopes, and preferences?
- As you go throughout your day and encounter many people, do you study them by trying to understand why they do what they do, or what led them to be who they are?

---

1. *The Merchant of Venice*, Act-IV, Scene-I, Lines 173-186.
2. Doctrine and Covenants 3, section heading; emphasis added.
3. David A. Bednar, "And Nothing Shall Offend Them," *Ensign*, November 2006.
4. James E. Faust, "The Weightier Matters of the Law: Judgment, Mercy, and Faith," *Ensign*, November 1997; emphasis added.
5. "Praise to the Man," *Hymns* (1985), no. 7.

CHAPTER 13

HE HONORS RELATIONSHIPS

Attribute 69: Obedient

Obedient: *Submissive to the restraint of command or authority.*

Obedience is a theme that is woven throughout the Savior's ministry. The Apostle Paul said of Jesus, "Though he were a Son, yet learned he obedience by the things which he suffered" (Hebrews 5:8). One thing Jesus suffered was for His will to be "swallowed up in the will of the Father" (Mosiah 15:7). He declared, "I am Jesus Christ; I came by the will of the Father, and I do his will" (D&C 19:24). While speaking at the temple in the land of Bountiful, Jesus said, "I came into the world to do the will of my Father, because my Father sent me" (3 Nephi 27:13).

One Sabbath day in Judea, Jesus went to the pool of Bethesda and healed an infirm man. Many accused Him of healing on the Sabbath, but Jesus responded by saying, "My Father worketh hitherto, and I work" (John 5:17). He further explained that "The Son can do nothing of himself, but what he seeth the Father do: for what things soever he doeth, these also doeth the Son likewise" (John 5:19). All that Jesus did, and now does, is done by obedience to His leader. It is done consistently with the pattern and directions He has been given.

When speaking to the righteous in Bountiful, Jesus showed obedience to His leader. That obedience demonstrated personal restraint. He said, "This is the land of your inheritance; and the Father hath given it unto you. And not at any time hath the Father given me commandment that I should tell it unto your brethren at Jerusalem. Neither at any time hath the Father given me commandment that I should tell unto them concerning the other tribes of the house of Israel, whom the Father hath lead away out of the land. This much did the Father command me, that I should tell unto them, That other sheep I have which are not of this fold" (3 Nephi 15:13–17).

Jesus told those in attendance only what His leader would have Him say. He did not divulge more than the Father permitted. Jesus then followed by saying, "I was commanded to say no more of the Father concerning this thing unto them" (3 Nephi 15:18). Speaking to the Jews shortly before the Crucifixion, Jesus taught, "For I have not spoken of myself; but the Father which sent me, he gave me a commandment, what I should say, and what I should speak" (John 12:49).

When approached by those who came to take Jesus while in Gethsemane, Peter drew his sword "and smote the high priest's servant and cut off his right ear" (John 18:10). "Then said Jesus unto Peter, Put up thy sword into the sheath: the cup which my Father hath given me, shall I not drink it?" (John 18:11). Jesus had the power and the agency to avoid the difficulties ahead, but He remained obedient in completing His mission. He then could say, "Father, it is finished, thy will is done" (Joseph Smith Translation, Matthew 27:54).

Examples of Righteous Leaders

The Apostle Paul taught the Hebrews the importance of being obedient to their leaders. He also cautioned against earning an unfavorable report from them. He said, "Obey them that have the rule over you, and submit yourselves: for they watch for your souls, as they that must give account, that they may do it with joy, and not with grief: for *that is unprofitable for you*" (Hebrews 13:17, emphasis added).

Being obedient is inherently difficult for mortal man, but it is made easier when those to whom we are obedient truly "watch for [our] souls" (Hebrews 13:17). However, our obedience needs to be genuine, for as the Lord warned, "He that receiveth my law and doeth it, the same is my disciple; and he that saith he receiveth it and doeth it not, the same is not my disciple, and shall be cast out from among you" (D&C 41:5).

Examples of obedience are found in the lives of most leaders throughout the scriptures. One of the most familiar is Abraham who was asked to sacrifice his son Isaac. Other examples are the Apostles who left their nets to become "fishers of men" (Mark 1:17); Lehi who left his gold, silver, and all other worldly possessions and comforts to lead his family into the wilderness (1 Nephi 2:4); Nephi, who obtained the plates of brass as he obediently went forward "not knowing beforehand" (1 Nephi 4:6) what to do; Nephi again, as he obediently built a ship in the manner he was told to build; Jacob, who did as Nephi directed, in recording only that which was sacred upon his plates (Jacob 1:1–3); Mosiah, who followed a prompting and led many of his people to find safety in Zarahemla (Omni 1:12); and Alma, who "returned speedily to the land of Ammonihah" (Alma 8:18) after being directed by an angel to do so.

On the other hand, there are examples of disobedience where leaders fell from their positions because of their actions. For example, Saul was commanded to destroy the Amalekites and all their possessions, but instead, he saved some of their animals for a sacrifice (1 Samuel 15:1–11). As a result, the Lord rejected Saul as king. His replacement, King David, also fell because of disobedience, as did some of his children who followed his immoral ways. In the book of Ether, the account tells how Jared desired their people to be ruled by a king. However, the brother of Jared, who was their spiritual leader, said that having a king would "Surely . . . leadeth into captivity" (Ether 6:23). Jared prevailed, a king was appointed, and soon the people lived in captivity as was foretold.

Summary of Examples

- Honorable leaders are obedient by following the directions and desires of their leader, as Jesus does.
- Honorable leaders are obedient as they restrain themselves from going beyond the bounds set by their leader, as demonstrated by Jesus when He withheld knowledge of the Nephites from the Jews.
- Honorable leaders are obedient even when asked to do difficult things, as demonstrated by Abraham who was asked to sacrifice Isaac; the Apostles who left their nets; Lehi who

took his family into the wilderness; Nephi who obtained the plates; Mosiah who fled wickedness; and Alma who immediately returned to Ammonihah.

- Leaders lose their positions and influence through disobedience, as did Saul and David.

Questions for Personal Reflection

- Are you obedient to your leaders because of love, respect, and a sincere desire to serve them?
- Are you outwardly obedient but inwardly resentful of your leaders?
- Do you model obedience to your family or do they see you finding ways to bypass laws whenever possible?
- Are you willingly obedient to civil authority?
- If your leader puts you in a compromising situation, how far will your obedience go?

Attribute 70: Submissive

Submissive: *Yield to the power or authority of another.*

Being submissive involves a deeper level of commitment than simply being obedient. One can be obedient by doing the will of another, but being submissive implies giving your heart as well as your effort. Following the healing of the infirm man at Bethesda, Jesus said, "I can of mine own self do nothing . . . because *I seek not mine own will*, but the will of the Father which hath sent me" (John 5:30, emphasis added). It is important to note the word *seek*. Again, going beyond simple obedience, Jesus sought to align His actions and desires to that of His Father. As Mosiah taught, "the will of the Son being swallowed up in the will of the Father" (Mosiah 15:7).

Perhaps the greatest example of His submission was in the Garden of Gethsemane where, under great distress and suffering, Jesus plead, "O my Father, if it be possible, let this cup pass from me: nevertheless not as I will, but as thou *wilt*" (Matthew 26:39). What better example could there be for us to put off natural man tendencies described by King Benjamin than that of the Savior who was "willing to submit to all things . . . as a child doth submit to his father" (Mosiah 3:19).

When we look at the example of the Savior being submissive to His Father, we may tend to minimize His actions because being submissive to the God of Heaven may seem only natural. However, for mortal man to be submissive to another mortal man, there are a number of human weaknesses that seem to get in the way. Being submissive to a leader who is honorable, kind, capable, and respectable can be difficult enough for most people, but it can seem almost impossible when the leader is not respected.

The Apostle Peter taught, "Servants, be subject to your masters . . . not only to the good and gentle, but also to the froward" (1 Peter 2:18). The word *froward* as used in the Bible is defined as being oppositional.[1] In these cases, we can and should use our influence to lead our situation to a better place. Although we need to have tolerance for individual personalities and varying levels of experience in our leaders, we do not need to submit to unrighteous behavior.

Examples of Righteous Leaders

President Brigham Young was a powerful leader who led thousands of refugees into the unknown regions of the American Mountain West. Yet this great leader demonstrated a submissive spirit to his leader, Joseph Smith. Bishop Richard Edgley said the following of Brigham: "A story is told of an encounter between the Prophet Joseph Smith and Brigham Young. In the presence of a rather large group of brethren, the Prophet severely chastised Brother Brigham for some failing in his duty. Everyone, I suppose somewhat stunned, waited to see what Brigham's response would be. After all, Brigham, who later became known as the Lion of the Lord, was no shrinking violet by any means. Brigham slowly rose to his feet, and in words that truly reflected his character and his humility, he simply bowed his head and said, 'Joseph, what do you want me to do?' The story goes that sobbing, Joseph ran from the podium, threw his arms around Brigham, and said in effect, 'You passed, Brother Brigham, you passed.'"[2]

Great leaders need to be great followers, and Brigham Young demonstrated that he was both. This helps keep themselves and the organization in balance and models the behavior the leader would like to see in his followers.

Elder Dieter F. Uchtdorf further explained the concept of being submissive when he taught that we should be as submissive and useful to our leaders as his favorite pen was to him. He said, "I once owned a pen that I loved to use during my career as an airline captain. By simply turning the shaft, I could choose one of four colors. The pen did not complain when I wanted to use red ink instead of blue. It did not say to me, 'I would rather not write after 10:00 p.m., in heavy fog, or at high altitudes.' The pen did not say, 'Use me only for important documents, not for the daily mundane tasks.' With greatest reliability it performed every task I needed, no matter how important or insignificant. It was always ready to serve."[3]

Likewise, leaders should "always be ready to serve." They willingly submit themselves to the needs of their own leaders and their followers, either in great tasks or mundane. They do so as a shepherd does for his sheep, as Jesus does for each of us.

Summary of Examples

- Leaders are submissive as they actively and willingly seek to do the will of their leader and not their own will or agenda, as demonstrated by Jesus when He said, "I seek not mine own will" (John 5:30).
- Leaders are submissive as they seek to do the will of their leader, even if he or she is less than perfect, as taught by Peter regarding "froward" leaders.
- Great leaders are great followers, as demonstrated by Brigham Young who yielded to the chastening of Joseph Smith.

Questions for Personal Reflection

- Are you submissive in your heart as well as your external actions?
- Can you be submissive to a peer who has been called to be your leader?
- Do you seek for and follow advice from your leader?
- Do you fully carry out the intent of your leader's agenda without regard to your own agenda?
- How well do you submit to better ideas presented by others?
- Do you handle disagreements with your leader in private rather than inciting dissent among your associates?

Attribute 71: Loyal

Loyal: *Giving or showing firm and constant support or allegiance to a person or institution.*

If being loyal is giving constant support or allegiance, then the Savior demonstrated loyalty from the very beginning. In the Council in Heaven, when God the Father presented His plan for the salvation of His children, Jesus was first to offer His loyal support. He willingly accepted His role as the sacrificial lamb. As significant as that was, Jesus still directed all of the glory back to His Father.

The Savior's loyalty continued during His mortal ministry as He showed allegiance to His Father by declaring, "my Father is greater than I" (John 14:28). The scriptures record many occasions where Jesus reaffirmed that loyalty by teaching, "I seek not mine own will, but the will of the Father which hath sent me" (John 5:30). All that Jesus did and taught reflected a firm allegiance to His Father and the mission given to Him.

Throughout His mission, Jesus consistently taught, "I must work the works of him that sent me" (John 9:4). As a result, there could not have been any doubt as to His loyalty. Even when His very life hung in the balance, when evil men mocked Him, scourged Him, and spit upon Him. Even when "Pilate therefore said unto him, Art thou a king then? Jesus answered, Thou sayest that I am a king. To this end was I born, and for this cause came I into the world, that I should bear witness unto the truth" (John 18:37). While standing before His enemies, Jesus boldly proclaimed His continuing love and loyalty to His Father and to the mission He had been sent to perform.

In addition to being loyal to His Father and His mission, the Savior declares His loyalty to those who follow Him. He said, "For them that honour me I will honour" (1 Samuel 2:30). This promise has application throughout our life as Jesus helps us along our mortal journey. When we fall short, the Savior's loyalty will continue for as John explained, "And if any man sin, we have an advocate with the

Father, Jesus Christ the righteous" (1 John 2:1). This He does because as He said, "Ye are my friends" (John 15:14). This friendship was never more on display than when Jesus proclaimed those beloved words, "Greater love hath no man that this, that a man lay down his life for his friends" (John 15:13). It was a proclamation that Jesus would soon personally demonstrate.

Examples of Righteous Leaders

The scriptures contain many examples of loyalty to God, to the truth, to another person, and to one's own beliefs. There are examples of shifting loyalty such as Moses who once was loyal only to Pharaoh. Then after Mount Sinai, he was loyal only unto Jehovah. Then there is the example of a split loyalty as with Daniel. Daniel had tried to be loyal to the king, but when the king forbade prayer, Daniel had to choose between God and the king. By remaining loyal to God, Daniel was thrown into the lions' den where God then manifested His loyalty to Daniel by preserving him.

There are examples where someone has multiple loyalties such as Joseph who served in the household of Potiphar. Because of Joseph's loyalty, Potiphar "committed all that he hath to my [Joseph's] hand" (Genesis 39:8). Then, when Potiphar's wife made inappropriate advances to him, Joseph's loyalties to God, to Potiphar, and to his own beliefs led him to flee her outstretched arms. His loyalty and ability earned Pharaoh's trust that gave him the influence needed to save a starving nation.

The house of Israel was led for many years by judges rather than kings. One of these judges was the prophetess Deborah. She served because of her wisdom and her ability to be guided by the Holy Ghost. On one occasion, Deborah received revelation that told her that Barak, the military commander of Israel, had received divine direction to lead his army into battle, yet he refused. In response, she said to him: "Hath not the Lord God of Israel commanded, saying, Go and draw toward mount Tabor, and take with thee ten thousand men of the children of Naphtali and of the children of Zebulun? And I will draw unto thee to the river Kishon Sisera, the captain of Jabin's army, with his chariots and his multitude; and I will deliver him into thine hand" (Judges 4:6–7).

A reluctant Barak responded to Deborah that he would go, but not without her. "And Barak said unto her, If thou wilt go with me, then I will go: but if thou wilt not go with me, then I will not go" (Judges 4:8). Deborah, ever loyal to him and her people, simply said, "I will surely go with thee" (Judges 4:9). These two leaders united together, and with an army of ten thousand men, were victorious over their enemies.

The story of Naomi and Ruth is one of the most beloved stories recorded in the scriptures. It is a story of losing much and gaining much more. It is a story of famine, death, and loneliness but also of hope, love, and loyalty. It begins with Elimelech, Naomi, and their two sons leaving their famine–plagued homeland of Beth–lehem–judah and moving to Moab. There they hoped to find food and a place to raise their family. In time, the two sons married Orpah and Ruth, and they all continued living in Moab for another ten years. Tragedy then came upon the family when Elimelech and the two sons died. Naomi then decided to return to her homeland. Her two daughters–in–law traveled with her for a while, but then Naomi encouraged them to return to Moab. In response, the loyal Ruth uttered some of the most touching and tender words in all scripture. She said:

"Entreat me not to leave thee, or to return from following after thee: for whither thou goest, I will go; and where thou lodgest, I will lodge: thy people shall be my people, and thy God my God:

"Where thou diest, will I die, and there will I be buried: the Lord do so to me, and more also, if ought but death part thee and me" (Ruth 1:16–17).

The loyalty and concern Ruth had for her mother–in–law turned out to be a great blessing for both beloved women. The influence of Ruth's actions went far beyond their immediate relationship. By returning with Naomi, Ruth married Boaz, and out of their posterity came the future leadership of Israel, including David, Solomon, and the Messiah.

We see a unique example of loyalty in King David where loyalty is to a position rather than to a person. Following David's defeat of Goliath, King Saul was favorable toward David. However, as David's fame increased, so did Saul's jealousy. On many occasions, Saul sought David's life, but David remained loyal. At one point, David and his men came upon Saul who lay sleeping in a trench. Abishai, one of David's men, encouraged him to have Saul killed and become free from his wrath. David responded, "Destroy him not: for who can stretch forth his hand against the Lord's anointed, and be guiltless?" (1 Samuel 26:9). Regardless of David's personal feelings for Saul and the hardship Saul had caused him, David had a firm allegiance to the position of king of Israel, and he remained loyal regardless of the personal cost.

Another example of unusual loyalty comes years later and an ocean apart. During the great final battle between the Nephites and the Lamanites, Mormon was placed in charge of the entire Nephite army. Mormon fought with them and loved them as a shepherd loves his sheep, but his sheep chose to be evil and, therefore, faced annihilation. Because of their wickedness, Mormon resigned as their leader, but only for a time. Because of his loyalty and love for them, Mormon consented to again lead them in what he knew would be a failed cause. "And it came to pass that I did go forth among the Nephites, and did repent of the oath which I had made that I would no more assist them; and they gave me command again of their armies, for they looked upon me as though I could deliver them from their afflictions. But behold, I was without hope, for I knew the judgments of the Lord which should come upon them; for they repented not of their iniquities" (Mormon 5:1–2).

At first, it may seem odd that Mormon would be loyal to a wicked people. They were not worthy of his leadership, his guidance, or his love. Yet he did love them and fought for them and then died for them. All because they were *his* people to the very end. In this gesture, Mormon demonstrated the greatness of his character and the depth of his loyalty as he laid down his life for the people he loved. Mormon did just as the Savior did, who laid down His life for the people He loved, despite their imperfections.

In more modern times, Elder Neil L. Anderson of the Quorum of the Twelve Apostles tells a story of loyalty that spans almost two hundred years. He said: "In 1830, Frederick G. Williams, a prominent medical doctor, was baptized. He immediately gave of his talents and prosperity to the Church. He became a leader in the Church. He donated property for the Kirtland Temple. In 1837, caught up in difficulties of the times, Frederick G. Williams made serious mistakes. The Lord declared in a revelation that 'in consequence of [his] transgressions [his] former standing [in the leadership of the Church had] been taken away from [him].'

"The beautiful lesson we learn from Frederick G. Williams is that 'whatever his personal weaknesses, he had the strength of character to [renew] his loyalty to the [Lord,] the Prophet and . . . to the Church, when it would have been so easy to have disintegrated in bitterness.' In the spring of 1840, he presented himself at a general conference, humbly asking forgiveness for his past conduct and expressing his determination to do the will of God in the future. His case was presented by Hyrum Smith, and he was freely forgiven. He died a faithful member of the Church.

"I recently met the president of the Recife Brazil Temple, whose name is Frederick G. Williams. He recounted how his great–great-grandfather's decision of character had blessed the family and hundreds of his posterity."[4]

These examples, like hundreds more, show the far–reaching effects of loyalty and the powerful influence it yields in the lives of others. Generations can be blessed or hurt by how well this attribute is employed. Leaders who are loyal to their own leaders and to their followers will find that their influence can bring about tremendous good.

Summary of Examples

- Loyalty is a deep commitment based on love and respect, as when Jesus said, "My Father love me, because I lay down my life" (John 10:17).

- Loyalty is giving your whole self to someone or something you believe in, as demonstrated by Jesus who did His Father's will for His Father's children.
- The depth of loyalty is manifest in times of great distress, as demonstrated by David who was loyal to Saul even though he sought his life; by Joseph of old who fled the reaching arms of Potiphar's wife; and Daniel who was sentenced to the lion's den.
- Loyalty drives one to service even in an unpopular or failing cause, as demonstrated by Mormon who again took command of the Nephite army.
- Honorable leaders can allow a breach of loyalty to be healed, as demonstrated by Frederick G. Williams.

Questions for Personal Reflection

- When have you stuck with a seemingly losing effort because of loyalty to your fellow laborers?
- How are you being a loyal defender of those you lead?
- Do those you lead feel your loyalty to them?
- Are you an example to your associates by being loyal to governing bodies?
- How much remorse would you feel if you disappointed your leader?

Attribute 72: Trusted

Trust: *Assured reliance on the character, ability, strength or truth of someone or something.*

What greater trust could there be than that shown by God the Father in His Son Jesus Christ? He placed in the Savior's hands the eternal well–being of all His children who number in the billons. Moses records, "And the Lord said: Whom shall I send? And one answered like unto the Son of Man: Here am I, send me. And another answered and said: Here am I, send me. And the Lord said: I will send the first" (Abraham 3:27) for the second "sought to destroy the agency of man" (Moses 4:3).

The trust that the Father showed in Jesus helped influence most of the Father's children to put their eternal happiness in Jesus's hands (D&C 29:36). No one has ever been trusted more. We believed Jesus was right. He adhered to the truth. He was united with His leader, and He had the strength and capability to do what He said He would do. When the Palmist said, "Our fathers trusted in thee: they trusted, and thou didst deliver them" (Psalms 22:4), it is as though he was speaking for each of us who have put our trust in Jesus to deliver us as well.

As trust is placed in Jesus, so Jesus places trust in us. Despite our mortal weaknesses and imperfections, He leads us by trusting us. Without that trust, we may not trust ourselves to act for ourselves. A leader who trusts his or her followers provides an environment of growth. Consider the trust Jesus placed in His chief Apostle, Peter. Even though Peter's weaknesses were manifest as his feet slipped below the surface of the Sea of Galilee, still the Master trusted him to lead His Church. Even though Peter would thrice deny Him, still the Master trusted him to lead His Church. Finally, even though Peter returned to fishing after the Crucifixion rather than feeding the Savior's sheep, still the Master trusted him to lead His Church.

The Apostle Peter is not alone in being trusted by Jesus. The Prophet Joseph Smith was continually trusted to restore the Gospel of Christ despite mortal failings. When 116 pages of the Book of Mormon were lost by failing to heed the Savior's direction, still the

Master trusted Joseph and used him to do a great work. In these two examples, and millions of others similar in nature, Jesus demonstrates that trust and weaknesses are essential characteristics of the growth process. Too often a leader withholds trust because of the weaknesses of those he or she leads. The Savior's leadership demonstrates great trust, despite weaknesses, because His goal is for our growth, not His.

Examples of Righteous Leaders

Trust is something that is slowly earned and powerful when mature. Consider the growth of trust in Joseph of old as explained by President James E. Faust: "Joseph, the son of Jacob and Rachel, was sold into slavery in Egypt. Because of treachery in the house of Potiphar, Joseph went to prison. Pharaoh had two troubling dreams. Hearing of Joseph's discernment from the captain of the prison guard, he sent for him to interpret the dreams. Joseph told him, through inspiration, that seven years of plenty would be followed by seven years of famine. Pharaoh not only recognized this true interpretation, but he trusted Joseph and appointed him to be second only to Pharaoh in power. The years passed and the famine came. In time Joseph rescued all of his brothers and his father from starvation. Because he earned the implicit trust of those who were over him, Joseph enjoyed a great amount of freedom."[5]

Joseph lived a life of integrity that earned him the trust of his leaders and associates. With that trust came freedom and the ability and power to bless a whole nation.

The scriptures tell of many leaders who did great things because of their trust in their leader, Jesus Christ. Peter trusted Jesus enough to walk towards him on the water. Moses trusted that Jehovah would support him before Pharaoh to let Israel go free. Moses trusted Him when Israel was backed against the Red Sea. David trusted Him when he stood before Goliath. Daniel trusted Him in the lions' den. Job trusted Him as he suffered sickness, abandonment, and poverty. The brother of Jared trusted Him that He could make stones produce light. Lehi trusted Him as he left all worldly possessions and took his family into the wilderness. Nephi trusted Him that he could build a ship.

Mosiah trusted Him that his sons would be safe on their mission to the Lamanites. When people trust their leader and the leader trusts his or her people, great power is unleashed and marvelous things can be accomplished for the benefit of man.

Summary of Examples

- People develop trust in their leaders who do what they say they will do, as the Psalmist testified of their fathers being delivered as promised; "Our fathers trusted in thee: they trusted, and thou didst deliver them" (Psalms 22:4).
- People trust their leaders who trust them, as demonstrated between Joseph and Pharaoh when Joseph interpreted the dreams and Pharaoh acted on that interpretation.
- People can do great things if they trust in the strength, support, and protection of their leader, as demonstrated by Peter, Moses, David, the brother of Jared, Lehi, Nephi, and Mosiah.

Questions for Personal Reflection

- Do you recognize that your associates trust there is no weakness in your character that will jeopardize their loyalty to you?
- Have your associates developed a trust for you based on extensive daily interactions?
- Is there anything you are doing to undermine the trust others have in you?
- What are you doing to earn the trust of your leader?
- How are you leading others to trust their leaders?

Attribute 73: United

United: *Made one, being in agreement. Relating to or produced by joint action.*

Jesus acknowledged His unity with His leader by declaring, "I and *my* Father are one" (John 10:30) "and *that* I do nothing of myself . . . for I do always those things that please him" (John 8:28–29). He continued this theme when He prayed, "That they all may be one; as thou, Father, *art* in me, and I in thee, that they also may be one in us" (John 17:21). Even in rejection, Jesus remained united with His leader, for He declared, "but now have they both seen and hated *both me and my Father*" (John 15:24, emphasis added).

Jesus taught His followers to be united with Him when He declared, "I say unto you, be one; and if ye are not one ye are not mine" (D&C 38:27). He explained, "Every kingdom divided against itself is brought to desolation; and every city or house divided against itself shall not stand" (Matthew 12:25). He also stated, "He that is not with me is against me" (Matthew 12:30). Both religious and civic history shows that infighting and disunity often begins small but, left unchecked, can grow into great wars and terrible suffering. The Savior taught that the attentive leader continually calls for unity to avoid such outcomes.

Jesus also taught His followers to be united among themselves, for His doctrine was one of inclusion. Paul taught this to the Ephesians as he welcomed them into the fold of God, "Now therefore ye are no more strangers and foreigners, but fellowcitizens with the saints, and of the household of God" (Ephesians 2:19). A leader who looks upon those who belong to his or her organization as fellow citizens, instills a feeling of unity and equality where the collective energy of each member can be harnessed to achieve great objectives.

Unfortunately, the collective energy of a group can fracture quickly. As discussed earlier, Jesus teaches that counseling together is productive even if people disagree with one another. However, if that disagreement turns into personal attacks from contentious people, then great harm can occur. Jesus warned, "Behold, this is not my doctrine, to stir up the hearts of men with anger, one against another; but this is my doctrine, that such things should be done away" (3 Nephi 11:30). He further declared, "there shall be no disputations among you" (3 Nephi 11:28) for "blessed are ye if ye have no disputations among you" (3 Nephi 18:34). Jesus preached of unity—a unity of heart, of purpose, of vision; a unity that binds people together in strength.

In the Doctrine and Covenants, the Lord taught a parable of a nobleman who asked his servants to plant twelve olive trees in his "choice piece of land" (D&C 101:44). He said to "set watchmen round about them, and build a tower, that one may overlook the land . . . that mine olive trees may not be broken down when the enemy shall come to spoil and take . . . the fruit" (D&C 101:45). The servants did as they had been directed but then "consulted for a long time, saying among themselves: What need hath my lord of this tower, seeing this is a time of peace? Might not this money be given to the exchangers? For there is no need of these things" (D&C 101:48–49). These servants disagreed with their leader because they did not have the vision, wisdom, or investment he had. And during their little rebellion while in a weakened state, the enemy came.

"And while they were at *variance one with another they became very slothful,* and they hearkened not unto the commandments of their lord. And the enemy came by night, and broke down the hedge; and the servants of the nobleman arose and were affrighted, and fled; and the enemy destroyed their works, and broke down the olive trees" (D&C 101:50–51, emphasis added).

This parable perfectly describes the causes and effects of dissension. The servants disagreed with their leader, they argued among themselves, they became slothful, they became weak, and they ultimately failed in their assignment. Again, that is why the Lord said, "If ye are not one ye are not mine" (D&C 38:27).

In one of Aesop's Fables, the ancient Greek storyteller taught the power that unity can have. In his fable, "*The Bundle of Sticks,*" he said, "An old man on the point of death summoned his sons around him to give them some parting advice. He ordered his servants to bring in a faggot of sticks, and said to his eldest son: 'Break it.' The son strained and strained, but with all his efforts was unable to break the Bundle. The other sons also tried, but none of them was successful. 'Untie the faggots,' said the father, 'and each of you take a stick.' When they had done so, he called out to them 'Now, break,' and each stick was easily broken. 'You see my meaning,' said their father. 'Union gives strength.'"[6]

This concept that "union gives strength" is true for a bunch of sticks as well as for families, sports teams, universities, businesses, and nations, etc. Unity forms a cohesive strength that creates the force necessary to accomplish things individual effort never could. The development of that unity starts with the leader and his relationship with his leader, and then is strengthened as he fosters unity between them and those he leads. This is the pattern established by the Father and His Son and is the foundation upon which we can become united with them.

Examples of Righteous Leaders

How do you unite a group of people as diverse as the Church of Jesus Christ of Latter-day Saints? From its earliest beginnings, the Church has been a collection of diverse races, cultures, nationalities, religious backgrounds, political perspectives, educational attainment, economic strength, gender, age, and maturity. They even have diverse levels of commitment, endurance, resilience, optimism, pessimism, and determination to lift themselves and others.

The Prophet Joseph Smith answered this question of how to unite a diverse membership by focusing them on common objectives. In the early 1840s, there was probably no other place on earth as diverse or as united as Nauvoo. This collection of people that reached an estimated 20,000 citizens came from the cultured eastern United States to the wild, wild West. They spoke a variety of languages, representing their homelands both far and near. They had belonged to many religions, but now they united together in one religion, one language, one culture, and one purpose. That purpose was to build Zion by building each individual person.

To assist in developing the Saints into a Zion people, Joseph organized the brethren of the Church around the priesthood and its power to bless lives. He then organized the sisters of the Church around the purpose of providing relief to those in need. This began by organizing the Nauvoo Female Relief Society which united the sisters in meeting the physical, spiritual, intellectual, and social needs of others. Joseph taught, "All must act in concert or nothing can be done."[7] By organizing and unifying the brethren and sisters while the Church was still in its infancy, Joseph established a firm foundation upon which future prophets could build.

In April 1936, the First Presidency created a Churchwide welfare program that built upon the foundation set almost a hundred years earlier in Nauvoo. President Heber J. Grant explained that this welfare program was "a system under which the curse of idleness would be done away with . . . and independence, industry, thrift and self respect be once more established amongst our people. The aim of the Church is to help people help themselves."[8] Later, President Harold B. Lee taught, "The most important object that is to be achieved by [the Church welfare program] is the promoting of a spirit of cooperation and *unity* throughout the entire Church."[9] This unity comes when leaders such as Joseph Smith, Heber J. Grant, and Harold B. Lee, focus their people on a common worthwhile purpose.

Summary of Examples

- An honorable leader who is united with his or her leader forms a solid foundation to build their organization, as Jesus did when He said, "I and *my* Father are one" (John 10:30).
- Honorable leaders and followers stay united with each other even when rejected, as Jesus did when people hated both Him and His Father for doing as His Father asked.
- Honorable leaders do not divide themselves from their people, but consider them as "fellowcitizens," as Paul taught the Ephesians.
- Honorable leaders build unity by eliminating disputations among their people lest enemies come in and destroy their work, as taught by Jesus with the broken–down olive trees.

- Honorable leaders unite their followers around a common objective, as Joseph did in focusing on building a Zion society and caring for one another.

Questions for Personal Reflection

- How do you bring diverse personalities and opinions together around a common objective?
- In your conversations with others, do you help foster unity rather than sowing seeds of dissent?
- Does your leader believe you are united with those you lead?
- Do your followers believe you are united with your leader?
- Are you leading your family, friends, neighbors and acquaintances to be fully united together?

Attribute 74: Respectful

Respectful: *A feeling of deep admiration for someone or something elicited by their abilities, qualities, or achievements.*

In all recorded scripture, there is no instance where Jesus tried to lift Himself above His leader or was disrespectful of Him. In fact, just the opposite is true. For example, during the Feast of Dedication, while Jesus was walking at Solomon's porch of the temple, He told the Jews, "My Father . . . is greater than all" (John 10:29). Later He said, "My Father is greater than I" (John 14:28). With all the wisdom Jesus displayed and the miracles He performed, He could have lifted Himself up in the sights of man. Instead, Jesus continually lifted up His Father with great respect.

In all His ministering around Jerusalem and in the Americas, Jesus always stated that He acted under the direction of His Father and desired to please Him. He stated, "My Doctrine is not mine, but his that sent me" (John 7:16) and "I do always those things that please him" (John 8:29). He showed the ultimate respect by saying, "I love the Father" (John 14:31). This love and respect were demonstrated during His ministry to the Nephites as Jesus continually quoted or referenced His Father in all His teachings. He prayed to His father in full view of His disciples so they could see His relationship with Him, and He explained that He was leaving them to be with His Father.

Before Jesus began His formal ministry in Jerusalem, His mother Mary put Him in a challenging situation. It was the third day of a marriage celebration in Cana of Galilee. These celebrations customarily continued for seven to fourteen days, but on the third day, Mary ran out of wine. Elder Bruce R. McConkie states: "Mary seemed to be the hostess at the marriage party, the one in charge, the one responsible for the entertainment of the guests . . . . Considering the customs of the day, it is a virtual certainty that one of Mary's children was being married."[10]

With some urgency and possible desperation, Mary approached Jesus and said, "They have no wine" (John 2:3). Since Jesus had not begun His ministry, He had not yet revealed His power over the temporal elements. Therefore, there may have been a reluctance to do so now for He said, "mine hour is not yet come" (John 2:4). In a gesture of respect for His mother, He simply asked, "Woman, what *will thou have me to do for thee? that will I do"* (Joseph Smith Translation, John 2:4). Miraculously, Jesus then turned the collected water into about 150 gallons of wine.[11]

Examples of Righteous Leaders

While it is important to speak respectfully of our leaders, we must also refrain from speaking ill of them. Even if what we have to say may be true, there is "a time to speak," and there is also "a time to keep silence" (Ecclesiastes 3:7). We are told to avoid "evil speakings" (1 Peter 2:1) and to "Let all bitterness, and wrath, and anger, and clamour, and evil speaking, be put away from you" (Ephesians 4:31). Further, modern revelations counsel us to avoid "backbiting," "evil speaking" (D&C 20:54), and "find[ing] fault one with another" (D&C 88:124).

Murmuring or speaking disrespectfully of our leaders undermines their influence and is often misdirected. Regarding the complaining children of Israel, Moses asked, "What are we, that ye murmur against us?" He continued, "The Lord heareth your murmurings which ye murmur against him: and what are we? your murmurings are not against us, but against the Lord" (Exodus 16:7–8). In a similar situation, the Lord told the prophet Samuel, "They have not rejected thee, but they have rejected me" (1 Samuel 8:7). These actions by unholy people reflect the true nature of their dissent and the weaknesses of their character.

During the difficult persecution–filled days in Kirtland, Ohio, many Saints had their faith severely tested as financial difficulties gripped the community. Several of the Saints blamed Joseph Smith directly, for if he truly was a prophet, he would have guided them to become affluent. Even Brigham Young lost confidence in Joseph's financial abilities, but he would not allow his doubts to destroy his confidence in Joseph as a Prophet. Brigham Young concluded: "Though I admitted in my feelings and knew all the time that Joseph was a human being and subject to err, still it was none of my business to look after his faults . . . He was called of God; God dictated him, and if He had a mind to leave him to himself and let him commit an error, that was no business of mine. . . . He was God's servant, and not mine."[12] Brigham Young simply chose to not speak ill of his leader. He remained loyal despite the significant challenges they now faced.

Parley P. Pratt, a fellow Apostle with Brigham Young, also showed his determination to avoid the consequences of speaking ill of his leader. While laboring in New Portage, fifty miles from Kirtland, Parley received letters from W. W. Phelps who was then President of the Church in Missouri. These letters censured Parley for not resolving his financial obligations. In February 1835, Parley went to Joseph Smith to explain the truth and defend himself from these false accusations. Joseph responded, "Walk such things under your feet; it was a trick of Satan to hinder your usefulness; God Almighty shall be with you."[13] The Prophet Joseph's counsel, which was basically to leave it alone, removed a stumbling block that surely would have brought about more disharmony.

Another example of speaking respectfully occurred during the pioneer migration. The trek across America's heartland was uneventful for many pioneers, but others had tribulations which sorely tested them. Great character was often revealed during those tests. On the evening of August 13, 1856, a group of pioneers from the Willie handcart company met in Florence, Nebraska, to decide if they should continue their journey to the Salt Lake Valley. Levi Savage, who was one of the sub-captains, warned of the difficult journey that lay ahead for the late–traveling Saints. His journal states:

"I then related to the Saints the hardships that we should have to endure. I said that we were liable to have to wade in snow up to our knees and shovel at night, lay ourselves in a thin blanket and lie on the frozen ground without a bed. [I said it] was not like having a wagon that we could go into and wrap ourselves in as much as we liked and lie down. No, said I, we are without wagons, destitute of clothing, and could not carry it if we had it. We must go as we are.

The handcart system I do not condemn. I think it preferable to unbroken oxen and inexperienced teamsters. The lateness of the season was my only objection to leaving this point for the mountains at this time. I spoke warmly upon the subject, but spoke truth."[14]

Levi, with tears running down his cheeks, pleaded with the Saints to winter in Florence, but most of the other leaders favored moving on. In a display of loyalty with the Saints whom he loved, Levi pledged his support to them with these noble words: "Brethren and sisters, what I have said I know to be true; but seeing you are to go forward, I will go with you, will help you all I can, will work with you, will rest with you, will suffer with you, and, if necessary, I will die with you. May God in his mercy bless and preserve us."[15]

It would have been an understandable response if Levi had chosen to walk away and let them press forward alone. From his earlier experience in finding the remains of the ill-fated Donner Party, it would have been tempting for him to condemn the decision of his leaders, but he offered nothing short of his full support. That support never wavered even as he continued to be criticized for his apparent faithless remarks.

There will come opportunities in the lives of each of us to take a stand against disrespectfulness. During those moments, we can use our influence to lead others to a better path. President Spencer W. Kimball has given us a wonderful example of speaking respectfully. He recounts: "In the hospital one day I was wheeled out of the operating room by an attendant who stumbled, and there issued from his angry lips vicious cursing with a combination of the names of the Savior. Even half-conscious, I recoiled and implored: 'Please! Please! That is my Lord whose names you revile.' There was a deathly silence, then a subdued voice whispered: 'I am sorry.'"[16]

President David O. McKay taught that fault-finding is associated with the spirit of envy. He counseled that when the feeling comes to find fault, we should sing the following hymn titled, "Nay, Speak No Ill."[17]

Nay, speak no ill; a kindly word
Can never leave a sting behind;
And, oh, to breathe each tale we've heard
Is far beneath a noble mind.

Full oft a better seed is sown
By choosing thus the kinder plan,
For, if but little good is known,
Still let us speak the best we can.

Then speak no ill, but lenient be
To other's failings as your own.
If you're the first a fault to see,
Be not the first to make it known,
For life is but a passing day;
No lip may tell how brief its span;
Then, O the little time we stay,
Let's speak of all the best we can."[18]

The wisdom of this poem can guide our actions and refine our character. President Gordon B. Hinckley continued this theme when he counseled: "What I am suggesting is that each of us turn from the negativism that so permeates our society and look for the remarkable good among those with whom we associate, that we speak of one another's virtues more than we speak of one another's faults."[19]

We gain respect as we respect our leaders, spouse, parents, coaches, teachers, and followers. It does not lift us up to tear others down. Someone once said, "When you throw mud, you only lose ground." Leaders who publicly disagree with or dislike their leaders weaken the respect they could have received had they withheld criticism. The adage of "compliment in public, disagree in private" is still wise counsel. President Henry B. Eyring said that one "principle of unity . . . is to speak well of each other."[20] If we can follow this counsel to speak of the virtues of another person, to build them up rather than to tear them down, we will warrant the attending influence of the Holy Ghost. We will foster loyalty, harmony, unity, and respect that will strengthen our relationships and help our endeavors to be more successful.

Summary of Examples

- Honorable leaders gain respect as they speak respectfully of their leaders to their followers, as demonstrated by Jesus when He said, "My Father is greater than I" (John 14:28).
- Honorable leaders speak respectfully with their actions when they submit to the out–of–the–ordinary requests of their leader, as Jesus did for creating wine from water for His mother.
- Honorable leaders speak respectfully when they remain silent when there is an opportunity to criticize, as demonstrated by Brigham Young's refusal to criticize Joseph. Also, Levi Savage for refraining to criticize the handcart leaders who criticized him for being faithless.
- Honorable leaders help their followers avoid speaking ill of another person, as Joseph did when he counseled Parley P. Pratt to let go of his frustration toward W. W. Phelps who censured him.
- Honorable leaders use their influence to stop others from being disrespectful, as President Kimball did in the hospital.

Questions for Personal Reflection

- Do you convey to your associates a feeling of admiration for the abilities, qualities, and achievements of your leader?
- Have your associates ever heard you being disrespectful of your leaders?
- Have you used your influence to change a conversation that is speaking disrespectfully of others?
- Do you help family members avoid speaking disrespectfully of coaches, teachers, leaders, or each other?
- How do you discuss concerns about political leaders without being disrespectful?

Attribute 75: Reports Back

Report: *To give an account.*

An integral part of accountability is giving an accounting to whom we are accountable. Just prior to His death, Jesus offered a prayer to His Father which has been termed the great intercessory prayer. In a very real sense, it was the Son giving an accounting to His Father. Below are statements He made in that prayer which gave a report or accounting of His mission on earth.

1. "I have glorified thee on the earth."
2. "I have finished the work which thou gavest me to do."
3. "I have manifested thy name unto the men which thou gavest me."
4. "They have kept thy word. "
5. "They have known that all things whatsoever thou hast given me are of thee."
6. "I have given unto them the words which thou gavest me; and they have known surely that I came out from thee, and they have believed that thou didst send me."
7. "I pray for them."
8. "While I was with them in the world, I kept them in thy name: those that thou gavest me I have kept, and none of them is lost, but the sons of perdition."
9. "I have given them thy word."
10. "For their sakes I sanctify myself."
11. "The glory which thou gavest me I have given them; that they may be one, even as we are one" (John 17:1–26).

Jesus gave an accounting or report to the Father during each of His major missions. He reported back during the Creation, at the end of His mortal ministry, as just noted, and after His Crucifixion. When He appeared to Mary, "Jesus saith unto her, Touch me not, for I am not yet ascended to my Father: but go to my brethren, and say unto them, I ascend unto my Father, and your Father; and to my God, and your God" (John 20:17). He also prepared to report back to the Father while visiting the Nephites. He said, "And now I go unto the Father, because it is expedient that I should go unto the Father for your sakes" (3 Nephi 18:35). How pleased His Father must have been for the perfect offering rendered by the perfect Son.

In the parable of the talents, Jesus teaches that we need to account for our use of resources given us. In that parable, "a man travelling into a far country" (Matthew 25:14) called his servants together and "unto one he gave five talents, to another two, and to another one; to every man according to his several ability; and straightway took his journey" (Matthew 25:15). "After a long time the lord of those servants cometh, and reckoneth with them" (Matthew 25:19). He asked for an accounting from each of his servants and rewarded them accordingly. As with all parables, there are multiple lessons to be learned. Clearly, an important one is the need to report back and give an accounting of our labors.

Jesus used this reporting back with the brother of Jared while He helped him prepare barges to take his family across the great deep. Jesus instructed him to build the barges, and then He waited for that step to be completed before giving additional instruction. When the barges were built:

"The brother of Jared cried unto the Lord, saying: O Lord, I have performed the work which thou hast commanded me, and I have made the barges according as thou hast directed me.

"And behold, O Lord, in them there is no light; whither shall we steer? And also we shall perish, for in them we cannot breathe, save it is the air which is in them; therefore we shall perish.

"And the Lord said unto the brother of Jared: Behold, thou shalt make a hole in the top, and also in the bottom; and when thou shalt suffer for air thou shalt unstop the hole and receive air. And if it be so that the water come in upon thee, behold, ye shall stop the hole, that ye may not perish in the flood.

"And it came to pass that the brother of Jared did so, according as the Lord had commanded" (Ether 2:18–21, emphasis added).

A similar pattern of reporting back was used in getting light for the barges. Once the brother of Jared had prepared sixteen small stones, he went back to the Lord to show Him what he had done. He then asked the Lord to do what he could not do: touch the stones that they radiate light (Ether 2:22–3:6). The Lord follows this pattern throughout our entire lives—He gives a little information then asks us to do with it what we can. When we report back, He will give more instruction if needed.

Examples of Righteous Leaders

Much has been said over the centuries about the leadership of Moses. It can be difficult to lead willing men and women, but to lead thousands of undisciplined people into the inhospitable wilderness of Sinai would have been impossible for most leaders. However, Moses had great natural skills that Jehovah, Jethro, and others magnified. One of the attributes of Moses was his willingness to report back to his leader. When Moses had received the tablets containing the law of God, he returned to the camp of Israel and found them living in sin. And *"Moses returned unto the Lord"* (Exodus 32:31, emphasis added) and gave a report of what he had encountered. He told the Lord, "Oh, this people have sinned a great sin, and have made them gods of gold" (Exodus 32:31). The Lord received this report and then gave Moses additional instructions to follow. Undoubtedly, the pattern of returning and reporting, now established, would continue throughout his life.

President Thomas S. Monson taught, "A cardinal principle of industrial management teaches: 'When performance is measured, performance improves. When performance is measured *and reported*, the rate of improvement accelerates.'"[21] This truth was demonstrated so well in a story told earlier in this book of how a high councilor, Brother Ralph Christensen, reported back monthly to his stake president, President Bill Marriott. In this story, President Marriott simply took the role of listening to what Brother Christensen planned to do, then a month later he asked for a report on how well he did. A simple process that produces great results.

Being accountable keeps one disciplined, productive, and aids in personal growth. Reporting back helps measure that level of accountability. Giving this accounting does more than just update our leader on the status of assigned tasks. It closes the cycle that began when someone trusted us enough to empower us to act. Reporting back is a courtesy conveying to our leader a measurement of our obedience, submission, loyalty, ability, and dependability. It gives them confidence that this cycle of giving responsibility and receiving a report back is working between them and us. This cycle usually starts small, with less important assignments. As confidence grows through the reporting back process, we are often entrusted with more significant responsibilities. This is the mentoring process used by the Savior as He builds each of us.

Summary of Examples

- Honorable leaders ensure they report to their own leader on each significant assignment, as Jesus did when creating the world; when finishing His mortal mission; and when visiting the Nephites.
- Those who have been made accountable will be called upon to give a report of the results they achieved and the manner of getting those results, as did the servants of the man traveling into a far country.
- Honorable leaders use the reporting back process to determine what has occurred and what additional support they need to give, as Jesus did with the brother of Jared as he constructed barges.
- Followers use the reporting back process to counsel with their leader and to receive additional instructions, as Moses did with Jehovah regarding the wickedness of Israel.

Questions for Personal Reflection

- Do you give an accounting of the use of resources invested in you to both your leader and those you lead?

- When you give a report, are you filled with a sense of loyalty rather than a feeling of resentment toward a higher power?
- Do you voluntarily report back to your leaders on a regular basis?
- How accurate and true are the facts and the spirit of your report?
- How often do you give an accounting to those who support you financially, emotionally, or in any other way?
- Have you established the practice of reporting in your family?

---

1. Merriam Webster's Collegiate Dictionary Tenth Edition, 1998, "Froward."
2. Richard C. Edgley, "*The Empowerment of Humility,*" *Ensign*, November 2003; See Truman G. Madsen, "*Hugh B. Brown—Youthful Veteran,*" *New Era*, April 1976, 16.
3. Dieter F. Uchtdorf, "*Pride and the Priesthood,*" *Ensign*, November 2010.
4. Neil L. Andersen, "Never Leave Him," *Ensign*, November 2010.
5. James E. Faust, "Obedience: The Path to Freedom," *Ensign*, May 1999.
6. Aesop Fables, retold by Joseph Jacobs. Vol. XVII, Part 1. The Harvard Classics, New York: P.F. Collier & Son, 1909-14; Bartleby.com, 2001.
7. *Relief Society Minute Book,* Nauvoo Illinois, Mar. 30, 1842, 22.
8. *Daughters in My Kingdom,* 72.
9. *Daughters in My Kingdom,* 73; emphasis added.
10. Bruce R. McConkie, *Doctrinal New Testament Commentary,* Volume 1 135.
11. McConkie, Volume 1 136.
12. Brigham Young, *Journal of Discourses,* 4:297.
13. Joseph Smith, in *Autobiography of Parley P. Pratt,* ed. Parley P. Pratt Jr. (1938), 96.
14. Savage, journal, 13 Aug. 1856. Cited in Andrew D. Olsen, *The Price We Paid.*

15. Chislett, "Narrative," 331; Woodward, journal, 12 Aug. 1856; Cunningham, "Autobiography," 2. Cited in Andrew D. Olsen, *The Price We Paid.*

16. *The Teachings of Spencer W. Kimball,* ed. Edward L. Kimball (1982), 198.

17. David O. McKay, *Conference Report,* Oct. 1967, 7.

18. "Nay, Speak No Ill," *Hymns,* #233.

19. Gordon B. Hinckley, "The Continuing Pursuit of Truth," *Ensign,* April 1986, 3–4.

20. Henry B. Eyring, "Our Hearts Knit as One," *Ensign,* November 2008.

21. Thomas S. Monson, *Conference Report,* October 1970, General Priesthood Meeting, 107.

CONCLUSION

The seven-step process and the 75 attributes described in this book can change your life. First, they can aid in your personal growth by helping you become more like the Savior by enlarging and improving your character. You can become someone that other people will want to follow. Remember, the first person you need to lead is yourself. Second, with this expanded character and improved ability, you can have greater influence to affect change, to improve each situation you encounter each day, and to inspire others to improve themselves as well.

There is such a need for effective leaders in every aspect of life. In the home, community, work place, government, business, education, and so forth. In addition, each day we find ourselves in many various situations where we can use our influence to improve results. Whether we are traveling on our daily commute, working, volunteering, shopping, or being a spectator at some event, there are many situations where we can lead. Perhaps we can help someone find a solution to a problem, calm a strained situation, help find a desired location, or lend a hand with overactive children. There are so many opportunities to lead. Better leaders will find better solutions and achieve better results.

With better leaders, we can create a society where there is enough food and medicine, happiness and opportunity, and education and employment for everyone; a community where suffering is minimized, and hope is maximized. One great leader can have some influence, but many great leaders can have more. If everyone would lead and spread their influence to promote good, then greater things can occur. That is the essence of the gospel of Christ, to let our light shine and to improve lives.

Each person, whether young, middle-aged, or elderly, can begin this quest by selecting a few of these attributes to focus on. Then, as progress is made, other attributes can receive focus as well. As we face a pending decision or situation, a quick review of the 75 attributes will help guide our actions and our outcomes. To help in selecting which attributes to focus on, complete the self-evaluation form in The Appendix. This will help you rate yourself against each of the 75 attributes to identify where growth is currently needed. It may be helpful to have a trusted friend, coworker, spouse, or supervisor also complete an evaluation of you. Often, other people see us differently than we see ourselves.

Remember, a daily review only takes a few seconds and can help you make a difference by leading as Jesus leads.

Bibliography

A Disciple's Life: the Biography of Neal A. Maxwell, © 2002, Bruce C. Hafen, under license from Deseret Book

All That Was Promised, © 2013, Blaine M. Yorgason, under license from Deseret Book

Autobiography of Parley P. Pratt, Parley P. Pratt, under license from Deseret Book

Be of Good Cheer, © 1987, Marvin J. Ashton, under license from Deseret Book

Crusader for Righteousness, © 1966, Melvin J. Ballard, under license from Deseret Book

Daughters in My Kingdom - The History and Work of Relief Society, 2011, The Church of Jesus Christ of Latter-day Saints, © By Intellectual Reserve, Inc.

Discourses of Brigham Young, John A. Widstoe, under license from Deseret Book

Discourses of the Prophet Joseph Smith, Joseph Smith, under license from Deseret Book

Doctrinal New Testament Commentary, © 1965, Bruce R. McConkie, under license from Deseret Book

Encyclopedia of Mormonism, 4 vols. © 1992, Daniel H. Ludlow, under license from Deseret Book

George Washington A Life, 1997, Willard Sterne Randall, New York: Henry Holt and Company

Gospel Doctrine, 5th ed. © 1939, Joseph F. Smith, under license from Deseret Book

Gospel Symbolism, © 1985, Joseph Fielding McConkie, under license from Deseret Book

Heroines of the Restoration, © 1997, Barbara B. Smith & Blyth Darlyn Thatcher, under license from Deseret Book, p.27)

History of The Church of Jesus Christ of Latter-day Saints, vol. 4, B. H. Roberts, under license from Deseret Book

Hymns of the Church of Jesus Christ of Latter-day Saints, 1985, The

Church of Jesus Christ of Latter-day Saints, © By Intellectual Reserve, Inc.

Hyrum Smith: A Life of Integrity, © 2003, Jeffrey S. O'Driscoll, under license from Deseret Book

Jesus the Christ, James E. Talmage, under license from Deseret Book

Joseph of Egypt, © 1981, Mark E. Petersen, under license from Deseret Book

Joseph Smith the Prophet, © 1989, Truman G. Madsen, under license from Deseret Book

Joseph Smith, an American Prophet, © 1989, John Henry Evans, under license from Deseret Book

Journal of Discourses, Brigham Young, under license from Deseret Book

Henry V, William Shakespeare

Lectures on Faith, under license from Deseret Book

Life of Joseph F. Smith, Joseph Fielding Smith, under license from Deseret Book

Life Story of Brigham Young, Susa Young Gates, under license from Deseret Book

Merriam-Webster's Collegiate Dictionary, 11th edition, 2003, Massachusetts, Merriam-Webster, Incorporated, Springfield

Messages of the First Presidency, © 1966, James R. Clark, under license from Deseret Book

Pathways to Perfection, © 1973, Thomas S. Monson, under license from Deseret Book

Poems of Giles Fletcher, B.D.," 1868, Giles Fletcher, collected and edited by Rev. Alexander B. Grosart, St. George's, Blackburn, Lancashire.

Presidents of the Church, © 1991, Truman G. Madsen, under license from Deseret Book

Portrait of Courage, © 1966, Don Cecil Corbett, under license from Deseret Book

Relief Society Minute Book, 1868–79. Lehi Ward, Alpine Stake, Oct. 27, 1869, Church History Library. © By Intellectual Reserve, Inc.

Riverside Webster's II Dictionary, 1996, New York: Berkley

Teachings of Presidents of the Church: Joseph Smith, The Church of

Jesus Christ of Latter–day Saints, © By Intellectual Reserve, Inc.

The Art of War, 2000, Tzu, Sun, Boston: Shambhala

The Autobiography of Benjamin Franklin, 2003, Louis P. Masur, Boston: Bedford/St. Martin's

The Merchant of Venice, William Shakespeare

The Price We Paid, © 2006, Andrew D. Olsen, under license from Deseret Book

The Spirit Knows No Handicap, © 1980, Becky Reeve, under license from Deseret Book

The Teachings of Spencer W. Kimball, edited by Edward L. Kimball © 1982, Spencer W. Kimball, under license from Deseret Book

The Wentworth Letter, Joseph Smith, under license from Deseret Book

The Writings of Camilla Eyring Kimball, © 1988, Camilla Eyring Kimball, under license from Deseret Book

Things of the Soul, © 1996, Boyd K. Packer, under license from Deseret Book

Three Kings of Israel, © 1980, Mark E. Petersen, under license from Deseret Book

Understanding the Parables of Jesus Christ, © 2006, Jay A. and Donald W. Parry, under license from Deseret Book

Vital Quotations, © 1968, Emerson Roy West, under license from Deseret Book

INDEX

THE APPENDIX

Personal Attribute Assessment Form

	Attributes	1	2	3	4	5	Comments
	MOTIVES						
1.	Charity/Love						
2	Pure motives						
3.	Authentic						
4.	Selfless						
5.	Delights in the success of others						
	DEMEANOR						
6.	Optimistic						
7.	Cheerful						
8.	Dignified						
9.	Approachable						
10.	Inclusive						
11.	Friendly						
12.	Patient						
13.	Compassionate						
14.	Kind						
15.	Humble						
	ABILITY						
16.	Confident						
17.	Courageous						
18.	Durable						
19.	Capable						
20.	Knowledgeable						
21.	Accountable						
22.	Has integrity						
23.	Diligent						
24.	Perceptive						
	GOVERNS HIMSELF						
25.	Disciplined						
26.	Maintains confidentiality						

27.	Frugal						
28.	Consistent						
29.	Endures to the end						
30.	Prioritizes						
31.	Plans ahead						
32.	Prepares Himself						
33.	Rejuvenates Himself						
34.	Grows Personally						
35.	Labors also						
	LEADS OUT						
36.	Defines objectives						
37.	Lifts vision						
38.	Initiates action						
39.	Visible						
40.	Motivates with persuasion						
41.	Inspires with oratory						
42.	Has order						
43.	Gives clear direction						
44.	Counsels together						
45.	Serves others						
46.	Ministers to the one						
47.	Succors the weak						
	PREPARES FOLLOWERS						
48.	Knows followers						
49.	Defends followers						
50.	Delegates						
51.	Allows freedom						
52.	Avoids favoritism						
53.	Overcomes obstacles						
54.	Teaches						
55.	Nourishes						
56.	Sets an example						
57.	Mentors						
	OVERSEES FOLLOWERS'						
58.	Provides hands–on leadership						
59.	Places faith in followers						
60.	Expects results						

61.	Accepts people's best						
62.	Follows up						
63.	Steps in when needed						
	JUDGES						
64.	Is just and merciful						
65.	Judges righteously						
66.	Disciplines with kindness						
67.	Forgives						
68.	Looks on the heart						
	HONORS RELATIONSHIPS						
69.	Obedient						
70.	Submissive						
71.	Loyal						
72.	Trusted						
73.	United						
74.	Respectful						
75.	Reports back